ADVANCES
IN
ENVIRONMENTAL
PSYCHOLOGY
Volume 2
Applications of Personal Control

ADVANCES IN ENVIRONMENTAL PSYCHOLOGY

Volume 2
Applications of Personal Control

Edited by **ANDREW BAUM**
JEROME E. SINGER
*Uniformed Services University
of the Health Sciences*

LEA LAWRENCE ERLBAUM ASSOCIATES, PUBLISHERS
1980   Hillsdale, New Jersey

Lawrence Erlbaum Associates, Inc., Publishers
365 Broadway
Hillsdale, New Jersey 07642

Library of Congress Cataloging in Publication Data

Main entry under title:

Applications of personal control.

(Advances in environmental psychology; v. 2)
Includes bibliographies and indexes.
1. Control (Psychology) I. Baum, Andrew.
II. Singer, Jerome E. III. Series.
BF632.5.A66   362.1′01′9   79-25025
ISBN 0-89859-018-3

34,663

Printed in the United States of America

Contents

7. DEPRESSION MAINTENANCE AND INTERPERSONAL CONTROL
Dan Coates and Camille B. Wortman

Preface

How do people manage their environments? What processes are basic to the interactions between people and their environments? These questions are central to almost all areas of psychology but in a more narrow sense are the heart of environmental psychology. Some environmental studies focus on the antecedents of person-environment interactions, others on the effects of the environment on the individual, and others on outcomes. Still others focus on the processes by which people attempt to manipulate their surroundings. This volume, the second in a series, is concerned with one of these processes— control, actual and perceived, that individuals exercise over their environment.

Of all the basic processes offered to explain environmental coping, control is one of the most thoroughly explored, widely cited, and generally accepted. Control has been considered in a variety of studies and has been defined in a number of ways. Often an operant definition is used—control is seen as a positive relation between responses and outcomes, although this relationship is usually implicit rather than explicit. At other times, control is a concept that is implied rather than exercised. For example, in several studies in the literature, the subject has a switch that, if pressed, could terminate an experiment. Even though the subject chooses not to press the switch, and, in effect, elects to undergo some environmental stimulation, the existence of the switch is considered an illustration of environmental control—in this case perceived, not actual. Thus, control may be real or perceived, objective or subjective. Control may also be seen as freedom to choose among courses of action, outcomes, or situations and may refer to onset or offset of the person's actions or environmental events. In short, control refers to regulation of many things in many ways. It is not our intention to advocate a particular definition of control or to argue that it is better than, or even different from, competence, selective attention, effectance, or other mechanisms proposed to explain responses to environmental stress. Rather, we hope to show the variety of situations in which control has been applied, the factors that potentiate and vitiate it, and its relation to other psychological processes.

It has been several years since a comprehensive review of control has been published. There have been several volumes, conferences, and partial reviews since then. It now appears that, as with Humpty Dumpty, the concept has splattered over so wide an area that such an inclusive review may no longer be possible. In its place there may appear partial reviews of the control concept in various areas and at various levels, such as control and depression, control and effective learning, etc. The present volume represents a partial review that emphasizes those aspects of control that are relevant to what has been broadly termed environmental psychology.

This volume and the entire series of advances volumes is intended for the audience that reads the primary literature—professionals and students in the congeries of fields comprising environmental psychology. The primary literature in environmental psychology is more scattered than in most other subfields, and the application of control to this topic is a fairly recent phenomenon. Although many of the studies relating control and environment have appeared in the social psychological literature, the use of control to mediate environmental events has also been a theme in behavioral medicine and psychopathology as well. One aim of this book is to provide reviews of some of the primary literature from these diverse subareas.

Our efforts in preparing this volume were aided by a number of people: Joan Graefe, Karen Laue, and Wanda Waters provided a complete range of secretarial and clerical support services, and their help is gratefully acknowledged.

ANDREW BAUM
JEROME E. SINGER

ADVANCES
IN
ENVIRONMENTAL
PSYCHOLOGY
Volume 2
Applications of Personal Control

1 Perceived Control: A Review and Evaluation of Therapeutic Implications

Robert J. Gatchel
Uniformed Services University of the Health Sciences

In this chapter, evidence is reviewed that indicates that individuals react differently to stressful events that they perceive can be personally controlled than to those perceived not in their control. A rapidly growing literature has shown that perceived controllability/uncontrollability significantly affects self-report, overt motor, and physiological components of behavior elicited by a stressor. In the present discussion of this concept, perceived control is defined simply as the subject's perception of a contingency between the performance of some behavior and the ability to avoid or escape a stressful, unpleasant event. Perceived uncontrollability, in contrast, is the perception of no contingency between one's responding and avoidance/escape outcomes. After a review of the evidence of the important impact that this concept of perceived controllability/uncontrollability has on behavior, it is shown how this factor appears to be an active ingredient in behavior therapy techniques directed at the treatment of fear and anxiety.

EARLY STUDIES OF PERCEIVED CONTROL

Through the years, there has been anecdotal material reported in the literature to suggest that the lack of control over aversive events can lead to some rather dramatic negative consequences. For example, Bettelheim(1943) described the *Muselmaner*, or walking corpses, in Nazi concentration camps, who—due to an apparent sense of helplessness and lack of control over their aversive life situation—developed apathy and withdrawal, which many times culminated in death due to no known organic cause. Richter (1957), in an

1

investigation employing wild rats, suggested that the perception of noncontrol by these rats in an environment in which they were held captive was primarily responsible for their losing incentive for living and resulted in a phenomenon that he labeled "sudden death." Seligman (1975) has also more recently documented other apparent instances of this "sudden death" due to perceived uncontrollability over a stressful environment.

The fact that feelings of helplessness and lack of control appear to interfere significantly with the ability to respond adaptively to a stressful situation has often been pointed out by various investigators (e.g., Cofer & Appley, 1964; Janis, 1958; Janis & Leventhal, 1968; Lazarus, 1966). There have been a number of research studies attempting to document objectively the effects of perceived control on behavior, as well as to gain insight into the mechanisms of perceived control. The great bulk of these studies have demonstrated that reduced control over an aversive situation increases negative emotional responding associated with that situation. Averill (1973) and Lefcourt (1973) have provided excellent reviews of many of the early studies on this topic. I briefly review some of this work, after which some of the more recent studies are discussed.

In a classic study demonstrating the stressful effects of uncontrollable shock on rats, Mowrer and Viek (1948) shocked two groups of rats while they were eating. One group of rats could control the shock by performing an instrumental response—jumping into the air; the other group of rats were yoked controls who could not escape the shock by performing some behavior. It was found that the rats who could control the shock responded less fearfully to this aversive situation than the yoked controls.

In other research with animals, it has been demonstrated that persistent exposure of rats to stress (unpredictable or uncontrollable electric shock) led to a significant increase in the ulceration rate in these rats (e.g., Price, 1972; Weiss, 1968, 1971). In passing, it should be noted that a widely publicized earlier study by Brady, Porter, Conrad, and Mason (1958), which became known as the "executive monkey" study, reported that ulcers were not produced in rats exposed to uncontrollable electric shock but only in those who could actively control the occurrence of this stress. Brady and colleagues interpreted these results to suggest that the pressure and responsibility of actively responding and attempting to control stressful events produces ulceration. These data were used to support the popular but unsubstantiated notion that ulcers are more frequent in persons in responsible, high-level executive positions. However, there were a number of major methodological flaws in the design of the Brady study that seriously interfered with the interpretability of these results. Weiss (1968, 1971) has reviewed these problems in design and has demonstrated that the availability of coping responses, with immediate and positive feedback concerning their effectiveness, alleviates stress and produces less ulceration relative to no-control conditions. Thus, research to date indicates that exposure to uncontrollable emotional stress is associated with an increase in gastric secretion and, as a result, an increased probability that stomach ulcerations will occur.

With human subjects, there have been numerous studies also indicating that when subjects believe they can terminate an electric shock, they demonstrate less emotional stress than under conditions in which they are unable to terminate it (Champion, 1950; Corah & Boffa, 1970; Haggard, 1943). In one such study, Staub, Tursky, and Schwartz (1971) demonstrated that subjects who had no predictability or personal control of an electric shock judged a less intense shock as more uncomfortable than did subjects with controllability. They also tolerated significantly fewer shocks.

INVESTIGATIONS OF "LEARNED HELPLESSNESS"

During the past few years, there has been an enormous increase in this type of investigation, which examines the impact of a stressful situation as a function of the degree of personal control over it perceived by a subject. The bulk of this research has focused on a phenomenon that has come to be known as *learned helplessness*. The concept of learned helplessness was initially developed from a series of studies conducted by Seligman and colleagues on traumatic avoidance learning in dogs (Overmier & Seligman, 1967; Seligman & Maier, 1967). In these studies, it was found that inescapable aversive events presented to the animals resulted in profound interference with subsequent instrumental learning. Learned helplessness was interpreted as a phenomenon that develops when an organism learns that responding and reinforcement (escape) are independent. This learning is assumed to interfere with initiating instrumental responses.

Seligman (1975) has proposed a conditional probability theory to account for this learned helplessness effect. It is beyond the scope of this chapter to evaluate this theoretical account critically. It should be noted, however, that certain investigators have recently questioned the learning principles upon which the learned helplessness phenomenon is assumed to be based (e.g., Levis, 1976).

Regardless of the precise learning principles that underlie the effect, there can be no doubt from the research conducted to date that the lack of control has a significant impact upon cognitive, emotional, and motivational responding in subjects exposed to stressful situations (cf. Seligman, 1975). This has been demonstrated in a wide variety of studies employing both animal and human subjects. For example, in a series of studies from my own laboratory, it has been found that both self-report and physiological measures of emotion are significantly affected by the lack of control over an aversive event. In one study, Gatchel and Proctor (1976b) demonstrated that subjects exposed to a learned helplessness task (inescapable aversive noise) evidenced lower tonic and phasic skin conductance responding relative to nonhelpless and control group subjects. This response pattern was viewed as a concomitant of decreased task involvement and motivation in learned helplessness subjects, which was prompted by their learning that responding and reinforcement (escape) were independent. At the same time, they demonstrated a greater frequency of spontaneous skin conductance fluctuations. Thus, there was evidence for both deactivation responses (lower tonic and phasic skin conductance responses) as well as activation responses (greater spontaneous electrodermal activity). We interpreted these findings of *fractionation* of electrodermal responses in terms of an explanation suggested by Kilpatrick (1971) and, more recently, by Schwartz (1974). They have suggested that skin conductance level may be more responsive to cognitive and vigilance tasks, or what Schwartz refers to as "cortical arousability." Spontaneous electrodermal fluctuations, on the other hand, may be more expressive of emotional or limbic system stress, referred to by Schwartz as "subcortical reactivity." Although Schwartz indicates that this is an oversimplified explanation, we viewed it as consistent with the data from our study. Subjects in the escapable condition, who would be expected to have greater vigilance and task involvement during the experimental task than subjects in the inescapable condition because of the probability of escaping, had higher skin conductance levels. At the same time, these subjects had a smaller number of spontaneous electrodermal fluctuations than the subjects who could not escape. This would be expected due to the greater emotional stress in the inescapable-condition subjects prompted by their inability to escape the noise. Indeed, it has also been shown by Hokanson, DeGood, Forrest, and Brittain (1971) that the lack of any control over a stressful task (performance of a symbol-matching task with shocks being delivered for poor performance) produced significantly greater increases in blood pressure than a condition in which subjects could personally control the time course of this experimental task. Blood pressure is a common physiological correlate of increased arousal.

Along with the foregoing physiological evidence of emotional stress in the learned helplessness subjects, we have also found an increase in self-reported affect in subjects exposed to the learned helplessness task. In studies both by Gatchel, McKinney, and Koebernick (1977b) and by Gatchel, Paulus, and Maples (1975), it was found that there was an increase in depression, anxiety, and hostility—as measured by the Multiple Affect Adjective Check List (Zuckerman & Lubin, 1965)—in subjects exposed to a learned helplessness task. Similar results have also been reported by Miller and Seligman (1975).

THE EFFECTS OF PERCEIVED CONTROL
IN "REAL-LIFE" SITUATIONS

Thus, the negative emotional impact of an aversive event appears to be a function of the degree to which a subject can control it. Personal control appears to decrease significantly the negative emotional impact of a stressor. In "real-life" situations, there have been some recent studies to suggest the importance of perceived control over a stressful situation in reducing the aversive emotional impact of that situation. Langer, Janis, and Wolfer (1975) reported a study in which it was found that when the perception of control over stress was induced in hospital patients by a method that emphasized to these patients their ability to exert cognitive control over the situation, these subjects required fewer pain-relief drugs and sedatives and were also viewed by nurses as evidencing less anxiety.

In another study, Langer and Rodin (1976) demonstrated that enhanced personal responsibility and choices given to a group of nursing home residents resulted in a marked improvement, relative to a comparison group, in factors such as general alertness, active participation, and a general sense of well-being. Many residents in nursing homes experience an adverse reaction to this institutionalization, probably due to their inability to manipulate and control their environment, which results in feelings of helplessness and the development of physical symptoms (Schulz & Aderman, 1973). Providing these residents with some sense of control apparently will alleviate some of these negative reactions and lead to a better adjustment. Schulz (1976) has also found that the introduction of predictable and controllable positive events produces a significant therapeutic impact on the well-being of institutionalized aged.

Another area of growing interest in which perceived control appears to play an important role is research on crowding. Rodin (1976) has suggested that one result of chronic crowded living is the development of a feeling that one is at the mercy of one's environment. Because high-density living appears to decrease an individual's opportunity to exert control over that environment, it is assumed that feelings of perceived uncontrollability are developed under such conditions. Individuals come to perceive that they cannot control the contingency between their responses and outcomes. This perception, according to Rodin (1976), appears to affect significantly the performance of those persons on a variety of tasks.

In a recent study, Langer and Saegert (1977) examined the aversive effects produced by a high-density condition in a naturalistic situation—shopping at a crowded supermarket. It was found that the aversiveness of this crowded condition could be significantly ameliorated by information that gave individuals cognitive control of the situation, in the form of data about the expected effects of crowding before exposure to it. There was an increase in complex task performance and better emotional responding produced by this cognitive control condition. It thus appears that perceived control may play a significant role in a very prevalent environmental condition—crowding. It should be pointed out, though, that this viewpoint is still very speculative and requires a great deal of additional research.

THE EFFECTS OF
NONVERIDICAL PERCEIVED CONTROL

In the majority of studies that demonstrated that the emotional impact of an aversive event appears to be a function of the degree to which a subject can control it, the stress-inducing effects were produced by the experimenter's arrangement of experimental events, with little attention being paid to the subject's belief or perception of control. There have been, however, some studies that specifically examined whether these stress-reducing effects are produced by merely creating the *belief* in subjects that they can control the amount of stress, even though they actually cannot. The first widely cited study that experimentally manipulated the *perception* of effective control over a stressor where there actually was none was conducted by Geer, Davison, and Gatchel (1970). There were two parts to the experiment. In the first part, all subjects were instructed to press a microswitch at the onset of a 6-second, painful electric shock, so that their reaction time could be measured. Following 10 such trials, half the subjects (perceived-control group) were told that by decreasing their reaction times during the second part of the experiment, which would also consist of 10 trials, they could reduce shock duration in half. These subjects were thus led to believe that they could actually exert control during the next 10 trials. The remaining subjects (no-perceived-control group) were simply told that the shock would be of shorter duration during the next 10 trials. All subjects, however, regardless of group assignment or reaction-time speed, received 3-second shocks on all 10 trials during this second part of the experiment. Thus, the actual amount of aversive stimulation was held constant across the two groups. A major finding of this study was that the no-perceived-control-group subjects had a significantly greater frequency of spontaneous skin conductance fluctuations during the second half of the study than did the perceived-control-group subjects. These results indicate that the perception of effective control, even if not veridical, can significantly decrease the electrodermal component of autonomic arousal produced by an aversive situation. As the reader will recall from the earlier reviewed learned-helplessness study by Gatchel and Proctor (1976b), the no-control learned-helplessness group in that study also demonstrated a greater frequency of spontaneous fluctuations. It therefore appears that actual control, or merely the perception of control even if it is not really present, can significantly ameliorate the effects of aversive stimulation. As we stated in discussing the results of our early study (Geer, Davison, & Gatchel, 1970):

Man creates his own gods to fill in gaps in his knowledge about a sometimes terrifying environment...creating at least an illusion of control which is presumably comforting. Perhaps the next best thing to being master of one's fate is being deluded into thinking he is [pp. 737–738].

There have been a number of other studies indicating that the nonveridical control over an impending event reduces the aversiveness of that event (Bowers, 1968; Glass & Singer, 1972; Kanfer & Seidner, 1973). In the investigation by Glass and Singer (1972), which showed the importance of perceived control over aversive stimulation as a means of ameliorating its effects, these investigators played to two groups of subjects a loud, aversive noise tap (108-db. noise level). The noise was unpredictable for both groups. One group was told it had potential control over the noise (perceived-control group); its members were informed that they could at any time terminate the noise for the remainder of the session by pressing a button attached to the side of the chair. In relating these instructions, the experimenters also stated that they would prefer the subject not to press the switch and to complete the entire experiment. Thus, subjects were given the feeling that even though the experimenter preferred that they not press the switch, they could do so and thus stop the experiment if they so desired. Few subjects used the switch to terminate the experiment. The other group of subjects received no instructions that gave them the perception of control.

In a number of experiments using the foregoing paradigm, Glass and Singer found that the unpredictable stressful noise perceived as controllable, compared to the no-perceived-control condition, caused no disruption of later performance measures on various tasks such as tolerance for postnoise frustration and proofreading effectiveness. There was also a tendency toward reduced physiological reactions to the initial loud noise bursts under the condition of perceived personal control. Thus, the results of their research suggest that the perception of control significantly reduces the aversive impact of unpredictable noise. In a recent study by Pennebaker, Burnam, Schaeffer, and Harper (1977), which used an unpredictable-noise task similar to that employed by Glass and Singer, it was found that lack of control over noise led to a subsequent report of a higher incidence of physical symptoms relative to a perceived-control situation.

THE RELATIONSHIP BETWEEN CONTROLLABILITY AND PREDICTABILITY

Many times, it is not clear whether the reduction in reported aversiveness of a stressor is due to personal control or merely to the increase in predictability of the occurrence of that stressor. This is because controllability is usually confounded with predictability. When individuals have control over a stimulus, they usually also have a greater ability to predict when that stimulus might occur. It is extremely difficult to make an uncontrollable stimulus as predictable as a controllable stimulus. There have been only a couple of studies designed to examine whether controllability adds anything significant to the ability to predict the onset of a stressful event. In a study by Reim, Glass, and Singer (1971), which employed the unpredictable-noise task used in the Glass and Singer (1972) studies, it was found that subjects in a predictable-only noise group and a perceived-control noise group performed much better on a proofreading task after their noise exposure in comparison to unpredictable-noise-group subjects. More importantly, subjects who perceived that they had control over the termination of the aversive noise demonstrated less automatic responding (peripheral vasoconstriction) than subjects in either the predictable-noise or unpredictable-noise conditions. Thus, at least in terms of physiological responding, there appear to be different consequences produced by predictability and controllability.

In another study exploring this distinction, Geer and Maisel (1972) employed three groups of subjects: (1) a perceived-control group, which could escape an aversive stimulus (photographs of dead bodies) by pressing a button; (2) a predictability group, which knew when and for how long the photographs would be presented but could not actively control when they would be terminated; (3) a no-control, no-predictability group, which could neither control nor predict the occurrence of the aversive stimuli. Throughout the experiment, electrodermal responding was recorded. Results of this experiment indicated that subjects in the perceived-control group demonstrated lower electrodermal reactivity (i.e., less electrodermal arousal) to the aversive stimuli than subjects in the other two groups. Thus, these results again suggest that, at least with respect to the physiological component of behavior, perceived control appears to be more than just predictability. However, as Geer and Maisel (1972) and, more recently, Seligman (1975) indicate, a number of additional studies need to be conducted in order to differentiate more precisely between these two factors and to explicate better the different mechanisms underlying them.

INDIVIDUAL DIFFERENCES
AND PERCEIVED CONTROL

Averill (1973) has delineated three major forms of personal control: (1) behavioral, which involves some direct action on the environment; (2) cognitive, which involves the interpretation of events; and (3) decisional, which involves having a choice among various alternative courses of action. Each type can be beneficial in alleviating the aversive effects of a stressor, although Averill (1973) notes that the specific relationships are quite complex and depend on the situation as well as the person. In this section, I would like to review some "person" variables that appear to affect the impact of perceived controllability/uncontrollability significantly.

One personality variable that appears to determine partially the effects of perceived controllability/uncontrollability is *locus of control*. Locus of control is a personality construct originally hypothesized by Rotter (1966). Rotter holds that the effects of reinforcement on behavior partially depend on whether individuals habitually perceive events as contingent on their behavior or independent of it. The Internal–External Locus of Control Scale was developed for social psychology research to measure the degree to which individuals feel they can control their environments. At one end of the personality dimension are internal locus of control subjects, who perceive rewards as being contingent on their own behavior. They have a high degree of perceived personal control. At the opposite pole are external locus of control subjects, who perceive rewards as independent of their behavior— that is, due to chance. This locus of control construct has been found to differentiate significantly between subjects on a variety of performance tasks (e.g., Rotter, 1966).

In a learned-helplessness study by Hiroto (1974), half the subjects in each experimental group were internal locus of control subjects; the other half were external locus of control subjects. Hiroto found that external locus of control subjects who were exposed to inescapable noise became helpless, as measured on a performance task, more easily than internals exposed to the same condition. Thus, this personality characteristic signficantly affects the degree to which perceived uncontrollability impairs performance.

Another personality-type factor that has been demonstrated to affect the impact of perceived controllability/uncontrollability is the *coronary-prone behavior pattern* (Friedman & Rosenman, 1974). The Type A coronary-prone behavior pattern consists of such attributes as a competitive and achievement-directed orientation, a great sense of time urgency, and the demonstration of hostility in response to inappropriate environmental precipitation. Type B behavior consists of attributes opposite to these. It has been suggested by Friedman and Rosenman (1974) that Pattern A behavior is associated with the occurrence of coronary heart disease.

Glass (1977) has provided an excellent review of recent research on the effects of Pattern A behavior on performance, including performance on tasks perceived as controllable or uncontrollable. In summarizing a number of studies conducted in his laboratory, Glass found that Pattern A behavior initially *enhanced* performance in response to uncontrollable stress. This was interpreted as a general strategy by Type A subjects to cope with uncontrollable stress by trying to assert control over a situation that threatens them with uncontrollability. After prolonged exposure to uncontrollable stress, however, there is a dramatic decrement in efforts at control. Type A subjects eventually demonstrate more learned-helplessness behavior than

Type B subjects. It should be noted that this relationship is somewhat complicated by another factor—the salience of the environmental cues that signify the uncontrollable nature of the stress. As Glass (1977) found, Type A subjects demonstrate excessive helplessness only under conditions of high salience. The reader is referred to Glass (1977) for a more detailed discussion of this salience factor.

Thus, the foregoing research demonstrates the importance of the subject's A–B classification on both the short- and long-term impact of perceived lack of control. Future research should further elucidate the exact nature of this relationship.

THE ROLE OF PERCEIVED CONTROLLABILITY IN THE TREATMENT OF ANXIETY

On the basis of the preceding review, there is little doubt that the perception of control, whether it be veridical or not, can significantly reduce the impact of stressful events. In the next section, I review some therapy-evaluation research conducted in my laboratory during the past few years that demonstrates the significant role that perceived controllability has in reducing anxiety. In this research, we have found the important impact that the *placebo effect* has in eliminating anxiety. Before reviewing this research in detail, a brief discussion of the placebo effect will familiarize the reader with this phenomenon and will indicate how perceived personal control appears to be a significant psychological factor contributing to the effect.

The placebo effect was originally shown to be an important factor in medical research when it was found that inert chemical drugs, which had no direct effect upon physical events underlying various medical disorders, were often found to produce symptom reduction. An extensive literature on the placebo effect in medicine undeniably demonstrates that a patient's belief that a prescribed medication is active, even if it is in fact chemically inert, often leads to significant symptom reduction (Honigfeld, 1964; Shapiro, 1971). Indeed, as Shapiro (1959) notes: "The history of medical treatment until relatively recently is the history of the placebo effect [p. 303]." Even response to a chemically active drug depends to some degree on a belief in the drug's action and faith in the doctor prescribing it.

The placebo effect has also been found to be an active ingredient in psychotherapy (e.g., Wilkens, 1973), especially when anxiety is being treated (Shapiro, 1971). As Shapiro (1971) indicates, the effect appears to be a "multidetermined phenomenon" that is not yet completely understood. One important psychological factor contributing to the placebo effect that has been shown to affect the outcome of psychotherapy is generalized expectancy of improvement (Wilkens, 1973). This factor has also been implicated to be important in analogue therapy research (Borkovec, 1973).

How does perceived control relate to the placebo effect? Merely the expectancy or belief that a treatment is going to be therapeutic and effective, that it is going to provide a means of coping with a stressful symptom or array of symptoms, will often lead to that very state of affairs—symptom reduction. People suffering from a significant amount of anxiety often feel at the mercy of this aversive emotional state, with no effective means of alleviating or personally controlling it. One of the chief attractions of tranquilizers, besides the reduction of the physiological components of anxiety, is the comforting perception they allow the individual that he or she now has a means of actively controlling the anxiety—by ingesting a drug.

This dimension of perceived controllability has been suggested by Seligman (1975) to be an active ingredient in systematic desensitization, which is a very effective form of behavior therapy used in the treatment of anxiety. For example, muscle relaxation, which is a major component of systematic desensitization, works best when it is presented as a voluntary and active process, leading individuals to believe they can actively control anxiety. In one study, Goldfried and Trier (1974) demonstrated the effectiveness of muscular relaxation training in reducing anxiety when presented as an active self-control coping skill. This self-control concept has recently been reviewed as an important component in behavior therapy techniques (e.g., Goldfried & Merbaum, 1973; Mahoney, 1976). Goldfried and Trier found that subjects who were given relaxation training presented as an active coping skill over which they exerted personal control demonstrated a significantly greater reduction in anxiety than subjects who were given identical training presented as an "automatic" procedure for passively reducing anxiety.

Of course, the concept of personal control is not the entire reason why systematic desensitization and relaxation work. Indeed, the techniques are still effective when relaxation is passively induced. There is little doubt, however, that the cognitive factor of controllability plays a significant role in the anxiety-reduction process.

Seligman (1975) has also reviewed some research on drug-induced relaxation that suggests the importance of perceived controllability. Because certain patients encounter difficulty learning how to relax effectively, a number of clinicians have attempted to induce relaxation by means of chemical muscle relaxants such as the drug *methohexitone*. However, it is generally found that such drug-induced relaxation by itself is not effective. Patients appear to need a sense of personal control in accomplishing the relaxation. In summarizing these studies, Seligman (1975) concludes: "Relaxation by itself does not inhibit anxiety as much as relaxation that an individual produces himself [p. 130]."

Seligman (1975) goes on to indicate that not only actual control but also perceived control may play an important role in a technique such as systematic desensitization:

> Phobics often panic at the mere thought of the phobic object or an anxiety-provoking situation. This helplessness-induced panic precludes their using any available coping response. The perception of potential control, which arises once the subject has learned that he can relax in the presence of the phobic object, prevents panic. Consider a client who has come to a behavior therapist for treatment of a phobia: After initial discussion the therapist decides to use systematic desensitization and explains to the client that he intends to use a proven technique that will enable him to master his fear and anxiety. A hierarchy is constructed and the client begins to work his way up; at every stage of the hierarchy the client's expectancy of gain is confirmed, that is, he is no longer afraid or anxious. As time goes on the client no longer panics at the sight of the phobic stimulus, but expects to be able to control fear. For the first time in his life the phobic has at his disposal the ability to short-circuit anticipatory panic and time to marshal his coping resources. He confirms this belief by successfully applying his newly learned mastery to realistic situations. So believing that one can control fear may reduce panic and allow more effective coping [p. 131].

Thus, the foregoing clinical observation suggests that perceived controllability plays an important role in therapy directed at anxiety reduction. It is this component that is an important factor contributing to the placebo effect in certain instances. I next review some recent research indicating the role that perceived control plays in biofeedback therapy directed at the treatment of fear and anxiety.

BIOFEEDBACK AND THE MODIFICATION OF FEAR AND ANXIETY

Gatchel and Proctor (1976a) examined whether learned control of heart-rate deceleration could be employed as a therapeutic strategy to alleviate anxiety in speech-anxious subjects. It was thought that it might prove to be a practical method for reducing aversive emotional responding through inhibition of sympathetic components of the stress response. Learning theorists such as Mowrer (1947) have suggested that a basic component of the fear response is autonomic activation. Indeed, a major goal of a number of therapies—such as progressive relaxation therapy (Jacobson, 1938), autogenic training (Schultze & Luthe, 1959), and systematic desensitization (Wolpe, 1958), which were developed to eliminate anxiety and tension states—is the production of a low state of sympathetic arousal that competes against the stress response and accompanying elevated arousal level. Until the Gatchel and Proctor (1976a) study, however, there was no controlled research demonstrating that anxiety can be directly restrained through inhibition of specific components of sympathetic arousal.

There were a number of factors that prompted Gatchel and Proctor (1976a) to focus on learned control of heart-rate slowing. First of all, Lang, Melamed, and Hart (1970) had shown that those individuals who demonstrated the steepest heart-rate habituation gradient gained the greatest profit from systematic desensitization. It was therefore thought that training subjects to slow heart rate might be a more direct and powerful tool for bringing about fear reduction. Second, it had been casually observed that subjects undergoing heart-rate biofeedback training often report feeling calm and relaxed at the end of heart-rate-slowing sessions, but they frequently report feeling anxious and tense at the end of speeding sessions (e.g., Headrick, Feather, & Wells, 1971). In a more systematic examination of this subjective phenomenon, Hatch (1977) recently completed a study in my laboratory in which he measured transitory anxiety state, with the State–Trait Anxiety Inventory (STAI) (Spielberger, Gorsuch, & Lushene, 1970), of subjects immediately before and again immediately following each of four separate heart-rate-control sessions. A comparison of STAI scores before and after the four slowing sessions indicated a slight decrease in perceived state anxiety. This change, however, was not statistically significant. For the speeding sessions, though, there was a large and statistically very significant increase in mean state anxiety scores following heart-rate-speeding performance. Thus, although a significant reduction in state anxiety was not found with heart-rate slowing, the results obtained for the heart-rate-speeding situation indicate that the direct manipulation of a physiological component (heart rate) of anxiety generalizes to a self-report component (STAI) of anxiety as well. It suggests that heart-rate restraint, through the use of biofeedback training, might be useful in inhibiting situational anxiety states.

In passing, it should be pointed out that speech anxiety was chosen as the target behavior in my research program for two major reasons. The primary reason was that this behavior occurs with great frequency in the general population and, therefore, is a highly relevant clinical concern. Data collected from the introductory psychology class at the University of Texas at Arlington during the years 1974 and 1975 ($N = 731$) indicated that 33% of the students experienced much fear, very much fear, or terror when speaking before a group, as assessed by the Fear Survey Schedule (Geer, 1965). A large population is therefore available on the basis of this usual fear survey criterion. This type of social anxiety is also generally more disruptive to daily functioning, and of greater concern to the individual, than the small-animal fears used as target behaviors in the great majority of past analogue therapy research that has been conducted. For example, in an analysis of patient responses to the Fear Survey Schedule conducted by Lawlis (1971), fear of small animals emerged as a minor factor, whereas a general social anxiety factor accounted for 87.3% of the variance. The second major reason for use of this target behavior is that it has been found to be uninfluenced by demand characteristics and suggestions of improvement, and it involves a strong physiological arousal component that fails to habituate rapidly (Borkovec, Stone, O'Brien, & Kaloupek, 1974). In contrast, the potent influence of demand characteristics in analogue studies employing small-animal fears, such as snake phobia, has been well documented (cf. Borkovec, 1973). These findings indicate that past experiments that employed analogue snake phobics may not permit valid cause-and-effect conclusions concerning the effectiveness of the therapeutic procedures utilized.

Results of the biofeedback study conducted by Gatchel and Proctor (1976a) demonstrated that learning to control heart-rate deceleration led to a significant reduction in self-report, physiological (heart rate and skin conductance level), and overt signs of anxiety in speech-anxious subjects, relative to a no-heart-rate-control condition. This was the first conclusive report in the scientific literature demonstrating that anxiety can be effectively inhibited through inhibition of the heart-rate component of sympathetic arousal. Case studies reported by Blanchard (1977), Blanchard and Abel (1976), and Gatchel (1977) have also demonstrated the therapeutic effectiveness of a heart-rate biofeedback procedure in reducing anxiety.

As a therapeutic technique, the heart-rate biofeedback training procedure employed in the foregoing studies by Gatchel and colleagues was viewed as a self-control skill for effectively coping with anxiety. As indicated earlier, this self-control concept has recently been reviewed as an important component in behavior therapy techniques (e.g., Goldfried & Merbaum, 1973; Mahoney, 1976). As a follow-up to the Gatchel and Proctor (1976a) study, an experiment by Gatchel, Hatch, Watson, Smith, and Gaas (1977a) investigated whether the muscle relaxation self-control technique used by Goldfried and Trier (1974) was as effective as the heart-rate biofeedback technique in bringing about fear reduction. Because heart rate is strongly associated with fear (Lang, Rice, & Sternbach, 1972), the use of learned control over this visceral response may be a more direct and powerful tool for reducing anxiety than the traditional muscular relaxation technique. This study directly compared the therapeutic effectiveness of these two techniques in reducing anxiety in speech-anxious subjects. In addition, a combined muscle relaxation/biofeedback treatment group was included in order to assess whether a combination of the two techniques produces greater therapeutic improvement than each separately administered technique. All three treatment groups were compared to a false-biofeedback control group. Members of this placebo group were led to believe that they were successfully learning to decrease heart rate voluntarily, which would later serve as an effective means of alleviating anxiety.

Results of this investigation indicated that all four experimental groups showed a decrease in the self-report component of public-speaking anxiety as the result of the treatment they received. There were no significant differences among the four groups. The fact that the false-biofeedback placebo group demonstrated as much improvement as the active treatment groups indicates that this placebo condition has a very powerful therapeutic impact. As mentioned previously, therapeutic expectancy/demand characteristics have been shown to be significant factors in analogue therapy research (cf. Borkovec, 1973). The great amount of publicity and exaggereated accounts of "cure-all" biofeedback techniques, which routinely appear in the news media, appear to make a false-biofeedback group an extremely powerful placebo condition because of the significant amount of therapeutic expectancy produced by this publicity. The perception, even if nonveridical, that one can now control a physiological response that is a major component of a fear response may play an extremely important role in eliminating that fear.

Another analogue therapy study has also demonstrated the significant impact of false-biofeedback training. Prigatano and Johnson (1972) assessed the effectiveness of learned control of heart-rate variability in treating college students who had a fear of spiders, comparing a veridical-biofeedback group to a false-biofeedback group. It was found that there was a significant amount of improvement in posttreatment approach behavior among the biofeedback-group subjects. This group, however, did not differ from the false-biofeedback subjects. Thus, again, a false-biofeedback condition produced some significant fear reduction. Indeed, Stroebel and Glueck (1973) had earlier implicated the importance of placebo factors in biofeedback treatment.

Although there were no significant differences found among groups for the self-report measure of anxiety in the Gatchel et al. (1977a) study, an evaluation of the physiological indices yielded some interestingly different findings. Results indicated that the three treatment groups showed significantly less heart-rate and skin conductance level increases during the posttreatment assessment of anxiety in comparison to the false-biofeedback control group. Moreover, among the three treatment groups, the combined relaxation/biofeedback group demonstrated the greatest amount of decrease in responding. In viewing these results, the intriguing question that arises is: What component(s) is the most valid and clinically useful measure of anxiety reduction? Of course, this is not a novel or recent concern. Over the years, there has been a great deal of interest and attention directed at the empirical fact that the component measures of behavior are not always highly correlated. Lang (1977) has been most articulate in suggesting that a construct, such as fear, is best considered to involve any or all of these separate but interacting response groups. Cognition, overt motor behavior, and physiological responses may be independently influenced by different situational factors at different points in time. They may even obey different learning principles. At the same time, however, due to their potential interaction, change in one behavioral component may affect subsequent change in responses of the other components. Moreover, individuals differ in their learning history associated with each response group, which results in individual differences in the intensity and functional importance of the components in reaction to a particular feared stimulus.

In passing, it should also be noted that some data reviewed by Hodgson and Rachman (1974) shed light on these findings of a low relationship between response systems. These investigators have proposed that *level of demand* is an important factor that affects the degree of discordance among the different response systems. They summarized a study by Miller and Bernstein (1972) that demonstrated that avoidance behavior is partially a function of this demand factor. In this study, claustrophobics were requested to remain in a darkened chamber while heart rate and respiration were recorded. According to Miller and Bernstein, in a low-demand condition, in which subjects were under no pressure to remain in the chamber longer than "a point at which you would usually want to leave the situation if it happened to you in your daily life [p. 207]," correlations were relatively high between time in chamber and self-reported anxiety (–.42), heart rate (–.56), and respiration rate (–.51). However, under high-demand conditions, in which subjects were instructed to remain in the chamber for 10 minutes and were told, "If you should become fearful please control it as best you can so that you can remain for this full period [p. 207]," correlations between systems dropped to zero (.00, .00, and .07, respectively). Thus, concordance between response systems is greater under low-demand conditions; high levels of demand produce discordance between systems. In explaining the results of discordance under high-demand conditions, Hodgson and Rachman (1974) note that it appears that "a highly motivated subject is able to control a tendency towards flight in spite of autonomic and experiential signs of fear [p. 321]."

In the earlier reviewed studies by Gatchel and colleagues, the false-biofeedback-group condition can be viewed as a high-demand condition. By subjects being told that the biofeedback technique was effective in reducing anxiety, it was likely that they may have become highly motivated to force themselves to control their anxiety even though physiological cues were still present. This may have contributed to the resultant discordance among response systems. These results again illustrate that the use of one measure alone to assess a construct such as anxiety is not recommended, because it can lead to erroneous conclusions. In assessing results, the response topography of the interaction of these various behaviors needs to be evaluated in the context of a specifically defined situation.

A major method of assessing the relative importance of the various components would be the determination of both the short-term *and* long-term effects on these components produced by a particular treatment modality. The study by Gatchel et al. (1977a) assessed only short-term improvement, measured immediately after therapy administration. It is of great importance to examine whether the improvement demonstrated by the various groups is maintained when speech anxiety is assessed at a later time and whether it generalizes to other speech situations dissimilar to that in which the anxiety assessment procedure was first conducted. One would expect that a truly effective and active therapeutic procedure would produce long-lasting clinical improvement that would maintain its strength and effectiveness over time and when applied to different situations. A recently completed study by Gatchel, Hatch, Maynard, Turns, and Taunton-Blackwood (1979) investigated these questions in a study comparing three groups: the combined muscle relaxation/biofeedback group, which was found to produce the greatest reduction in physiological responding in the earlier study; the false-biofeedback control group, which produced clinically significant reductions in speech anxiety in the earlier study; a systematic desensitization group, which was included in the study because—even though the active muscular relaxation group was demonstrated to produce therapeutic improvement greater than an attention-placebo group by Goldfried and Trier (1974)—no study had assessed whether the muscular relaxation technique is as effective as the standard systematic desensitization procedure.

Results of this study indicated that, again, the false-biofeedback placebo group demonstrated as much reduction in self-reported speech anxiety as the two treatment groups. Physiologically, it did not demonstrate as much reduction. One month later, however, when subjects were again tested for speech anxiety in a different speaking situation (a larger room with an audience of six individuals, rather than the smaller room with an audience of two observers used in the earlier speech evaluation), the self-report improvement was maintained in all groups including the false-biofeedback group. Thus, the improvement effects do not appear to be illusory or short-lived. Indeed, in an earlier study, Paul (1967) reported maintenance of gains over 2 years for treatment groups in his therapy-evaluation study, including an "attention-placebo" group. In the Paul study, however, the "attention-placebo" group did not improve as much as the desensitization group. In our study, though, the false-biofeedback group did improve as much as the active treatment groups. The perception by this group that they had active control over an anxiety-competing response—heart-rate deceleration—appears to have influenced significantly their self-report of anxiety.

Research is continuing in my laboratory on the impact of biofeedback and false-biofeedback placebo procedures in reducing anxiety. Individual differences in response to these techniques are being examined in order to more reliably predict who will benefit most from the procedures. This research should provide further insight into the mechanisms underlying the biofeedback technique, as well as those involved in the perceived-control/placebo phenomenon.

CONCLUSIONS AND SUMMARY

Evidence has been reviewed indicating that individuals react differently to stressful events that they perceive can be personally controlled than to those perceived not in their control. This dimension of perceived controllability/uncontrollability of a stressor has been shown to affect significantly self-report, overt motor, and physiological components of behavior. The effects of aversive stimulation are pronounced under conditions of uncontrollability; perceived controllability, even if nonveridical, can significantly reduce these debilitating effects. There are also at least two individual-difference variables that can affect the impact of perceived controllability/uncontrollability: internal–external locus of control, and coronary-prone personality characteristics.

This dimension of perceived controllability/uncontrollability appears to be a significant factor contributing to the placebo effect in psychotherapy. The placebo effect has been shown to be an active ingredient in psychotherapy, especially when anxiety is being treated. Recently, it has been shown to play a significant role in biofeedback therapy directed at the treatment of fear and anxiety. The perception, even if nonveridical, that one can control a physiological response that is a major component of a fear response appears to play an important role in eliminating certain behavioral components of that fear. It was pointed out that a construct such as fear or anxiety involves any or all of three separate but interacting response groups—cognition, overt motor behavior, and physiological responding—which may be independently influenced by different situational factors at different points in time. The placebo factor in biofeedback therapy appears to exert its effect on the self-report component of behavior. It was found that although subjects in a false-biofeedback placebo treatment group did not display as much of a reduction in physiological responding as did the other treatment groups, their self-report component of anxiety did show a significant reduction. This clinical improvement was not illusory or short-lived. Subjects in this placebo condition maintained their improvement when tested at a later time and in a different situation. These results clearly demonstrate the important role that perceived-control placebo factors play in producing and maintaining fear reduction.

ACKNOWLEDGMENT

The writing of this paper was supported in part by a grant to the author from the National Heart, Lung, and Blood Institute (Grant No. NIH HL21426-01).

REFERENCES

Averill, J. R. Personal control over aversive stimuli and its relationship to stress. *Psychological Bulletin*, 1973, *80*, 286–303.

Bettelheim, B. Individual and mass behavior in extreme situations. *Journal of Abnormal and Social Psychology*, 1943, *38*, 417–452.

Blanchard, E. Biofeedback and the modificaton of cardiovascular dysfunctions. In R. J. Gatchel & K. P. Price (Eds.), *Clinical applications of biofeedback: Appraisal and status*. New York: Biomonitoring Application, 1977, Catalog #MV-6.

Blanchard, E. B., & Abel, G. G. An experimental case study of the biofeedback treatment of a rape-induced psychological cardiovascular disorder. *Behavior Therapy*, 1976, *7*, 113–119.

Borkovec, T. D. The role of expectancy and physiological feedback in fear reduction: A review with special reference to subject characteristics. *Behavior Therapy*, 1973, *4*, 491–505.

Borkovec, T. D., Stone, N. M., O'Brien, G. T., & Kaloupek, D. G. Evaluation of a clinically relevant target behavior for analogue outcome research. *Behavior Therapy*, 1974, *5*, 503–513.

Bowers, K. Pain, anxicty, and perceived control. *Journal of Consulting and Clinical Psychology*, 1968, *32*, 596–602.

Brady, J. V., Porter, R. W., Conrad, D. G., & Mason, J. W. Avoidance behavior and the development of gastroduodenal ulcers. *Journal of Experimental Analysis of Behavior*, 1958, *1*, 69–72.

Champion, R. A. Studies of experimentally induced disturbances. *Australian Journal of Psychology*, 1950, *2*, 90–99.

Cofer, C. N., & Appley, M. A. *Motivation: Theory and research*. New York: Wiley, 1964.

Corah, N. L., & Boffa, J. Perceived control, self-observation, and response to aversive stimulation. *Journal of Personality and Social Psychology*, 1970, *16*, 1–4.

Friedman, M., & Rosenman, R. H. *Type A behavior and your heart*. Ne York: Knopf, 1974.

Gatchel, R. J. The therapeutic effectiveness of voluntary heart rate control in reducing anxiety: A case report. *Journal of Consulting and Clinical Psychology*, 1977, *45*, 689–691.

Gatchel, R. J., Hatch, J. P., Maynard, A., Turns, R., & Taunton-Blackwood, A. Comparative effectiveness of biofeedback, false-biofeedback, and systematic desensitization in reducing speech anxiety: Short- and long-term results. *Journal of Consulting and Clinical Psychology*, 1979, *47*, 620–622.

Gatchel, R. J., Hatch, J. P., Watson, P. J., Smith, D., & Gaas, E. Comparative effectiveness of voluntary heart-rate control and muscular relaxation as active coping skills for reducing speech anxiety. *Journal of Consulting and Clinical Psychology*, 1977, *45*, 1093–1100. (a)

Gatchel, R. J., McKinney, M. E., & Koebernick, L. F. Learned helplessness, depression, and physiological responding. *Psychophysiology*, 1977, *14*, 25–31. (b)

Gatchel, R. J., Paulus, P. B., & Maples, C. W. Learned helplessness and self-reported affect. *Journal of Abnormal Psychology*, 1975, *84*, 732–734.

Gatchel, R. J., & Proctor, J. D. Effectiveness of voluntary heart rate control in reducing speech anxiety. *Journal of Consulting and Clinical Psychology*, 1976, *44*, 381–389. (a)

Gatchel, R. J., & Proctor, J. D. Physiological correlates of learned helplessness in man. *Journal of Abnormal Psychology*, 1976, *85*, 27–34. (b)

Geer, J. H. The development of a scale to measure fear. *Behavior Research and Therapy*, 1965, *3*, 45–53.

Geer, J. H., Davison, G. C., & Gatchel, R. J. Reduction of stress in humans through nonveridical perceived control of aversive stimulation. *Journal of Personality and Social Psychology*, 1970, *16*, 731–738.

Geer, J. H., & Maisel, E. Evaluating the effects of the prediction–control confound. *Journal of Personality and Social Psychology*, 1972, *23*, 314–319.

Glass, D. C. Stress, behavior patterns, and coronary disease. *American Scientist*, 1977, *65*, 177–187.

Glass, D. C., & Singer, J. E. *Urban stress.* New York: Academic Press, 1972.

Goldfried, M. R., & Merbaum, M. (Eds.). *Behavior change through self-control.* New York: Holt, Rinehart & Winston, 1973.

Goldfried, M. R., & Trier, C. S. Effectiveness of relaxation as an active coping skill. *Journal of Abnormal Psychology,* 1974, *83,* 348–355.

Haggard, E. A. Experimental studies in affective processes: I. Some effects of cognitive structure and active participation on certain autonomic reactions during and following experimentally induced stress. *Journal of Experimental Psychology,* 1943, *33,* 257–284.

Hatch, J. P. *The effects of biofeedback schedules on the operant modification of human heart rate.* Unpublishd doctoral dissertation, University of Texas at Arlington, 1977.

Headrick, M. W., Feather, B. W., & Wells, D. T. Unidirectional and large magnitude heart rate changes with augmented sensory feedback. *Psychophysiology,* 1971, *8,* 132–142.

Hiroto, D. S. Learned helplessness and locus of control. *Journal of Experimental Psychology,* 1974, *102,* 187–193.

Hodgson, R., & Rachman, S. II. Desynchrony in measures of fear. *Behavior Research and Therapy,* 1974, *12,* 319–326.

Hokanson, J. E., DeGood, D. E., Forrest, M. S., & Brittain, T. M. Availability of avoidance behaviors in modulating vascular-stress responses. *Journal of Personality and Social Psychology,* 1971, *19,* 60–68.

Honigfeld, G. Non-specific factors in treatment. I. Review of placebo reactions and placebo reactors. *Diseases of the Nervous System,* 1964, *25,* 145–156.

Jacobson, E. *Progressive relaxation.* Chicago: University of Chicago Press, 1938.

Janis, I. L. *Psychological stress.* New York: Wiley, 1958.

Janis, I. L., & Leventhal, H. Human reactions to stress. In E. Borgatta & W. Lambert (Eds.), *Handbook of personality theory and research.* Skokie, Ill.: Rand McNally, 1968.

Kanfer, R., & Seidner, M. Self-control: Factor enhancing tolerance of noxious stimulation. *Journal of Personality and Social Psychology,* 1973, *25,* 381–389.

Kilpatrick, D. G. Differential responsiveness of two electrodermal indices to psychological stress and performance of a complex cognitive task. *Psychophysiology,* 1971, *9,* 218–226.

Lang, P. J. The psychophysiology of anxiety. In H. Akiskal (Ed.), *Psychiatric diagnosis: Exploration of biological criteria.* New York: Spectrum, 1977.

Lang, P. J., Melamed, B. G., & Hart, J. A psychophysiological analysis of fear modification using an automated desensitization procedure. *Journal of Abnormal Psychology,* 1970, *76,* 220–234.

Lang, P. J., Rice, D. C., & Sternbach, R. A. Psychophysiology of emotion. In N. Greenfield & R. Sternbach (Eds.), *Handbook of psychophysiology.* New York: Holt, Rinehart & Winston, 1972.

Langer, E. J., Janis, I. L., & Wolfer, J. A. Reduction of psychological stress in surgical patients. *Journal of Experimental Social Psychology,* 1975, *11,* 155–165.

Langer, E. J., & Rodin, J. The effects of choice and enhanced personal responsibility for the aged: A field experiment in an institutional setting. *Journal of Personality and Social Psychology,* 1976, *34,* 191–198.

Langer, E. J., & Saegert, S. Crowding and cognitive control. *Journal of Personality and Social Psychology,* 1977, *35,* 175–182.

Lawlis, G. F. Response styles of a patient population in the Fear Survey Schedule. *Behavior Research and Therapy,* 1971, *9,* 95–102.

Lazarus, R. S. *Psychological stress and the coping process.* New York: McGraw-Hill, 1966.

Lefcourt, H. M. The function of the illusions of control and freedom. *American Psychologist,* 1973, *28,* 417–425.

Levis, D. J. Learned helplessness: A reply and alternative S–R interpretation. *Journal of Experimental Psychology: General,* 1976, *105,* 47–65.

Mahoney, M. J. *Cognition and behavior modification.* Cambridge, Mass.: Ballinger, 1976.

Miller, B. V., & Bernstein, D. A. Instructional demand in a behavioral avoidance test for claustrophobic fears. *Journal of Abnormal Psychology,* 1972, *80,* 206–210.

Miller, W. R., & Seligman, M. E. P. Depression and learned helplessness in man. *Journal of Abnormal Psychology,* 1975, *84,* 228–238.

Mowrer, O. H. On the dual nature of learning: A re-interpretation of "conditioning" and "problem-solving." *Harvard Educational Review,* 1947, *17,* 102–148.

Mowrer, O. H., & Viek, P. An experimental analogue of fear from a sense of helplessness. *Journal of Abnormal and Social Psychology,* 1948, *43,* 193–200.

Overmier, J. B., & Seligman, M. E. P. Effects of inescapable shock upon subsequent escape and avoidance responding. *Journal of Comparative and Physiological Psychology,* 1967, *63,* 28–33.

Paul, G. L. Insight versus desensitization in psychotherapy two years after termination. *Journal of Consulting Psychology,* 1967, *31,* 333 348.

Pennebaker, J. W., Burnam, M. A., Schaeffer, M. A., & Harper, D. C. Lack of control as a determinant of perceived physical symptoms. *Journal of Personality and Social Psychology,* 1977, *35,* 167–174.

Price, K. P. The pathological effects in rats of predictable and unpredictable shock. *Psychological Reports,* 1972, *30,* 419–426.

Prigatano, G. P., & Johnson, H. J. *Biofeedback control of heart rate variability to phobic stimuli: A new approach to treating spider phobia.* Paper presented at the meeting of the American Psychological Association, Honolulu, September 1972.

Reim, B., Glass, D. C., & Singer, J. E. Behavioral consequences of exposure to uncontrollable and unpredictable noise. *Journal of Applied Social Psychology,* 1971, *1,* 44–56.

Richter, C. P. On the phenomenon of sudden death in animals and man. *Psychosomatic Medicine,* 1957, *19,* 191–198.

Rodin, J. Density, perceived choice and response to controllable and uncontrollable outcomes. *Journal of Experimental Social Psychology,* 1976, *12,* 564–578.

Rotter, J. B. Generalized expectancies for internal versus external control of reinforcement. *Psychological Monographs,* 1966, *80 (#1, Whole No. 609).*

Schultze, J. H., & Luthe, W. *Autogenic training: A psycho-physiologic approach in psychotherapy.* New York: Grune & Stratton, 1959.

Schulz, R. Effects of control and predictability on the physical and psychological well-being of the institutionalized aged. *Journal of Personality and Social Psychology,* 1976, *33,* 563–573.

Schulz, R., & Aderman, D. Effect of residential change on the temporal distance of terminal cancer patients. *Omega: Journal of Death and Dying,* 1973, *4,* 157–162.

Schwartz, G. E. *Meditation as an altered state of consciousness: Current findings on stress reactivity, attentional flexibility, and creativity.* Paper presented at the 82nd Annual Convention of the American Psychological Association, New Orleans, September 1974.

Seligman, M. E. P. *Helplessness.* San Francisco: W. H. Freeman, 1975.

Seligman, M. E. P., & Maier, S. F. Failure to escape traumatic shock. *Journal of Experimental Psychology,* 1967, *74,* 1–9.

Shapiro, A. K. The placebo effect in the history of medical treatment—implications for psychiatry. *American Journal of Psychiatry,* 1959, *116,* 298–304.

Shapiro, A. K. Placebo effects in medicine, psychotherapy, and psychoanalysis. In A. E. Bergen & S. L. Garfield (Eds.), *Handbook of psychotherapy and behavior change.* New York: Wiley, 1971.

Spielberger, C., Gorsuch, R., & Lushene, R. *State–Trait Anxiety Inventory Manual.* Palo Alto, Calif.: Consulting Psychologists Press, 1970.

Staub, E., Tursky, B., & Schwartz, G. E. Self-control and predictability: Their effects on reactions to aversive stimulation. *Journal of Personality and Social Psychology,* 1971, *18,* 157–162.

Stroebel, C. F., & Glueck, B. C. Biofeedback treatment in medicine and psychiatry: An ultimate placebo? In L. Birk (Ed.), *Biofeedback: Behavioral medicine.* New York: Grune & Stratton, 1973.

Weiss, J. M. Effects of coping responses on stress. *Journal of Comparative and Physiological Psychology,* 1968, *65,* 251–260.

Weiss, J. M. Effects of coping behavior with and without feedback signal on stress pathology in rats. *Journal of Comparative and Physiological Psychology,* 1971, *77,* 22–30.

Wilkens, W. Expectancy of therapeutic gain: An empirical and conceptual critique. *Journal of Consulting and Clinical Psychology,* 1973, *40,* 69–77.

Wolpe, J. *Psychotherapy and reciprocal inhibitions.* Palo Alto, Calif.: Stanford University Press, 1958.

Zuckerman, M., & Lubin, B. *Manual for the Multiple Affect Adjective Check List.* San Diego, Calif.: Education and Industrial Testing Service, 1965.

2 A Model of Life Crisis, Control, and Health Outcomes: Cardiac Rehabilitation and Relocation of the Elderly

David S. Krantz
Uniformed Services University of the Health Sciences

Richard Schulz
Institute on Aging, Portland State University

Medical and psychological investigators generally acknowledge that stressful life events may affect the incidence and outcomes of physical illness. One popular approach to the stress-illness problem has been to consider a range of recent life changes and illness susceptibility (Holmes & Rahe, 1967). A second approach focuses more intensively on single life events or crises and on the psychosocial variables that can mediate health-related outcomes. However, based on available evidence, it is fair to conclude that there is probably *not* a one-to-one relationship between the occurrence of specific life events and the incidence of physical illness. Rather, to better understand the links between life stress and illness, one must consider the individual's interpretation of these events and the success and failure of various psychological coping mechanisms (e.g., Lazarus, 1976). In particular, the concepts of uncontrollability and helplessness have figured prominently in psychosomatic research, with several investigators proposing that a state of helplessness or hopelessness is a general precursor of physical and psychic diseases (Engel, 1968; Seligman, 1975).

The General Model

In the present chapter our aim is to offer an integrative view of reactions to life crises based on the concepts of control and predictability. We make the assumption that responses to particular life events are mediated by the kinds of cognitive processes that operate in experimental research on stress. Simply put, we would expect that stressful life events and crises will generally have less of a negative impact on health to the extent that they are perceived to be predictable and/or controllable. Although this assumption may seem obvious or oversimplified, a necessary first step in applying this model to a particular life situation is to formulate specific operations or naturally occurring dimensions that correspond to the conceptual variables of interest—perceived control and predictability. Any single operational variable may be more relevant to some life crises than others; nevertheless, we would expect that variations of information or preparation, and degree of voluntariness or choice, would be among the most common ways of dimensionalizing perceived control. For example, we discuss the stress-reducing effects of making a particular crisis situation more predictable by providing preparatory information. This particular intervention has been shown to be effective in reducing complications following heart attack and in helping aged individuals react less negatively to relocating. In formulating our model, we also consider the fact that the situational context may alter the meaning of any specific operation to the individual (e.g., Averill, 1973; Mills & Krantz, 1979) and that the individual's interpretation of events moderates the impact of life stress.

Chapter Outline

Although we believe that a control analysis has applicability to a variety of life events and chronic diseases, we illustrate this approach by examining in depth two frequently and extensively studied traumas occurring across the life span: acute coronary disease and relocation of the elderly. Both events place heavy demands on the individual for radical and abrupt shifts in life-style, represent major sources of stress, and precipitate abrupt declines in the individual's control over the environment. Research has also shown that behavioral and psychosocial variables play an important role in determining the outcomes of both these crises.

This chapter reviews in turn existing research on psychosocial aspects of cardiac rehabilitation and relocation of the elderly. In the specific area of cardiac rehabilitation, several alternative perspectives have been advanced to understand the recovery process. We present these alternative views and discuss their strengths and weaknesses. With respect to relocation of the aged, relatively few attempts at theoretical integration are available. In our discussion of each area, we present a control perspective and describe the relevant operations that correspond to the controllability variable. We also suggest several testable hypotheses regarding the link between psychosocial variables and illness. Following these reviews, we discuss the more general implications of this perspective for understanding the relationship between life crises and health outcomes.

PSYCHOSOCIAL ASPECTS
OF CARDIAC REHABILITATION

Diseases of the cardiovascular system (e.g., arteriosclerosis, coronary heart disease, and hypertension) constitute a major health problem and account for over 40% of the mortality of those aged 45 and over (U.S. Public Health Service, 1975). Not only does this disorder represent an important social crisis for survivors and their families, but potential economic loss is also considerable, because the disease strikes individuals who are frequently at their peak in terms of occupational status and earning potential. Progress in the medical technology of acute coronary care has led to large increases in the percentages of individuals surviving an acute coronary event (cf. Garrity, 1975); yet many of the nonmedical problems resulting from the onset of symptomatic coronary disease—particularly heart attack or myocardial infarction (MI)—can be as distressing and debilitating as the primary illness itself. In this regard, considerable evidence in the last 15 years has documented the importance of behavioral and psychosocial variables in the process of recovery from coronary heart disease (CHD).

Dimensions of Recovery

A large number of predictor variables have been implicated and studied as possible determinants of post-MI adjustment (cf. Garrity, McGill, Becker, Blanchard, Crews, Cullen, Hackett, Taylor, & Valins, 1976). These include physical variables (e.g., severity of MI, intensity of symptoms, physical activity), psychological processes (e.g., perception of health, fear of reinfarction, anxiety or depression, locus of control), sociological and demographic characteristics (age, socioeconomic status, pre-MI work, money available for early retirement), and characteristics of the health care system (e.g., information or misinformation provided by the physician). Vocational adjustment (usually return to work) and morale of the patient during recovery (assessed through self-reports and clinical ratings) have been the most frequently studied outcome variables. A major problem with research on the recovery process has been the lack of standardized instruments for measuring outcome variables and their predictors. In addition, much research in this area has been descriptive or correlational, and there has been a notable lack of prospective investigation. These facts have made it difficult to establish firm cause-and-effect relationships.

Despite extensive research in the area of cardiac rehabilitation (for comprehensive reviews, see Croog & Levine, 1977; Croog, Levine, & Lurie, 1968; Doehrman, 1977) there is still no universally accepted definition of "recovery." Some investigations define recovery in terms of physical health status and others in terms of behavioral outcomes such as return to work and vocational adjustment. There is some agreement in dividing the course of illness temporally into an acute (in-hospital) phase and a convalescent/ recovery (posthospital) phase; however, there seems to be little uniform consensus about how medical and psychosocial processes are interrelated at each stage. Moreover, a given medical or psychological variable may affect some outcome variables associated with recovery and not others. For example, actual health status may be improved by medical intervention, whereas behavioral reactions to illness may remain poor (cf. Croog et al., 1968); and recovery defined in terms of return to work may have different determinants than recovery defined as achieving maximal physical capacity. This lack of complete correspondence between actual physical health status and various criteria of recovery and adjustment has posed major problems for attempts to conceptualize response to heart disease. Therefore, any useful conceptual approach to the recovery process must deal sucessfully with the interaction of medical and psychological processes at many levels.

Theories of the Recovery Process

To untangle the complexities of the recovery process, two theoretical models have previously been proposed to explain reactions to heart attack. One psychodynamically oriented view, proposed by Hackett, Cassem, and co-workers, stresses the importance of *denial* as a defense mechanism for coping with the stress of illness. A second, health-perception perspective emphasizes the patient's beliefs about his or her own health status and the role of these beliefs in guiding recovery-related decisions. The Hackett and Cassem denial perspective seems to account for outcomes in the acute (in-hospital) phase of heart attack better, whereas the health-perception approach seems to address itself to more long-term outcomes such as return to work. After reviewing relevant evidence and describing the benefits and shortcomings of each existing approach, we propose a third view based on a conceptualization of heart attack as a severe life crisis. In our approach, we emphasize environmental control and predictability as determinants of both behavioral and physiological health outcomes. We now proceed with a review of evidence bearing on each theoretical approach to recovery.

Denial as Defense Mechanism. Cassem and Hackett (1971) have developed a model for the time course of emotional reactions of the person who has an MI, and denial is implicated as the focal mechanism for the coronary patient. It is proposed that a patient feels heightened anxiety when first admitted to the coronary care unit. However, denial is soon mobilized, and the patient finds it difficult to believe that he or she has really had a heart attack. Anxiety therefore declines for a period; the patient often protests detention in the CCU, insists on returning to normal activities, and becomes difficult to manage. However, after several days the patient becomes more cognizant of the limitations of the true condition, and depression sets in. The Cassem and Hackett model implies that deniers will experience less anxiety than nondeniers and, because of the presumed stress-reducing effects of this defense mechanism, will show facilitated recovery. Therefore, Hackett and Cassem (1974) believe that deniers will have better survival records in the coronary care unit than nondeniers. In support of this model, several studies have found that deniers tend to be less anxious in *early* phases of illness than nondeniers (e.g., Froese, Hackett, Cassem, & Silverberg, 1974; Gentry, Foster, & Haney, 1972). However, long-term follow-up studies examining the relationship between denial and longevity have not used large samples to produce results conclusive enough to support or refute the hypothesis. Paradoxically, use of denial has been related to long-term resistance to compliance with medical regimens (e.g., Croog, Shapiro, & Levine, 1971; Garrity et al., 1976), as deniers indicate less willingness to follow medical instructions. In sum, use of denial may make for better coping with the early stress of illness in the coronary care unit. But in the long term, patients may endanger their chances of recovery by ignoring medical recommendations that are important for satisfactory rehabilitation.

Greene, Moss, and Goldstein (1974) and Simon, Feinleib, and Thompson (1972) offer a somewhat different view of denial. They believe that denial of symptoms may appear even before hospitalization and cause delay in seeking help. Instead of viewing denial as an unconscious defense mechanism, they instead emphasize the fact that patients may use denial as a (possibly conscious) instrumental cognitive coping strategy. These investigators report that many patients appreciate the seriousness of their symptoms but delay in seeking help because they cannot tolerate the helplessness entailed with interruption of ongoing activities and being sick (Moss & Goldstein, 1970; Moss, Wynar, & Goldstein, 1969). Greene et al. (1974) present the argument that defense mechanisms among heart patients are developed in order to counter the threat of helplessness that accompanies chronic illness.

Although Hackett and Cassem have developed a questionnaire instrument to measure denial (Hackett & Cassem, 1974), defense mechanisms are notoriously difficult to measure operationally. This problem makes the denial hypothesis a difficult one to test. Particularly with data gathered by face-to-face interview, it is difficult to distinguish denial (as a defense mechanism) from inability or conscious unwillingness to discuss emotionally laden issues (cf. Taylor & Levin, 1976). Inconsistencies in data linking denial to recovery outcomes have, for example, been attributed to differences in patient willingness to admit troublesome feelings in brief interviews with strangers as opposed to in-depth interviews with trusted hospital staff (Doehrman, 1977).

To sum up, evidence for the efficacy of the Hackett and Cassem denial notion is mixed, suggesting some benefits in the early stages of illness due to reduction of anxiety. However, other investigators have presented evidence implicating denial of symtoms as a source of delay in treatment and hospitalization. There is also the possibility, not yet thoroughly studied, that persistent deniers may be less likely to comply with medical regimens. As a conceptualization of the recovery process, the denial hypothesis seems best to explain short-term in-hospital reactions but is not sufficiently developed to account for long-term outcomes.

Perceptions of Health.   Another approach to understanding psychosocial aspects of cardiac rehabilitation assumes that *perceived* health status is a central variable. This view is based on the notion that illness-related behaviors are products of a series of decisions based on how patients view their current health situations (Garrity et al., 1976). Therefore, the patient's own understanding of his or her clinical status is seen as equally important in determining behavioral outcomes as the actual *physical* status. Mood and behavior in reaction to illness are seen as products of what people believe about the severity of their disorder; and within the physical limitations imposed by their disease, recovery-related variables are bound to health perceptions.

This view has received major impetus from research conducted by Garrity (1973a, 1973b) designed to explain why some individuals return to work and recreational activities and achieve acceptable levels of morale, whereas others do not. In this research, the study group consisted of male heart attack patients who had suffered their first MI. Perceived health was measured by rating scales during the hospital stay and 6 months later. Self-reported morale and resumption of activities were also measured after a 6-month period. Results indicated that patients who perceived their health to be poor were less likely to have returned to work or to community involvement and also rated their morale as lower. Health perceptions during and after hospitalization were related to each other and perceived health status was only weakly related to clinical measures of physical health status. Therefore, perceptions of health had, to a certain degree, an independent relationship to measures of recovery and adjustment; partialing out the influence of physical health variables, health perceptions were related to recovery outcomes.

It should be noted that the conclusions of this research are limited by the fact that no attempt was made to manipulate or alter patient health perceptions. Since this research was retrospective, it is also not clear to what extent reported poor health *reflects* rather than causes low morale. Self-reports of poor health may provide a justification for not returning to work and for withdrawing from outside involvements. Nevertheless, these findings highlight the importance of beliefs about the severity and nature of illness for the recovering heart patient. Self-perceived health status after heart attack is associated, in part, with perception of one's health before illness and with current clinical status. The health-perception model also suggests interventions to improve self-assessed health status. Personnel involved in acute coronary care may be able to affect behavioral rehabilitation several months later by altering patient perceptions and fostering a belief (which is usually veridical) in the optimistic aspects of physical recovery (cf. Garrity, 1975). Patient perceptions can be altered through instruction, education, and through various nursing care and rehabilitation procedures.

The health-perception model bears conceptual similarity to a more general health belief model used to study participation in preventative health behavior (Kasl & Cobb, 1966; Rosenstock, 1966). The emphasis in these models is on decision making to reduce threats posed by illness. It has recently been proposed (Garrity et al., 1976) that many physical, psychosocial, and sociological predictors of post-MI adjustment may be mediated by the patient's perception of personal health status. This decisional model has the benefit of linking together many different predictor and outcome variables in cardiac rehabilitation and also is intervention oriented (although we know of no intervention studies to date that have been designed to test the model specifically). The health-perception model moves in the right direction, we feel, because it emphasizes the patient's beliefs about illness rather than the objective medical facts and circumstances. Although this model explains how beliefs about physical health status may translate into behavior, it says little about how beliefs (or other psychological mechanisms) may directly influence clinical health status. In contrast, the *personal control* model we propose places even greater emphasis on cognitive appraisal processes and has the potential to explain mechanisms linking psychological interventions to physiological health outcomes.

Both the health-perception and denial perspectives already described have generated several studies directed specifically at testing propositions derived from each model. However, several investigators (e.g., Croog & Levine, 1977; Croog et al., 1968) have suggested that the recovery process in heart disease might be fruitfully conceptualized as a response to crisis. As a crisis, the emotional reaction to myocardial infarction has been likened to a grief process following other experiences of loss (Garrity, 1975). In addition to physical discomfort and fear of death, patients are confronted with multiple uncertainties regarding job, leisure, and life-style activities in the future; in short, patients are likely to feel that their ability to predict and control the environment are severely limited. Predictability and control, variables that have been demonstrated to affect reactions to stress in a wide variety of situations, seem particularly relevant to the setting of acute heart attack, and it is possible to organize a considerable amount of research on reactions to coronary disease in terms of these two variables.

A Control Perspective

A conceptual analysis of response to heart disease in terms of personal control seems particularly appropriate because of the sudden onset and wide-ranging behavioral effects of the illness. The applicability of this line of thought is further supported by reports of an association between the onset of symptomatic coronary disease and reactions to uncontrollable events (cf. Glass, 1977; Greene, Goldstein, & Moss, 1972), and a series of infrahuman studies by Lown and associates that implicate environmental stress (restraint and uncontrollable shock) as a factor in cardiac arrhythmia and sudden death (Lown, Verrier, & Corbalan, 1973; Lown, Verrier, & Rabinowitz, 1977).

In our approach, we hypothesize that adverse reactions occurring after acute myocardial infarction are in part mediated by feelings of helplessness induced by illness and potentially threatening hospital procedures. Our model would lead us to expect that:

1. Control-related cognitive processes will be linked to behavioral and physiological responses important for recovery. Holding medical status constant, we would expect that individuals who feel more competent, less depressed, and less threatened during the acute phase of illness will fare better at later points in the recovery process.

2. Procedures that enhance the patient's behavioral control (e.g., providing choices, encouraging participation) or cognitive control (providing information, increasing environmental predictability) should facilitate recovery from acute MI. We would expect, however, that in order for these various procedures to have the desired effect, they should be presented to the individual in a way that heightens sense of personal control.

Coping, Depression, and Recovery.   A study by Garrity and Klein (1971) provides evidence that coping processes evident in the early stages of acute illness may mediate long-term survival. Observations of patient's behavior were made during the first 5 days (acute phase) of illness. Patients were rated twice daily with respect to a variety of checklist dimensions from which two indices were constructed: one for positive behavior and one for behavior disturbance. On the basis of these indices, subjects were classified into two groups. One group (adaptors) manifested behavior indicating either little evidence of behavior disturbance or high evidence of positive behavior over the next 5 days. A second group (nonadaptors) showed either great behavioral disturbance and little positive behavior or an increase in disturbance over a 5-year period. A 6-month follow-up revealed considerably higher mortality in the nonadaptor group. Severity of heart attack (a medical variable) was also related to survival, but results showed that severity and behavioral response (i.e., attitudes toward illness) were not related to one another. Both had some independent predictive power for mortality. It is important to note that behavioral response to illness was related to prior health, with individuals in poorer health before the present attack reacting more poorly. However, prior health seemed to affect mortality through the agency of the patient's emotional reactions to illness. Although this study is not definitive in pinpointing the mechanisms whereby early reactions indicative of good or poor coping are associated with survival, it is nevertheless suggestive in linking cognitive processes during the acute phase of illness with mortality.

Some indication of the kinds of psychological processes relating to favorable medical outcomes comes from two studies of patients undergoing open-heart surgery. Kimball (1968) found that patients classified as least depressed and best adjusted based on an interview prior to surgery evidenced the lowest mortality and morbidity. Tufo and Ostfeld (1968) report that among an array of assessed preoperative states, only depression related to a high risk of operative death. These relationships could not be accounted for by cardiac status prior to surgery.

Other recent studies have also examined psychological characteristics of cardiac patients at various postinfarct time intervals. Pancheri, Bellaterra, Matteoli, Cristofari, Polizzi, and Puletti (1978) administered a battery of psychological tests and interviews to patients in the ICU on the 2nd or 3rd day following infarct. Approximately 8 days later, upon release, the clinical condition of the patients was evaluated based on medical parameters such as length of stay in coronary care unit (CCU) and electrocardiographic and laboratory test data. Subjects were divided into two groups—"improved" and "not improved"—based on these clinical parameters. Results indicated that several psychological measures given earlier during the stay in the CCU distinguished the two groups. Patients categorized as "not improved" evidenced higher anxiety and heightened emotional reactions on several scales, as well as more work-related frustration. Patients in grave medical condition at time of admission were not included in the study sample, but it is not entirely clear what medical variables distinguished the two groups in this study upon admission.

Obier, MacPherson, and Haywood (1977) found results only partially supportive of the notion that indices of coping ability may predict survival outcomes. Measures of depression and pessimism were taken in the CCU and at time periods 3, 6, and 12 months postinfarct. Out of a sample of 57 subjects, 12 died and 45 survived to participate in a final 2½-year follow-up. Results indicated higher depression and pessimism in nonsurvivors at 3-, 6-, and 12-month periods. However, the groups did not differ on these measures during their stay in the CCU.

Depression is considered to be one of the most formidable problems in cardiac convalescence and rehabilitation, and post-MI depression has been attributed to the threat of invalidism and loss of autonomy and control due to illness (Hackett & Cassem, 1973). It is at this time that patients must confront the realities of disability and deal directly with changes in life-style that are forced upon them. Moreover, after the period of hospitalization, many patients are reluctant to resume normal activities or return to work—often to an extent not justified by their medical disability. One common reaction, termed *cardiac invalidism*, is characterized by excessive dependency, helplessness, and restriction of activity. This reaction of physical inactivity may actually contribute toward worsening of medical status due to physiological effects of deconditioning (cf. Wenger, 1973).

In a successful attempt to counter these effects, a recent study by Gruen (1975) subjected a random sample of cardiac patients to brief cognitively oriented psychotherapy designed to facilitate coping with illness. Data collected showed that treated patients, compared to a matched control group, had shorter stays in the hospital, were less likely to develop medical complications in the form of arrhythmias, showed fewer manifestations of depression or anxiety, and were more able to return to normal activities at a 4-month follow-up.

The Hospital Environment and the Recovering Heart Patient.   Hospitalization constitutes a stressful event for most people, and many standard medical procedures, viewed as "routine" by the staff, are new and anxiety-provoking experiences to the patient. As medicine has become increasingly specialized, hospital units such as the coronary care unit (CCU) have been developed to allow for efficient care of patients in need of highly trained staff and special treatment. In the past, the hospital environment has been studied as a social system; only relatively recently have medical outcome variables been studied as a function of the physical characteristics of the hospital setting (cf. Kornfeld, 1972).

Several studies have observed the effects of various procedures occurring in the CCU on the physical and psychological well-being of recovering patients. Unfortunately, most of this research consists of observational reports of patient reactions characterized by biases in subject selection and the lack of relevant control groups. As a result, there is considerable variation in the results of these reports. For example, Hackett, Cassem, and Wishnie (1968) found little if any serious psychological upset caused by what might be considered provocative circumstances (e.g., witnessing the cardiac arrest of another patient, being hooked up to an EKG monitor). Graham (1969) also found that a substantial percentage of patients rated the CCU care as excellent and attributed their secure feelings to the monitoring equipment and nursing assistance. In contrast, Bruhn, Thurman, Chandler, & Bruce (1970) found differences in psychological and physiological reactions between patients who witnessed the sudden death of another patient and those who did not observe such an event. These apparently contradictory results may derive from the fact that the intensive medical and nursing care in the CCU creates a situation where two opposing forces are operative. First, the presence of monitoring equipment indicates to the patient how critically ill and close to danger he or she is. At the same time, the care of the CCU is reassuring at a time when patients feel their lives are threatened. Therefore, as noted by Klein, Kliner, Zipes, Troyer, and Wallace (1968), the threatening aspects of heart attack evoke a readiness in patients to accept intensive care, even though it requires extraordinary dependence on others beyond that usually acceptable to an adult. Whether the delicate balance of psychological forces shifts from reassurance to threat seems to vary with the particular nursing procedures in the CCU and also with individual differences in patient coping styles.

In earlier portions of this paper, we asserted that adverse reactions to acute myocardial infarction and hospitalization are mediated by feelings of helplessness induced by illness and threatening hospital procedures. We further asserted, then, that procedures that specifically enhance patients' behavioral and cognitive control or increase the predictability of the hospital environment should improve the progress of recovery from acute MI. Two studies (which were conceived independently of the present theoretical orientation) serve to illustrate this point and therefore are described in detail.

Transfer from a Coronary Care Unit: Effects of Increasing Predictability. As previously noted, the threatening aspects of heart attack evoke a readiness in most patients to accept the intensive care provided by the coronary care unit, even though it requires extraordinary passivity and dependence on others (cf. Klein et al., 1968). When a patient is ready for transfer from the CCU to the general medical ward, adverse reactions are frequently observed in some patients, accompanying the sudden disruption of physician–patient and nurse–patient relationships in the CCU. Klein et al. (1968) undertook a study to examine patient reactions to this transfer. Patients were observed for symptoms, changes in physical health status, and overt emotional responses. Daily urine samples were collected and examined for catecholamine excretion (cf. Frankenhaeuser, 1971). Results indicated that of the first seven patients followed after transfer, five showed emotional reaction to the transfer along with some form of cardiovascular complication. All five also exhibited an increase in catecholamine excretion coincident with or following departure from the coronary care unit.

Although transfer was intended as a sign of "recovery," the patients showing adverse reactions interpreted being moved as a sign of being rejected by the staff, as these patients were often transferred abruptly without choice or warning. In addition, there was a great deal of uncertainty over who was to be the patient's physician in his or her new location. Changes in treatment programs between CCU and ward were often abrupt; for example, fewer medications and increased physical activity were prescribed. Abrupt changes in diet were also frequent on the new ward, and other subtle changes included change in diagnoses from "acute myocardial infarction" to "coronary artery disease."

Klein et al. (1968) report there was evidence that these abrupt changes, many of which were occuring against the patient's will, were causing many of the adverse reactions. For example, whereas a gradual progression from bed rest to moderate physical activity was viewed favorably by the patient, sudden increments were often prescribed. In short, Klein et al. (1968) propose that adverse emotional and physiological reactions to transfer were the result of the uncontrollability of transfer and the unpredictability of the new ward environment.

Accordingly, Klein et al. (1968) instituted a number of changes in the procedures of the CCU and ward, and a second group of seven patients were studied. These changes included: (1) preparing the patient in advance for transfer and warning of the possibility of abrupt transfer; (2) having one nurse follow each patient through the CCU stay and the transfer; (3) having one physician follow the patient throughout hospitalization and assume an active, identifiable role in patient's care; and (4) after transfer, having the nurse visit the patient each day, provide illness information, and help him or her to make adjustments and future plans. Results of this intervention study showed that the second group of seven patients, in contrast to the first, evidenced no new cardiovascular complications accompanying transfer and a substantially lower incidence of elevated catecholamine excretion.

Unfortunately, the conclusiveness of the Klein et al. (1968) study must be tempered by the fact that the two sets of patients differed in severity of illness, duration of stay in the CCU, and level of physical activity. Nevertheless, these data provide a dramatic demonstration of the impact that unpredictable and uncontrollable changes in hospital environment can have on the recovering heart patient. They further suggest that instituting changes to increase environmental predictability can have profound medical and psychological effects.

Nursing Factors and Recovery. An implicit assumption made by practitioners of coronary treatment is that proper nursing and psychological care can reduce patient stress. A remarkable but rather complex study conducted by Cromwell and associates (see Cromwell, Butterfield, Brayfield, & Curry, 1977) manipulated patient care procedures that appear to represent, in part, mixtures of various types of control. The study was conducted in order to answer practical questions often asked by physicians and nurses concerning patient treatment during hospitalization for acute heart attack. Acute MI patients were randomly assigned to a given combination of three nursing care procedures in a 2 × 2 × 2 factorial design. The three factors were named, respectively, Information, Participation, and Diversion. Procedures differentiating the "high" and "low" levels of the nursing care dimensions were as follows.

High-information patients heard a recording and read literature explaining aspects of the causes, physiology, and treatment of myocardial infarction. By contrast, low-information subjects were given only a brief recording to listen to, and staff physicians agreed to keep their informative comments limited to support, reassurance, and generalities.

Participation was manipulated by varying the extent to which subjects initiated and engaged in activities related to their own treatment. High-participation subjects were given access to a switch to activate their own cardiac monitors to secure an EKG tracing whenever they felt some symptom. This recording was made available to the patient's physician for examination. In addition, these patients were taught mild isometric and foot-pedaling exercises that they performed under the close surveillance of the hospital staff. Low-participation subjects were given only the previously standard medical procedure of bed rest except for self-feeding.

Patients assigned to high-diversion treatments had access to television, newspapers, magazines, and liberal visitor privileges (unless the patient personally elected not to have company), and nurses were free to visit the patient and talk informally whenever they chose. By contrast, low-diversion subjects had none of these opportunities and were limited in the number of visitors they were allowed to receive. Nurses agreed to stay away from the patients' rooms except when carrying out duties of nursing care.

The major findings of the nursing care study concerned length of stay in the hospital and indicated that instead of producing simple effects, the three nursing care factors interacted with one another in a complex manner. In particular, the high-information treatment led to quick or slow discharge from both CCU and hospital, depending on the other factors with which it was paired. If patients were given high information but low levels of diversion and participation, hospital stay tended to be long. High information with high participation or high diversion, by contrast, led to short stays in the hospital. This effect, termed *information coupling*, indicated that if any acutely ill MI patient is told about the severity of his or her condition, that patient should also be given something to do about it or at least something to divert the mind from it.

A second finding of the study was that an intermediate level of physical activity was optimal for a short CCU and hospital stay. Specifically, intermediate amounts of participation and diversion (the two treatments associated with the most patient activity) were associated with short hospital stays; either high or low amounts of activity were associated with long stays in the hospital.

Practically speaking, patients in the Cromwell et al. (1977) study who received favorable psychological interventions tended to be released 2 to 3 days earlier from the coronary care unit and 7 to 8 days earlier from the hospital. As there was no indication that early-discharged patients had any more or less favorable medical outcome than those discharged later, the economic and psychosocial benefits of the favorable treatment combinations are self-evident. From a theoretical point of view, however, numerous questions are raised.

If we conceptualize the participation and information manipulations as forms of personal control, the Cromwell et al. (1977) study leads to the conclusion that the effects of various control treatments in this setting are dependent on the context in which they are administered. The information manipulation corresponds closely to the variable "cognitive control" (cf. Averill, 1973), as subjects were provided with information about the objective characteristics of the coronary disease stressor. However, the operations used to vary participation and diversion seem to have confounded personal control with other factors and are therefore less amenable to simple interpretation. For example, although the high-participation treatment probably resulted in heightened sense of responsibility (a variant of personal control), it also differed from low participation in amount of physical activity, which could affect healing processes of the vascular system independent of its psychological concomitants (e.g., Wenger, 1973). The diversion treatments are also subject to several interpretations, because in addition to directing attention away from fears and concerns connected with illness, high-diversion patients could control and regulate the amount of visitation they received (cf. Schulz, 1976).

It is important to note that Cromwell et al. (1977) measured quite a few recovery-related variables and that several important outcome variables were either unaffected or differently affected by the various treatment combinations. For example, heart-rate monitor alarms indicative of abnormal EKG activity showed weak trends paralleling the hospital stay findings, but cardiac symptoms were only minimally affected by the nursing care treatments. In addition, a pattern of results emerged suggesting that hospital stress was minimized to the extent that subjects received treatments congruent with measured personality characteristics, indicating that it is important to cater various treatment procedures to the individual for optimal health outcomes. In sum, the Cromwell et al. (1977) study highlights the fact that the meaning of control-related procedures in cardiac rehabilitation depends on the situational context in which these procedures are administered.

Personal Control and Cardiac Rehabilitation: Unanswered Questions and Implications for Health Care

In terms of a control model, results of the various studies reviewed should be viewed as preliminary and suggestive, rather than definitive. As these studies were not designed with this particular theoretical approach in mind, the procedures were often quite complex, and our interpretations required making liberal assumptions in order to apply the model. For example, we assumed that allowing patients to participate in or assigning them responsibility for their own treatment makes them feel that they can affect their health outcomes. Nevertheless, existing data are consistent enough to justify future research specifically designed to test this perspective. In addition, current research points to several unanswered questions regarding the applicability of personal control toward recovery from heart disease.

What Operational Variables Heighten Perceived Control, and How Much Control Is Optimal? The Cromwell et al. (1977) study suggests that the effects of control-related manipulations in a cardiac health care setting are context specific; that is, the meaning and effects of a given treatment depend on how it is presented and whether it enables the individuals to cope with threatening aspects of illness. The meaning of a particular treatment to the patient must be considered if we are to maximize favorable outcomes. For example, providing high levels of information but not permitting the patient to do anything about what he or she has learned may be undesirable. However, when information is paired with appropriate levels of participation or diversion, outcomes are favorable. In a similar manner, patients may neither prefer nor expect responsibility for medical decisions. Too much responsibility and choice or too much information may not be beneficial either psychologically or medically (e.g., Janis, 1958; Mills & Krantz, 1979). Recent research introducing control treatments in institutional settings has found these interventions to be effective, particularly when subjects in the research attribute enhanced control to stable factors that will persist over time (Langer & Rodin, 1976; Rodin & Langer, 1977; Schulz, 1976; Schulz & Hanusa, 1978). Other research in health care settings (Mills & Krantz, 1979) has shown that information and choice may sometimes be more beneficial *alone* than when combined. The Cromwell et al. (1977) study raises the issues that there may be an optimal degree or type of patient control to facilitate recovery from heart attack.

In health care settings, the patient's personal role in treatment is a major distinction between traditional medical model approaches to health care and newer, behavioral approaches that encourage the patient to become an active participant in his or her own treatment (cf. Schwartz & Weiss, 1977; Williams

& Gentry, 1977). Common sense suggests that a middle road be followed that maximizes patients' ability to cope with stressful aspects of illness without leading to unrealistic expectations or having patients make medical decisions beyond their realm of competence (cf. Johnson & Leventhal, 1974; Mills & Krantz, 1979). In a discussion of psychological aspects of breast cancer, Taylor and Levin (1976) favor this approach, which they label "informed participation." It appears that with respect to the cardiac rehabilitation setting, research is necessary to determine those treatment levels that are most effective. Moreover, recent research suggests that individuals differ in their receptiveness to self-care and information (Krantz, Baum, & Wideman, 1979). The most favorable outcomes may therefore result from matching individual patients with particular treatment interventions.

One type of participatory treatment that may be effective for the post-MI patient is physical exercise. An increasing body of data documents the effectiveness of regular, graduated programs of physical activity in convalescence of cardiac patients (cf. Naughton, Hellerstein, & Mohler, 1973); yet relatively little experimental attention has been paid to the psychological effects of exercise. Two studies (McPherson, Paivio, Yuhasz, Rechnitzer, Pickard, & Lefcoe, 1967; Naughton, Bruhn, & Lategola, 1968) report that participation in physical activity programs can lead to an increased sense of well-being and a decrease in anxiety and depression in postinfarction patients. Hackett and Cassem (1973) further consider physical exercise to be the most potent antidote for depression available to the cardiac patient and recommend an appropriate program of physical conditioning beginning while the patient is still in CCU. They propose that physical conditioning acts to counter depression by restoring self-esteem, sense of independence, and feelings of self-sufficiency and accomplishment—in short, to restore patients' feelings of control over relatively stable factors in their lives. This interpretation of exercise rehabilitation for the cardiac patient further links the concept of control to homecoming depression, which is an important outcome of the recovery process.

Mechanisms and Dimensions of Recovery. One of the benefits of conceptualizing the recovery process is to establish linkages between diverse outcome variables that have been shown to be influenced by psychosocial processes. There are many possible criteria that can be used to define recovery (cf. Croog et al., 1968). The most frequently studied outcome variable has been patient morale (e.g., Garrity, 1975; Gruen, 1975). Mortality, length of stay in the hospital, and physiological stress measures have also been examined (e.g., Cromwell et al., 1977; Gruen, 1975). Several studies reviewed in this chapter demonstrate that environmental interventions that enhance control and predictability can positively affect the health status of the recovering heart patient. The task of identifying precise mechanisms linking cognitive and physiological processes remains in preliminary stages; however, it is worthwhile to mention this research.

In our earlier discussion of denial, we alluded to the possibility that there may be separate mechanisms mediating short-term recovery and long-term recovery outcomes. That is, denial might enhance short-term recovery by reducing the stress associated with the acute phase of illness and impede long-term recovery by fostering noncompliance. Taking a somewhat broader conceptual approach, we might suggest parallel processes through which predictability and control could affect health outcomes. Focusing on short-term reacations during the acute phase of illness, cognitive treatments might directly affect internal physiological states. Beginning with Richter (1957) and Cannon (1957), investigators have sought to understand mechanisms linking emotional reactions to lethal cardiac electrical activity. Lown and associates have demonstrated that psychologically aversive situations can precipitate pathologic cardiac activity in dogs with previous myocardial damage (cf. Lown, Verrier, & Corbalan, 1973). In humans, cognitive interventions presumed to heighten control and predictability have been shown to affect cardiac electrical activity (e.g., Gruen, 1975) as well as catecholamine excretion related to physiological stress responses (e.g., Klein et al., 1968).

A second way that psychological interventions may be translated into physical health outcomes is by changing the individual's behavior in health-related areas. These relatively long-lasting behaviors might have their major effects after release from the hospital. In the case of the recovering heart patient, he or she may follow prescribed diet more closely, be more diligent in taking medicine and in stopping smoking, exercise with greater frequency or regularity, and so forth. Adherence to these regimens is of prime importance, as this constellation of behaviors contribute to risk of reinfarction and progressions of disease (see Fox, 1973; Heinzelmann, 1973). Several studies (e.g., Garrity & Klein, 1971; Gruen, 1975) indicate that cognitive processes evident in early phases of illness may affect long-term morale and resumption of activities. In addition, the concept of control has been implicated as an important element in compliance behavior (cf. Stokols, 1975). Most research linking personal control to compliance has relied on relatively global individual-difference measures (e.g., Wallston, Wallston, Kaplan, & Maides, 1976), with internal locus of control linked to increased compliance. Intervention studies examining the relationship between control-enhancing treatments and long-term health maintenance behaviors seem both theoretically desirable and practically feasible.

Last, there may be specific linkages between individual health-outcome variables and control-related cognitions. For example, Cromwell et al. (1977) suggest that their findings of reduced hospital stay may have been caused by stress leading to greater illness, selective reporting of relevant symptoms to the physician, reduced protest by patient or family, or combinations of these factors. Recent social psychological research has linked uncontrollable and unpredictable events to many of these processes, including symptom reporting (Pennebaker, Burnam, Schaeffer, & Harper, 1977; Weidner & Matthews, 1978). Systematic research is needed to explore these mechanisms in the case of cardiac rehabilitation.

Just as the heart disease recovery process may be viewed as a life crisis situation, whose outcomes are mediated by control-related cognitive processes, a similar conceptual analysis can be applied to the process of relocation of elderly individuals. Empirical data on relocation, presented next, support the notion that variables affecting environmental predictability and control can mediate health outcomes.

PSYCHOSOCIAL PERSPECTIVES
ON RELOCATION OF THE AGED

Of the many stressful events that ultimately affect the health status of aged individuals, few have been as thoroughly investigated as relocation. With the advent of urban renewal, change in government policy, debilitating physical decline, or decreased financial resources, aged individuals often find relocation a necessity. Some estimates indicate that no fewer than 20% (Kastenbaum & Candy, 1973) and perhaps as many as 40% (Shanas, 1962) of those over 65 years of age will have to relocate at least once before death. The emphasis of research on this problem has been on documenting the health outcomes attributable to relocation, with mortality rates frequently serving as the primary dependent measure (Lieberman, 1969).

The widespread interest in this topic reflects both the magnitude of the problem as well as the contradictory nature of the results in this area. Whereas many researchers (e.g., Aldrich & Mendkoff, 1963; Killian, 1970; Lieberman, 1961; Markus, Blenkner, Bloom, & Downs, 1972) have found that relocation has negative effects on the aged (e.g., increased mortality, decreased health status, depression, decreased activity), others have failed to find debilitating effects attributable to relocation (e.g., Carp, 1968; Lawton & Yaffe, 1970; Lieberman, Tobin, & Slover, 1971; Miller & Lieberman, 1965; Wittels & Botwinick, 1974). In one recent analysis, Tobin and Lieberman (1976) go so far as to argue that the debilitating effects of relocation occur long before the individual is actually moved. They believe, therefore, that it is not relocation per se that produces health declines but rather the decision to relocate and events associated with that decision that account for often observed health decline and increased mortality.

To untangle the inconsistent results of research on relocation, Schulz and Brenner (1977) have proposed a theoretical model that stresses the importance of control and predictability as mediators of relocation outcomes. Relocation is presumed to be a generally stressful experience, and negative response to relocation is thought to be lessened to the extent the individuals perceive it to be a predictable and/or controllable process.

In conceptual terms, environmental controllability corresponds directly to the voluntary–involuntary dimension in the relocation literature (degree of choice in electing to move.) Predictability is inversely related to the severity of environmental change experienced by relocatees and directly related to the amount of preparation given individuals before the move. Three specific hypotheses regarding relocation outcomes are derived from this theoretical perspective. Holding other variables constant:

1. The greater the choice the individual has, the less negative the effects of relocation. Therefore, voluntary relocatees should fare better than involuntary relocatees.

2. The more predictable a new environment, the less negative the effects of relocation. An individual who is prepared for a new environment by, for example, education programs or counseling should be less adversely affected by relocation than an individual who is not so prepared. In the absence of such a preparatory program, predictability should vary as a function of the severity of the environmental change. Thus, a move from home to an institution should be more devastating than a move from one institution to another.

3. Finally, an individual's response to relocation should also be influenced by personality-based expectancies for a predictable and controllable world. A person who views himself as one who controls his own fate should be relatively more devastated by an uncontrollable institutional environment than one who perceives himself to be ruled by the world around him. In addition, an individual's response to relocation should be mediated by the differences in environmental controllability between pre- and postrelocation environments; to the extent that relocation results in a decline in the controllability of the environment, the individual should be affected negatively by the move. This latter hypothesis is not unlike the several person–environment fit models proposed by Lawton (1975) and Kahana (1975). It differs from these models in that it identifies specific areas of congruity between the individual and the environment that are necessary for optimal functioning.

The settings of relocation studies vary in both the degree of *choice* the individuals had in electing to move and the degree of *environmental change* experienced as a result of the move. For example, Aldrich and Mendkoff (1963), Killian (1970), and Bourestom and Tars (1974) have investigated involuntary relocation within an institution or from one institution to another, whereas Zweig and Csank (1975) have analyzed this same move on a voluntary basis. Moves from home to an institution—both voluntary (Carp, 1968; Lawton & Cohen, 1974; Lawton & Yaffe, 1970; Storandt & Wittels, 1975; Wittels & Botwinick, 1974) and involuntary (Brand & Smith, 1974; Kasteler, Gray, & Carruth, 1968)—have also been examined. Based on our earlier conceptualization of relocation dimensions, the control model is best examined by classifying relocation studies according to type of move (institution to institution, home to institution, and home to home) and degree of choice (voluntary or involuntary).

In terms of the 2 × 2 organizational matrix already proposed (three types of moves and two levels of choice), we would, in general, expect more positive outcomes for voluntary than for involuntary relocatees and better outcomes for individuals being moved from one setting to a *similar* setting (home to home, institution to institution) than for individuals moved to a dissimilar setting (home to institution). More specifically, the model predicts that individuals moved involuntarily from home to an institution should show the greatest negative effects, with the outcomes being somewhat better for involuntary relocatees moved from institution to institution. Finally, the outcomes of individuals moving voluntarily from institution to institution and home to home should be the least negative compared to other groups.

Institution to Institution

Most studies in this category deal with involuntary relocation, with mortality rates serving as the major dependent measure in all cases. The range of independent variables examined in these studies make it possible to address each of three hypotheses presented earlier.

Aldrich and Mendkoff (1963) studied a sample of elderly persons moved involuntarily from one institution to another. The mortality rate (32%) was significantly higher than the anticipated rate of 19%. Killian (1970) matched two groups of elderly patients for age, sex, race, organic and functional diagnosis, length of hospitalization, and ambulatory facility. The group of patients transferred from Stockton State Hospital in California to other institutions had a higher death rate than a control group of patients allowed to remain at Stockton. Assuming there were no substantial differences in physical settings between the two institutions, we may conclude that the negative relocation effects are attributable primarily to the involuntary nature of the move.

Bourestom and Tars (1974) studied the effects of different degrees of environmental change and found, as predicted, that the more severe the change, the greater the negative effects of relocation. Two groups of involuntary relocatees were compared with nonrelocated controls. A higher mortality rate was found in both relocated groups, and a higher mortality rate was found for the radical-change relocatees than for the moderate-change ones.

The Modesto Study. Data strongly supportive of the personal-control model come from one of the most extensive involuntary institution relocation projects (Marlowe, 1974). Of the 1100 patients relocated when Modesto State Hospital in California was closed, almost half were 65 years of age or older. The elderly patients, who varied in physical and psychological status from extremely incapacitated to physically healthy and alert, were moved to either another state hospital or community residential facilities (i.e., nursing homes). One year later, mortality rates were significantly higher for this group both when compared to base rates for Modesto calculated for the years prior to its closure and when compared to rates of a control group of highly comparable but nonrelocated individuals.

In addition to the mortality data, Marlowe reports the extent of physical and cognitive deterioration or improvement among the survivors. Differential rates of change were found when different patient groups were compared, and in general, the physically and psychologically incapacitated patients exhibited significantly *less* deterioration than those who were more capable. Why should those with the strongest adaptive capacities deteriorate the most? One answer to this question is that these individuals are likely to experience the largest *decrease* in the opportunity to control their environment as a result of relocation. At Modesto, the patients in good condition typically occupied high-status positions, acting as "ward bosses" or "patient aides" on their hospital units. One consequence of relocation for these individuals was a substantial loss of control over their immediate environment.

The importance of environmental control is reiterated by another major finding of the Modesto study: Patients who were moved to environments that encouraged residents to be independent, to make their own decisions about the use of time and space, to try out new skills, and the like showed improvement. Patients denied these favorable conditions exhibited withdrawal and deterioration. It is important to note here that it is not the physical characteristics of the environment that determined patient outcomes but rather the psychological milieu vis-à-vis the control variable that accounted for deterioration or improvement among patients.

Effects of Preparatory Information. Three studies (Jasnau, 1967; Pastalan, 1976; Zweig & Csank, 1975) have examined the effects of prerelocation preparation programs. From a control perspective, we would predict that a new environment should be less stressful to the extent that it is predictable. Jasnau (1967) assessed the differences in postrelocation adjustment betwen a group of patients who were mass moved and a group given individualized preparatory treatment. Patients in the first group had an increased mortality rate after relocation, whereas persons in the second group had lower-than-expected mortality rates. Presumably, the use of individualized preparatory treatment served to increase the predictability and perceived controllability of the new environment. Zweig and Csank (1975) also instituted an extensive preparation program before moving chronic geriatric patients to a new institution. To assess the effectiveness of their program, Zweig and Csank compared mortality rates of patients in the same ward 3 years prior to relocation and 1 year after. From the year before relocation to 1 year after, there was a slight decrease in mortality.

Finally, Pastalan (1976) implemented a very extensive prerelocation preparation program for aged relocatees in the state of Pennsylvania. Some of the relocatees in his sample had the opportunity to participate in three different preparatory programs: (1) site visits to the receiving institution before relocation; (2) group discussions regarding the move; and (3) personal counseling consisting of discussions of the impending relocation between staff and patient. Comparisons in mortality were made between persons who did and did not participate in these programs. Preliminary data show that all three types of preparation effectively reduced mortality among relocatees, although significant differences were found only for certain subgroups of this population.

Home to Home

Numerous investigations have examined the effects of moving aged individuals from one home to another. For the most part these moves have been voluntary. As a result, we would expect little deterioration for persons undergoing this type of move.

In only two studies were individuals forced to move—in one case because of urban renewal (Brand & Smith, 1974) and in the other because of highway construction (Kasteler et al., 1968).

Kasteler et al. (1968) compared his sample of individuals moved because of highway construction with a matched sample of nonrelocated controls. The latter group scored significantly higher than the relocatees on measures of personal adjustment and amount of activity. The control groups scored significantly higher than the relocated group on a life satisfaction index. Presumably, the involuntary nature of the move represented a loss in decisional control, and the break with the familiar environment decreased predictability.

There have been several studies of voluntary relocation. Carp's (1968) well-documented research project was conducted at Victoria Plaza, an apartment building for the elderly, and compared relocatees and matched applicants. She found that relocated residents had less need for special services, had more memberships in clubs, and had more friends. Moreover, pre- and post-measures taken 12 to 15 months apart showed that nonresidents had decreased numbers of friends and level of happiness. The favorable outcome of the relocatees in this study is probably attributable both to the voluntary nature of the move and to the substantial improvement in living arrangements.

The pattern of findings reported by Carp has been replicated by Lawton and Cohen (1974). They studied voluntary relocation, comparing relocatees with controls, and found that the relocated were higher in morale and perceived more changes for the better than the control group. The relocatees, however, were poorer in functional health. The authors offer several explanations for these findings, including initial differences between applicants and nonapplicants that would make residents apply to a home for the elderly. They suggest, too, the possibility that the building provided conveniences (i.e., an elevator and nearby stores) that reduced the amount of functional health needed to survive well.

Lawton and Yaffe (1970) reported no differences in mortality rates between a voluntary relocated group and two matched groups. The relocatees moved to new housing that was a substantial improvement over the old. In explaining the results, the authors make note of the important voluntary–involuntary distinction. Wittels and Botwinick (1974) also found no differences in mortality rates between voluntary relocatees and controls. The controls consisted of applicants to the homes and the population at large.

Finally, Storandt and Wittels (1975) found no decrements in voluntarily relocated persons from pretest to posttest. In terms of our model, the move studied was ideal; it was voluntary, living conditions were improved, and the new housing was in the same neighborhood, allowing relocatees to maintain familiar life-styles. Decisional control was exercised, and a maximum of predictability was maintained.

Home to Institution

Many researchers have investigated the home-to-institution move, focusing either on mortality rates or adjustment as dependent measures. The major independent variables studied included the amount of choice people had in being moved, the severity of change experienced, and individual differences as predictors of institutional adjustment and survival. Given this array of independent variables, the validity of each of the three hypotheses presented earlier can be tested.

A study by Ferrari (1963) illustrates how choice contributes to differential patient outcomes. Two groups of aged individuals were compared, one entering an institution voluntarily and the other having no alternative. Those with no choice had a much higher mortality rate than those with choice. The actual rates were sobering: Within the first 10 weeks of residence in the institution, 16 out of 17 persons (94%) in the involuntary group died, whereas 1 out of 38 (2.6%) in the voluntary group died within the same period.

Severity of environmental change as a determinant of health-related outcomes among the elderly has been investigated in three different studies. Schulz and Aderman (1973) examined the effects of change on the temporal distance to death of terminal cancer patients. The authors hypothesized that length of survival would vary as a function of the disparity between the patient's preadmission living arrangement and the institutional life-style. The major finding was that those patients who came to the institution from similar institutions survived nearly 1 month longer, on the average, than patients who came from a dissimilar home environment. The two groups of patients were identical in health status at the time of admission.

In a similar study, Shrut (1965) investigated the effects of relocation on two groups: one from home to traditional institutional housing and the other from home to an apartment house for the elderly. As predicted by the model, individuals who moved to institutional housing were more afraid of and preoccupied with death, less socially alert, less productive, and less cooperative than the other relocatees.

The effects of decreased environmental predictability on the elderly were convincingly demonstrated in a study by Blenkner (1967), one of the few studies in the relocation literature using a random assignment procedure. Blenkner randomly assigned persons living in the community to service programs providing minimal, moderate, or maximal care. Minimal care consisted of information about available services, whereas maximal care provided direct intensive aid. At the 6-month follow-up, persons in the maximal-care group had the highest mortality rate, and persons in the minimal group had the lowest. These unexpected results can be understood from a predictability perspective: Persons in the maximal-care group were often uprooted from their familiar surroundings in order to be provided "better" medical care (Kasl, 1972).

Researchers who have attempted to determine those characteristics that predict institutional adaptation also report data consistent with the model. Sherwood, Glassman, Sherwood, and Morris (1974) used discriminant function analysis to divide voluntary relocatees into two groups characterized as more or less suitable for institutionalization. The *more* suitable group consisted of individuals who were accustomed to exerting little control over their environment and should therefore adapt well to institutionalization. Persons who exercised considerably more control over their environment were classified as *less* suitable for institutionalization. They were typically white-collar workers, functionally healthy, living alone or with spouse, and needing no financial aid. As expected, the former group adapted better to, and was more satisfied with, its institutional environment than the latter.

Although most institutions place a high value on the passivity of their residents, Turner, Tobin, and Lieberman (1972) have suggested that relocation environments vary in their adaptive demands and that successful institutionalization depends on congruence between the demands of the institution and the personality characteristics of the individual. Thus, an institution that values and reinforces high levels of interaction, activity, and aggressiveness would be better suited for an individual accustomed to exercising a great deal of control over his or her environment than for one who is relatively passive. The results of a study reported by Turner et al. (1972) support this view.

An Alternative View of Home-to-Institution Moves. The personal control analysis of the data on home-to-institution moves stands in contrast to a theory recently proposed by Tobin and Lieberman (1976). They agree that the characteristics of an institutional environment and the environmental discontinuity produced by the move may have deleterious effects but argue that the impact of these variables may be exaggerated because of selection biases. They further argue that particular types of older people (e.g., those already deteriorated or possessing psychological attributes typical of institutional populations) seek institutional care, and as a result any comparison between institutionalized persons and community residents will show the former to be more deteriorated. Thus, results typically attributed to institutionalization may in fact be due to selection bias. Tobin and Lieberman suggest instead that the factors causing negative effects are set into motion *prior* to actually entering and living in the institution. That is, shortly after the individual has been accepted by an institution and before the move actually occurs, the resident-to-be undergoes rapid and severe changes involving psychological withdrawal from his or her independent living arrangements. These investigators propose that the older person in the "anticipatory institutionalization phase" already looks like an institutionalized older person.

Tobin and Lieberman tested their hypothesis by collecting longitudinal and cross-sectional data from three different groups at three different times. The major sample consisted of persons interviewed initially while on the waiting list of one of three institutions for the aged. At the same time, data were collected from two additional groups intended to serve as controls. One consisted of residents of the receiving institutions who had lived there from 1 to 3 years and who had not undergone debilitating change since admission. The other consisted of community residents matched on demographic variables to the institutionalized group.

Comparisons between the three groups at the initial time of measurement were made on indicators of cognitive functioning, affective responsiveness, emotional state, and self-perceptions. These comparisons showed the waiting-list group to be more similar to the institutionalized group than to the community residents. Because the waiting-list group exhibited the same deficits observed in the institutional group and the community resident group was relatively intact, the authors conclude that the deterioration typically associated with relocation actually occurs during the preadmission phase.

The validity of this conclusion rests on the conceptual and methodological appropriateness of these comparisons. In particular, we must question the comparison between the waiting-list group and the institutionalized group, because the latter consisted of a biased sample of survivors of the institutionalization process. In addition, the comparison between the waiting-list group and the community residents was subject to strong alternative interpretation. Clearly, aged persons seek institutionalization for a reason, most notably physical and psychological decline, and it seems straightforward that there are large differences between those who decide to seek institutionalization and those who do not.

Tobin and Lieberman's perspective is introduced here, primarily, because if correct, it would have important practical implications. These investigators imply that future interventions should be aimed at the preadmission rather than the relocation or postrelocation phases of the institutionalization process. We propose instead that the available evidence indicates that we should focus our efforts on reducing the stress of relocation via predictability- and control-enhancing interventions.

The Predictability Experiment.   We have reviewed the majority of the relocation literature with the aim of showing that the individual's response to the stress of relocation is largely determined by: (1) the perceived controllability and predictability of the events surrounding a move; and (2) differences in environmental controllability between pre- and postrelocation environments. However, none of the research reviewed was specifically designed to test this model, and it was often necessary to make assumptions about the details of some studies in order to apply the model. Furthermore, a close examination of the methodologies renders the validity of some findings questionable. The most notable problem with several of the studies reviewed is the possibility of a self-selection confound. Given methodological flaws and the post hoc nature of this analysis, it is necessary to carry out controlled experiments before the model can be accepted.

A study recently completed by Schulz and Hanusa (1977) was designed to assess one aspect of this model using a random assignment procedure and experimental methodology. It was hypothesized that enhancing the predictability of an institutional environment for new admissions to a long-term care facility for the aged would facilitate adaptation and decrease some of the physical and psychological deficits typically associated with relocation.

Psychologically alert old persons recently admitted to a long-term care facility were assigned to one of three treatment conditions. One-third of the subjects were exposed to a treatment designed to enhance the predictability of the new environment. Subjects in this condition (*relevant information*) received an individualized orientation program that included detailed information about facilities and services available to them, their location within the institution, and directions on how to get to different areas of the hospital.

To control for the effects of increased attention given the relevant-information group, individuals assigned to a second group (*irrelevant information*) were given the same amount of personal attention but did not receive information designed to make their environments more predictable. These patients were told about the facilities within the hospital that were irrelevant to their functioning, such as the bakery and laundry. A third group (*no treatment*) received treatment as usual, which included a short orientation to the hospital provided by the social services staff.

Data assessing patients' level of activity and their physical and psychological status were collected from patients before and after the interventions were completed, and from the nursing staff after the interventions were completed. It was expected that the relevant-information group would be superior on indicators of health and psychological status to the irrelevant-information and no-treatment groups.

All subjects were asked to indicate whether or not they felt they had improved in physical and emotional health since their arrival at the institution and since the beginning of the manipulations. Subjects in the relevant-information group were more likely to say their emotional health had improved since their arrival than the no-treatment group, and subjects in the irrelevant-information group were more likely to say that their physical health had improved in the last 2 weeks than the no-treatment group.

Four different nurses were used to rate seven or eight subjects each; deviation scores were therefore derived by averaging the assessments made by each nurse and computing each subject's deviation from the mean of that nurse's group. Analysis of these scores on the two dependent measures yielded a significant effect for "Health Status" ($p < .06$) and "Zest for Life" ($p < .06$). Further analysis of the group means indicated that the relevant-information group was perceived to be healthier than the no-treatment group ($p < .06$). The means indicated that both relevant- and irrelevant-information groups were superior to the no-treatment group on ratings obtained on the "Zest for Life" scale.

Activity level for each subject was assessed by summing the total number of activities a subject indicated he or she had participated in since coming to the geriatric hospital. Two types of activity scores were computed for each subject: passive and active. Passive activities required little physical exertion from the subject and included such behaviors as watching television, talking to the person in the adjacent bed, reading and so on. Behaviors were classified as active activities when they required some physical effort on the part of the subject in order to engage in that activity. Thus, behaviors such as going to the snack bar, the library, the movies, or visiting someone in the hospital were classified as active behaviors.

A planned comparison indicated that the relevant-information group engaged in significantly more active activities than subjects in the no-treatment group. There was no effect of treatment on passive activities. In short, the experimental treatments increased participation in active but not passive activities.

Taken as a whole, these data are consistent with the findings of Schulz (1976) showing that predictable positive events have powerful positive impact upon the well-being of the institutionalized aged. Together, they lend credence to one aspect of the model proposed earlier; namely, enhancing the predictability of a new environment facilitates adaptation to that environment. Clearly, much additional research is needed to unambiguously validate other aspects of the proposed model.

Implications for Intervention and Some Unanswered Questions

Our analysis of the relocation literature has emphasized three aspects of the relocation process: (1) the decision to move; (2) the move itself; and (3) characteristics of the receiving environment (especially the differences between the sending and receiving environments on the controllability dimension). Practical implications of this analysis and examples of control- and predictability-enhancing interventions have already been described.

Summarizing supporting data, interventions that enhance feelings of control and predictability throughout the relocation process were shown to facilitate positive relocation outcomes. Personal control is maximized to the extent that persons perceive themselves to have a choice in moving and/or several alternative environments to choose from. The disruptive impact of the move itself may therefore be attenuated by giving the individual the option of choosing (within limits) the day and time of day he or she is to be moved, informing the individual exactly how the move will be carried out, and, if possible, arranging for the presence of significant others who may provide support and continuity for the relocatee. Increasing the predictability of a new environment can be accomplished in a variety of ways, including prelocation visits to the new environment and thorough orientations once the individual arrives. Control can be fostered by allowing the individual to determine a personal daily routine and by giving him or her responsibilities equivalent to those exercised in the sending environment.

Given the conceptual similarity between this and the preceding analysis of cardiac rehabilitation, it is not surprising that the important unanswered questions concerning relocation are similar to those raised earlier. As with cardiac rehabilitation, levels of control should be matched to individual expectations for control and the individual's realistic ability to exercise control in his or her current environment (cf. Felton & Kahana, 1974; Kahana, 1975; Krantz & Stone, 1978). Too much control in the form of increased responsibilities or a large number of choices may be intimidating to the individual who has had few choices in the past.

It is also probably safe to say that there are context-specific optimal levels of control for maximizing health-related outcomes for both cardiac patients and relocatees. How to match individual expectations for control and environmental opportunities for exercising control remains one of the important unanswered questions for future research. Pursuit of this topic will undoubtedly require an investigation of individual differences and relevant past-history information (cf. Krantz, Baum, & Wideman, 1979).

An additional major unanswered question concerns the mechanism of the translation of psychological interventions into physical health outcomes. It was suggested earlier that control-enhancing interventions may alter health-related behaviors and/or directly affect internal physical states. Although there is some direct evidence that the latter mechanism may apply to cardiac patients, there is as yet little data on the mechanisms intervening between a psychological intervention and health outcomes among the aged. Answers to this question should expand our understanding of the relationship between control and health status and should facilitate the design of effective psychological interventions.

INTEGRATION AND CONCLUSIONS

We have reviewed the research on psychosocial aspects of recovery from heart attack and relocation of the aged, two potentially severe life events that threaten the health and well-being of middle-aged and aged adults. Coverage of each area has been selective, rather than exhaustive, and the aim has been to suggest a theoretical structure to explain varied data. Each event has been conceptualized as a crisis, and environmental predictability and control have been identified as key psychological mechanisms influencing health outcomes of both these life events. In support of this view, research has been cited indicating that loss of control and helplessness often lead to heightened physical and mental distress in heart patients and in the elderly who are victims of relocation.

There are obvious differences between these two crises as psychosocial stressors, and the assumptions made to reinterpret existing empirical data suggest that conclusions be viewed as preliminary. However, applying a similar conceptual approach to two complex life events has several advantages. First, it is possible to begin to draw some general conclusions about the impact of psychosocial stressors on human health. Second, data from one area can be used to supplement research gaps in the other and to suggest directions for future investigation. To illustrate these benefits, consider several points of overlap between the two lines of research.

A benefit of a control interpretation is that it provides specific types of interventions to lessen adverse reactions and to maximize favorable outcomes. With respect to the stress of relocation, one study described earlier demonstrates that an orientation program providing relevant information to new admissions to an old-age home was effective in decreasing physical and psychological deficits typically associated with relocation (Schulz & Hanusa, 1977). A parallel finding emerges from a study (reported earlier) conducted with heart patients about to undergo transfer from a coronary care unit to the hospital ward (Klein et al., 1968). Increasing the predictability of the hospital environment resulted in fewer medical complications.

A related point of contact between research in the two areas concerns the mechanisms whereby control-enhancing interventions may affect health outcomes. We have suggested that these interventions may directly affect internal physiological states (e.g., Klein et al., 1968) or that they may act indirectly as they influence health-related behaviors such as self-care or compliance with medical regimens. Although there is presently little evidence regarding the effect of control interventions on preventative health behaviors, studies with the institutionalized aged (e.g., Langer & Rodin, 1976; Schulz, 1976) indicate that these treatments can influence activity level and the perception of one's own health—two factors that have been identified as predictors of subsequent actions concerning health care (cf. Garrity, 1975; Rosenstock, 1966).

In sum, increasing numbers of investigators are coming to recognize that life stress can exact a price in physical and psychic health (cf. Dohrenwend & Dohrenwend, 1974) and that predictability and control appear to be important psychological variables that mediate the outcomes of important life crises (e.g., Engel, 1968; Schulz, 1976). In the present chapter we have offered an analysis of reactions to heart attack and relocation that has combined these principles. Further pursuit of these research areas should provide valuable insights into the influence of psychosocial processes on human health.

ACKNOWLEDGMENT

Preparation of this paper was supported in part by grants HL23674 and AG00525 from the National Institutes of Health.

REFERENCES

Aldrich, C., & Mendkoff, E. Relocation of the aged and disabled: A mortality study. *Journal of American Geriatrics Society,* 1963, *11,* 185-194.

Averill, J. R. Personal control over aversive stimuli and its relationship to stress. *Psychological Bulletin,* 1973, *80,* 286-303.

Blenkner, M. Environmental change and the aging individual. *Gerontologist,* 1967, *7,* 101-105.

Bourestom, N., & Tars, S. Alterations in life patterns following nursing home relocation. *Gerontologist,* 1974, *14,* 506-510.

Brand, F., & Smith, R. Life adjustment and relocation of the elderly. *Journal of Gerontology,* 1974, *29,* 336-340.

Bruhn, J. G., Thurman, A. E., Jr., Chandler, B. C., & Bruce, T. A. Patients' reactions to death in a coronary care unit. *Journal of Psychosomatic Research,* 1970, *14,* 65-70.

Cannon, W. B. "Voodoo" death. *Psychosomatic Medicine,* 1957, *19,* 182-190.

Carp, F. Effects of improved housing on the lives of older people. In B. Neugarten (Ed.), *Middle age and aging.* Chicago: University of Chicago Press, 1968.

Cassem, N. H., & Hackett, T. P. Psychiatric consultation in a coronary care unit. *Annals of Internal Medicine,* 1971, *75,* 9-14.

Cromwell, R. L., Butterfield, E. C., Brayfield, F. M., & Curry, J. J. *Acute myocardial infarction: Reaction and recovery.* St. Louis, Mo.: C. V. Mosby, 1977.

Croog, S. H., & Levine, S. *The heart patient recovers.* New York: Human Sciences Press, 1977.

Croog, S. H., Levine, S., & Lurie, Z. The heart patient and the recovery process: A review of directions of research on social and psychological factors. *Social Science and Medicine,* 1968, *2,* 111-164.

Croog, S. H., Shapiro, D. S., & Levine, S. Denial among male heart patients. *Psychosomatic Medicine,* 1971, *33,* 385-397.

Doehrman, S. R. Psycho-social aspects of recovery from coronary heart disease: A review. *Social Science and Medicine,* 1977, *11,* 199-218.

Dohrenwend, B. S., & Dohrenwend, B. P. *Stressful life events: Their nature and effects.* New York: Wiley, 1974.

Engel, G. L. A life setting conducive to illness: The giving-up given-up complex. *Annals of Internal Medicine,* 1968, *69,* 293-300.

Felton, B., & Kahana, E. Adjustment and situationally bound locus of control among institutionalized aged. *Journal of Gerontology,* 1974, *29,* 195-301.

Ferrari, N. Freedom of choice. *Social Work,* 1963, *8,* 105-106.

Fox, S. M. Relationship of habits to coronary heart disease. In J. P. Naughton, H. K. Hellerstein, & I. C. Mohler (Eds.), *Exercise testing and exercise training in coronary heart disease.* New York: Academic Press, 1973.

Frankenhaeuser, M. Behavior and circulating catecholamines. *Brain Research,* 1971, *31,* 241-262.

Froese, A., Hackett, T. P., Cassem, N. H., & Silverberg, E. L. Trajectories of anxiety and depression in denying and nondenying acute myocardial infarction patients during hospitalization. *Journal of Psychosomatic Research,* 1974, *18,* 413-420.

Garrity, T. F. Social involvement and activeness as predictors of morale six months after myocardial infarction. *Social Science and Medicine,* 1973, *7,* 199-207. (a)

Garrity, T. F. Vocational adjustment after first myocardial infarction: Comparative assessment of several variables suggested in the literature. *Social Science and Medicine,* 1973, *7,* 705-717. (b)

Garrity, T. F. Morbidity, mortality, and rehabilitation. In W. D. Gentry & R. B. Williams, Jr. (Eds.), *Psychological aspects of myocardial infarction and coronary care.* Saint Louis, Mo.: C. V. Mosby, 1975.

Garrity, T. F., & Klein, R. F. A behavioral predictor of survival among heart attack patients. In E. Palmore & F. C. Jeffers (Eds.), *Prediction of life span.* Lexington, Mass.: Heath, 1971.

Garrity, T. F., McGill, A., Becker, M., Blanchard, E., Crews, J., Cullen, J., Hackett, T. P., Taylor, J., & Valins, S. Report of the task group on cardiac rehabilitation. In S. M. Weiss (Ed.), *Proceedings of the National Heart and Lung Institute Working Conference on Health Behavior,* 1976. (DHEW Publication No. 76-868).

Gentry, W. D., Foster, S., & Haney, T. Denial as a determinant of anxiety and perceived health status in the coronary care unit. *Psychosomatic Medicine,* 1972, *34,* 39.

Glass, D. C. *Behavior patterns, stress, and coronary disease.* New York: Wiley, 1977.

Graham, L. E. Patients' perceptions in the CCU. *American Journal of Nursing,* 1969, *69,* 1921.

Greene, W. A., Goldstein, S., & Moss, A. J. Psychosocial aspects of sudden death. *Archives of Internal Medicine,* 1972, *129,* 725-731.

Greene, W. A., Moss, A. J., & Goldstein, S. Delay denial and death in coronary heart disease. In R. S. Eliot (Ed.), *Stress and the heart.* Mount Kisco, N.Y.: Futura Publishing, 1974.

Gruen, W. Effects of brief psychotherapy during the hospitalization period on the recovery process in heart attacks. *Journal of Consulting and Clinical Psychology,* 1975, *43,* 232-233.

Hackett, T. P., & Cassem, N. H. Psychological adaptation to convalescence in myocardial infarction patients. In J. P. Naughton, H. K. Hellerstein, & I. C. Mohler (Eds.), *Exercise testing and exercise training in coronary heart disease.* New York: Academic Press, 1973.

Hackett, T. P., & Cassem, N. H. The impact of myocardial infarction. *Rhode Island Medical Journal,* 1974, *57,* 327-331.

Hackett, T. P., Cassem, N. H., & Wishnie, H. A. The coronary care unit: An appraisal of its psychologic hazards. *New England Journal of Medicine,* 1968, *279,* 1365.

Heinzelmann, F. Social and psychological factors that influence the effectiveness of exercise programs. In J. P Naughton, H. K. Hellerstein, & I. C. Mohler (Eds.), *Exercise testing and exercise training in coronary heart disease.* New York: Academic Press, 1973.

Holmes, T., & Rahe, R. The social readjustment rating scale. *Journal of Psychosomatic Research,* 1967, *11,* 213-218.

Janis, I. L. *Psychological stress.* New York: Wiley, 1958.

Jasnau, K. F. Individualized versus mass transfer of nonpsychotic geriatric patients from mental hospitals to nursing homes, with special reference to death rate. *Journal of American Geriatrics Society,* 1967, *15,* 280-284.

Johnson, J. E., & Leventhal, H. Effects of accurate expectations and behavioral instructions on reactions during a noxious medical exam. *Journal of Personality and Social Psychology,* 1974, *29,* 710-718.

Kahana, E. A congruence model of person–environment interaction. In P. G. Windley, T. O. Byerts, & F. G. Ernst (Eds.), *Theory development in environment and aging.* Manhattan, Kans.: Gerontological Society, 1975.

Kasl, S. V. Physical and mental health effects of involuntary relocation and institutionalization on the elderly—A review. *American Journal of Public Health,* 1972, *62,* 377-383.

Kasl, S. V., & Cobb, S. Health behavior, illness behavior, and sick role behavior. *Archives of Environmental Health,* 1966, *17,* 246-266.

Kasteler, J., Gray, R., & Carruth, M. Involuntary relocation of the elderly. *Gerontologist,* 1968, *8,* 276-279.

Kastenbaum, R., & Candy, S. E. The 5% fallacy: A methodological and empirical critique of extended care facility population statistics. *International Journal of Aging and Human Development,* 1973, *4,* 15-21.

Killian, E. Effects of geriatric transfers on mortality rates. *Social Work,* 1970, *15,* 19-26.

Kimball, C. P. The experience of open-heart surgery: Psychological responses to surgery. *Psychosomatic Medicine,* 1968, *30,* 552. (Abstract).

Klein, R. F., Kliner , V. A., Zipes, D. P., Troyer, W. G., & Wallace, A. G. Transfer from a coronary care unit. *Archives of Internal Medicine,* 1968, *122,* 104–108.

Kornfeld, D. S. The hospital environment: Its impact on the patient. *Advances in Psychosomatic Medicine,* 1972, *8,* 252–270.

Krantz, D. S., Baum, A., & Wideman, M. V. *Assessment of preferences for self-treatment and information in medical care.* Unpublished manuscript, Uniformed Services University of the Health Sciences, 1979.

Krantz, D. S., & Stone, V. Locus of control and the effects of success and failure in young and community-residing aged women. *Journal of Personality,* 1978, *46,* 536–551.

Langer, E. J., & Rodin, J. The effects of choice and enhanced personal responsibility for the aged: A field experiment in an institutional setting. *Journal of Personality and Social Psychology,* 1976, *34,* 191–198.

Lawton, M. P. Competence, environmental press and the adaptation of older people. In P. G. Windley, T. O. Byerts, & F. G. Ernst (Eds.), *Theory development in environment and aging.* Manhattan, Kans.: Gerontological Society, 1975.

Lawton, M. P., & Cohen, J. The generality of housing impact on the well-being of older people. *Journal of American Gerontology,* 1974, *29,* 194–204.

Lawton, M. P., & Yaffe, S. Mortality, morbidity, and voluntary change of residence by older people. *Journal of American Geriatrics Society,* 1970, *18,* 823–831.

Lazarus, R. S. Psychological stress and coping in adaptation and illness. In S. M. Weiss (Ed.), *Proceedings of the National Heart and Lung Institute Working Conference on Health Behavior,* 1976. (DHEW Publication No. 76–868).

Lieberman, M. Institutionalization of the aged: Effects on behavior. *Journal of Gerontology,* 1969, *24,* 330–340.

Lieberman, M., Tobin, S., & Slover, D. *The effects of relocation on long-term geriatric patients* (Final Rep. Proj. No. 17–1328). Chicago: University of Chicago, Illinois Department of Health and Committee on Human Development, 1971.

Lieberman, M. Relationship of mortality rates to entrance to a home for the aged. *Geriatrics,* 1961, *16,* 515–519.

Lown, B., Verrier, R., & Corbalan, R. Psychological stress and threshold for repetitive ventricular response. *Science,* 1973, *182,* 834–836.

Lown, B., Verrier, R., & Rabinowitz, S. H. Neural and psychologic mechanisms and the problem of sudden cardiac death. *American Journal of Cardiology,* 1977, *39,* 890–902.

Markus, E., Blenkner, M., Bloom, M., & Downs, T. Some factors and their association with post-relocation mortality among the aged persons. *Journal of Gerontology,* 1972, *27,* 376–382.

Marlowe, R. A. *When they closed the doors at Modesto.* Presented at National Institute of Mental Health Conference on the Closure of State Hospitals, Scottsdale, Ariz., 1974.

McPherson, B. D., Paivio, A., Yuhasz, M. S., Rechnitzer, P. A., Pickard, II. A., & Lefcoe, N. M. Psychological effects of an exercise program for post-infarct and normal adult men. *Journal of Sports Medicine and Physical Fitness,* 1967, *7,* 95–102.

Miller, D., & Lieberman, M. A. The relationship of affect state and adaptive capacity to reactions to stress. *Journal of Gerontology,* 1965, *20,* 492.

Mills, R. T., & Krantz, D. S. Information, choice, and reactions to stress: A field experiment in a blood bank with laboratory analogue. *Journal of Personality and Social Psychology,* 1979, *37,* 608–620.

Moss, A. J., & Goldstein, S. The pre-hospital phase of acute myocardial infarction. *Circulation,* 1970, *41,* 737.

Moss, A. J., Wynar, B., & Goldstein, S. Delay in hospitalization during the acute coronary period. *American Journal of Cardiology,* 1969, *24,* 659.

Naughton, J. P., Bruhn, J. G., & Lategola, M. T.   Effects of physical training on physiologic and behavioral characteristics of cardiac patients. *Archives of Physical Medicine and Rehabilitation,* 1968, *49,* 131–137.

Naughton, J. P., Hellerstein, H. K., & Mohler, I. C. (Eds.).   *Exercise testing and exercise training in coronary heart disease.* New York: Academic Press, 1973.

Obier, K., MacPherson, M., & Haywood, J. L.   Predictive value of psychosocial profiles following acute myocardial infarction. *Journal of the National Medical Assocation,* 1977, *69,* 59–61.

Pancheri, P., Bellaterra, M., Matteoli, S., Cristofari, M., Polizzi, C., & Puletti, M.   Infarct as a stress agent: Life history and personality characteristics in improved versus not-improved patients after severe heart attack. *Journal of Human Stress,* 1978, *4,* 16–26.

Pastalan, L.   *Report on Pennsylvania nursing home relocation program: Interim research findings.* Institute of Gerontology, University of Michigan, Ann Arbor, 1976.

Pennebaker, J. W., Burnam, A. M., Schaeffer, M. A., & Harper, D. C.   Lack of control as a determinant of perceived physical symptoms. *Journal of Personality and Social Psychology,* 1977, *35,* 167–174.

Richter, C. P.   On the phenomenon of sudden death in animals and man. *Psychosomatic Medicine,* 1957, *19,* 191–198.

Rodin, J., & Langer, E. J.   Long-term effects of a control-relevant intervention with institutionalized aged. *Journal of Personality and Social Psychology,* 1977, *35,* 897–902.

Rosenstock, I. M.   Why people use health services. *Milbank Memorial Fund Quarterly,* 1966, *44,* 94–124.

Schulz, R.   The effects of control and predictability on the psychological and physical well-being of the institutionalized aged. *Journal of Personality and Social Psychology,* 1976, *33,* 563–573.

Schulz, R., & Aderman, D.   Effect of residential change on the temporal distance to death of terminal cancer patients. *Omega: Journal of Death and Dying,* 1973, *4,* 157–162.

Schulz, R., & Brenner, G. F.   Relocation of the aged: A review and theoretical analysis. *Journal of Gerontology,* 1977, *32,* 323–333.

Schulz, R., & Hanusa, B. H.   *Facilitating institutional adaptation of the aged: Effects of predictability-enhancing intervention.* Paper presented at a meeting of the American Gerontological Society, San Francisco, November 1977.

Schulz, R., & Hanusa, B. H.   Long-term effects of control and predictability-enhancing interventions: Findings and ethical issues. *Journal of Personality and Social Psychology,* 1978, *36,* 1194–1201.

Schwartz, G. E., & Weiss, S. M.   What is behavioral medicine? *Psychosomatic Medicine,* 1977, *39,* 377–381.

Seligman, M. E. P.   *Helplessness.* San Francisco: W. H. Freeman, 1975.

Shanas, E.   *The health of older people: A social survey.* Cambridge, Mass.: Harvard University Press, 1962.

Sherwood, S., Glassman, J., Sherwood, C., & Morris, J. N.   Pre-institutional factors as predictors of adjustment to a long-term care facility. *International Journal of Aging and Human Development,* 1974, *5,* 95–105.

Shrut, S.   Attitudes toward old age and death. In R. Fulton (Ed.), *Death and identity.* New York: Wiley, 1965.

Simon, A. B., Feinleib, M., & Thompson, H. K.   Components of delay in the pre-hospital phase of acute myocardial infarction. *Cardiology,* 1972, *30,* 476.

Stokols, D.   The reduction of cardiovascular risk: An application of social learning perspectives. In A. J. Enelow & J. B. Henderson (Eds.), *Applying behavioral science to cardiovascular risk.* Seattle: American Heart Association, 1975.

Storandt, M., & Wittels, I.   Maintenance of function in relocation of community-dwelling older adults. *Journal of Gerontology,* 1975, *30,* 608–612.

Taylor, S. E., & Levin, S. *Psychological aspects of breast cancer: Theory and research.* San Francisco: West Coast Cancer Foundation, 1976.

Tobin, S., & Lieberman, M. *Last home for the aged.* San Francisco: Jossey-Bass, 1976.

Tufo, H. M., & Ostfeld, A. M. A prospective study of open heart surgery. *Psychosomatic Medicine,* 1968, *30,* 552. (Abstract).

Turner, B., Tobin, S., & Lieberman, M. Personality traits as predictors of institutional adaptation among the aged. *Journal of Gerontology,* 1972, *27,* 61–68.

U.S. Public Health Service. *Proceedings of the National Heart and Lung Institute Working Conference on Health Behavior,* 1975. (DHEW Publication No. 76-868).

Wallston, K. A., Wallston, B. S., Kaplan, G. D., & Maides, S. A. Development and validation of the health locus of control (HLC) scale. *Journal of Consulting and Clinical Psychology,* 1976, *44,* 580–585.

Weidner, G., & Matthews, K. A. Reported physical symptoms elicited by unpredictable events and the type A coronary-prone behavior pattern. *Journal of Personality and Social Psychology,* 1978, *36,* 1213–1220.

Wenger, N. K. Early ambulation after myocardial infarction: Grady Memorial Hospital–Emory University School of Medicine. In J. P. Naughton, H. K. Hellerstein, & I. C. Mohler (Eds.), *Exercise testing and exercise training in coronary heart disease.* New York: Academic Press, 1973.

Williams, R. B., & Gentry, W. D. (Eds.). *Behavioral approaches to medical treatment.* Cambridge, Mass.: Ballinger, 1977.

Wittels, I., & Botwinick, J. Survival in relocation. *Journal of Gerontology,* 1974, *29,* 440–443.

Zweig, J., & Csank, J. Effects of relocation on chronically ill geriatric patients of a medical unit: Mortality rates. *Journal of American Geriatics Society,* 1975, *23,* 132–136.

3 Environmental Stress and the Type A Response

David C. Glass
City University of New York

Charles S. Carver
University of Miami

Coronary heart disease, a major cause of death in this country, is a result of damage to the coronary arteries. This arterial damage is termed coronary artery disease or atherosclerosis (Friedberg, 1966) or, less technically, hardening of the arteries. Epidemiological data (e.g., Brand, Rosenman, Sholtz, & Friedman, 1976; Dawber & Kannel, 1961) indicate that high risk of coronary heart disease is associated with advancing age, being male rather than female, elevated levels of cholesterol and related fats in the blood, hypertension, heavy cigarette smoking, diabetes mellitus, parental history of heart disease, obesity, and physical inactivity. As might be expected, the likelihood of heart disease increases along with the number of risk factors present. But, somewhat surprisingly, the best combination of these factors still fails to identify most new cases of the disease (Jenkins, 1971). Most cardiac patients do not have excessive levels of serum cholesterol, only a small number are hypertensive, and even fewer are diabetic. Moreover, there is considerable controversy surrounding some of the risk factors that are widely assumed to be important (Friedman, 1969). For example, it is not at all clear that obesity directly increases the risk of heart disease, as is commonly believed.

In part because traditional medical risk factors have had limited success in predicting cardiovascular disease, a sizable body of research has begun to emerge that is aimed at determining what *psychological* factors enhance the risk of developing cardiac disorders (Jenkins, 1971, 1976). Two promising variables that have received a good deal of attention in recent years are psychological stress and the Type A coronary-prone behavior pattern.

PSYCHOLOGICAL STRESS

Psychological stress is often defined as an internal state that occurs when an individual confronts a threat to his or her physical or psychological well-being (e.g., Lazarus, 1966). This definition includes the implicit assumption that the internal stress state can be inferred through physiological, self-report, and overt behavioral measurements—for example, changes in heart rate, an inability to concentrate, or impairments in interpersonal relations.

Stressful life events, including such things as job dissatisfactions, economic frustrations, excessive work, and burdensome reponsibility, can occur in anyone's life. And it appears to be the case that such events increase the risk of coronary heart disease (House, 1975; Jenkins, 1971). People at high risk often have jobs with a good deal of responsibility for subordinates, excessive work loads, and role conflicts. Unhappiness in nonoccupational areas—for example, marital and family relations—has also been implicated in the occurrence of coronary disease. Finally, acute stressors over which the person has no control—for example, the death of a spouse—have been correlated with the subsequent onset of cardiac disorders in the person exposed to those stressful events (e.g., Parkes, Benjamin, & Fitzgerald, 1969).

The contribution of psychological stress to the pathogenesis of cardiovascular disease probably occurs via two types of pathways. One is the set of physiological and neurohumoral mechanisms that are involved in the initiation and development of atherosclerotic plaques and/or sustained elevations in blood pressure. Recent research seems to implicate specific mechanisms (see Eliot, 1974; Friedman, 1969; Rosenman & Friedman, 1974), including increases in cholesterol level as a function of stress; damage to the inner layer of the coronary arteries; and facilitation of the aggregation of blood platelets (substances important in coagulation), which are then incorporated into arterial plaques, thereby contributing to narrowing of the coronary vessels and subsequent myocardial infarction.

A specific illustration of this physiological mediation comes from research showing an association between cholesterol level in the blood and stressful life events. More specifically, this research showed that tax accountants had significantly higher serum cholesterol levels during the first two weeks of April (immediately prior to the April 15 tax deadline) than during the months of February and March. Moreover, their average cholesterol level fell sharply after April 15 (Friedman, Rosenman, & Carroll, 1958). This sort of finding has been replicated several times, using a variety of procedures for inducing stress (see Rosenman & Friedman, 1974, for a summary of these studies).

The second way in which stress may contribute to coronary disease is by repeatedly engaging the body's nonspecific reactions to aversive stimulation. It is widely agreed that such stimulation leads to discharge of the sympathetic nervous system and to increases in hormones such as adrenaline and noradrenaline (see e.g., Mason, 1972). There is evidence that high levels of these hormones, which are collectively termed catecholamines, may have special significance in the development of coronary disease. For example, it is well known that these substances elevate blood pressure. Some research indicates further that they can accelerate the rate of arterial damage, and in fact, induce myocardial lesions (e.g., Raab, Chaplin, & Bajusz, 1964; Raab, Stark, MacMillan, & Gigee, 1961). Catecholamines also potentiate the aggregation of blood platelets, which is considered to be an important factor in atherogenesis as well as in the genesis of thrombosis (Ardlie, Glew, & Schwartz, 1966; Duguid, 1946; Theorell, 1974). It follows from this that any psychological factor—such as stress—that serves to increase catecholamines in the blood may be a potential pathogen for cardiovascular functioning.

TYPE A BEHAVIOR PATTERN

A second psychological factor that has important implications for coronary heart disease is what has been termed the Type A coronary-prone behavior pattern. This pattern has three principal components: competitive achievement striving, a sense of time urgency, and aggressiveness. (We should note, however, that the assumption that these components are fully integrated within individuals remains to be validated.) Pattern A has been linked to the occurrence of coronary disease in several studies. For example, one major research project has shown that Type A men had more than twice the incidence of heart disease as did Type B men (defined by relative absence of A-type characteristics) during an 8½-year follow-up period (Rosenman, Brand, Jenkins, Friedman, Straus, & Wurm, 1975). This was the case even when statistical adjustments were made for such traditional risk factors as cigarette smoking, serum cholesterol, and hypertension. This latter point is an important one. It means that the predictive relationship of Pattern A to coronary disease cannot be accounted for entirely by the presence of other risk factors, even though there does tend to be a relationship between Pattern A and some of those risk factors (see following). The Type A behavior pattern exerts an independent pathogenic influence. Indeed, another study (Jenkins, Zyzanski, & Rosenman, 1976) has found that an objective measure of this behavior pattern was the strongest single predictor of recurring heart attacks, from among a set of variables that included cigarette smoking and serum cholesterol level. There is also evidence of an association between Pattern A and the atherosclerotic process that precedes heart attacks, with Type A's showing more pronounced occlusion of arteries than Type B's (e.g., Blumenthal, Williams, Kong, Thompson, Jenkins, & Rosenman, 1975; Zyzanski, Jenkins, Ryan, Flessas, & Everist, 1976).

Although Pattern A does make an independent contribution to coronary disease, its influence is probably mediated in part by certain more traditional risk factors. For example, some research indicates that fully developed Type

A's over 35 have significantly higher serum cholesterol levels than do Type B's (Friedman & Rosenman, 1959). Similar A–B differences have been reported for other fats and related substances in the blood (e.g., Rosenman & Friedman, 1974). In fact, even among subjects as young as 19 years of age, extreme Type A's have been found to have greater serum cholesterol concentrations than extreme Type B's (Glass, 1977).

Interestingly, there is little evidence of a relationship between hypertension and Pattern A (e.g., Shekelle, Schoenberger, & Stamler, 1976). On the other hand, recent research from a number of sources indicates that Type A's display greater transient increases in systolic blood pressure than do Type B's when both types of subjects are confronted with challenging environmental situations. For example, one study showed that college-aged A's responded to a difficult reaction-time task with greater increases in systolic blood pressure and heart rate than did B's (Dembroski, MacDougall, & Shields, 1977). Similarly, coronary patients have been found to display greater blood pressure elevations than matched controls when undergoing a stressful interview (Dembroski, MacDougall, & Lushene, in press), despite the presence of beta-adrenergic blocking medication among the coronary patients. This latter study also demonstrated a difference in blood pressure elevation between Type A's and Type B's. Differences in blood pressure elevation as a function of challenging tasks have also been demonstrated in a variety of other paradigms (e.g., Dembroski, MacDougall, Shields, Petitto, & Lushene, 1978; Manuck, Craft, & Gold, 1978; Manuck & Garland, in press). This research all seems to indicate that there is a subtle association between Pattern A and elevated blood pressure, but one that involves greater lability of blood pressure rather than hypertension per se.

As was argued earlier regarding the effects of stress, the relationship of Pattern A to coronary disease may be mediated by the sympathetic-adrenal medullary system. This hypothesis is supported by a variety of data, including the finding that after stressful treadmill exercise, Type A men show less decrease than do B's in platelet aggregation in response to noradrenaline (Simpson, Olewine, Jenkins, Ramsey, Zyzanski, Thomas, & Hames, 1974). Other studies indicate that blood clotting among Type A's is hastened during periods of stress to a greater degree than is true of Type B's (Rosenman & Friedman, 1974). Of greater significance, perhaps, is the finding that the elevation of plasma levels of noradrenaline immediately before, during, and after a stressful competition are greater among A's than B's (Friedman, Byers, Diamant, & Rosenman, 1975). Simpson et al. (1974) have also shown that physically fit Type A's have the largest increase in noradrenaline immediately after a treadmill test, whereas the least fit among the Type B's exhibited the lowest increase in noradrenaline. In addition, there is evidence that extreme Type A's excrete considerably more noradrenaline in their urine during active working hours than do Type B's. The potential mediation of the relation between Pattern A and coronary disease by the catecholamines is taken up again in a later section of this chapter.

Assessment of the Type A Behavior Pattern

Classification of persons as Type A or Type B is customarily based on a structured interview (Friedman, 1969; Jenkins, Rosenman, & Friedman, 1968).[1] The person being interviewed is asked questions dealing with the intensity of his or her ambitions, competitiveness, time urgency, and hostile feelings. The content of the person's answers is an important determinant of the classification of his or her behavior pattern, but the manner and tone in which the individual answers are given more weight in the classification. For example, Type A's use explosive vocal intonations more than Type B's do. Indeed, a recent study has shown that an index of volume of voice and speed of speech yields much the same classifications as does the more standard technique that utilizes content as well as vocal style (Schucker & Jacobs, 1977).

Another approach to classification is embodied in a self-administered questionnaire called the JAS, or the Jenkins Activity Survey for Health Prediction (Jenkins, Rosenman, & Zyzanski, 1972). It consists of a series of items such as the following: (1) "How would your wife (or closest friend) rate you?" where "Definitely hard-driving and competitive" is an extreme Pattern A response and "Definitely relaxed and easy-going" is a Pattern B response; (2) "Do you ever set deadlines or quotas for yourself at work or at home?" where "Yes, once per week or more often" is a Pattern A response and "No" and "Yes, but only occasionally" are Pattern B responses. The JAS provides a continuous distribution of A–B scores.

This instrument has recently been modified for use with college students (Glass, 1977). Most of the research described later used this student version. In many studies subjects were separated into A's and B's by division at the median of a distribution of scores obtained over a 3-year period. In some experiments, however, subjects were deliberately selected from the extremes of the JAS distribution (e.g., upper and lower thirds). These two criteria yielded similar patterns of results. Not surprisingly, though, the effects were usually somewhat stronger with extreme A's and B's.

---

[1]Descriptions of Type A and Type B individuals represent extremes of a bipolar continuum that presumably is normally distributed in the United States. Indeed, classification based on the interview was originally made on a 4-point scale: fully developed A's, incompletely developed A's, incompletely developed B's, and fully developed B's. It is therefore probably more accurate to speak of Pattern A and Pattern B than Type A and Type B, because we are not really dealing with a typology. For ease of exposition, however, the terms *type* and *pattern* are used interchangeably throughout this chapter.

As already discussed, Pattern A can be measured reliably, it has good validity for prediction of coronary disease, and there is even evidence regarding some of the mechanisms by which it contributes to cardiovascular pathology. Only recently, however, has systematic evidence been gathered that Type A's do indeed exhibit the behavioral characteristics that define the pattern: achievement striving, time urgency, and hostility. This evidence was amassed as the first stage of a program of research that had as its goal the elucidation of the interplay between Pattern A and psychological stress in the genesis of coronary disease (see Glass, 1977, for a complete report of the research). The behavioral characteristics of the Type A were assessed in this research by use of the kinds of controlled experimental procedures that have been developed by research psychologists.

Construct Validation Research

In both laboratory and field settings, studies have shown the Type A to be an achievement-oriented person who often works at near-maximum capacity. For example, college-aged A's and B's were asked to solve a series of arithmetic problems under one of two instructional sets: There was no time limit, or there was a 5-minute time limit (Burnam, Pennebaker, & Glass, 1975). Type A subjects worked at an elevated level irrespective of the presence or absence of an explicit deadline. Type B's worked at a comparable pace only when the deadline had been made explicit.

Other findings suggest that achievement striving is part of the day-to-day orientation of Type A's. For example, college student Type A's earned reliably more academic honors than did their Type B counterparts. Furthermore, when asked about their "plans after college," approximately 60% of the Type A's said that they intended to "go on to graduate or professional school," whereas 70% of the Type B's said that they intended to "go to work, get a job."

This achievement orientation is consistent with the description of the Type A as a person who believes that with sufficient effort, any obstacle can be overcome (e.g., Friedman, 1969). An interesting question that follows from this is whether Type A's might suppress subjective states that threaten their best efforts, in order to achieve task mastery. An example of such a potentially debilitating state is fatigue. The possibility that Type A's would suppress fatigue in order to persist at a tiring but challenging task was investigated using a paradigm designed to produce veridical fatigue (Carver, Coleman, & Glass, 1976). Subjects were required to walk continuously on a motorized treadmill at increasingly sharp angles of incline (cf. Balke, 1954; Balke, Grillo, Konecci, & Luft, 1954). Subjects completed this treadmill test while rating their fatigue at 2-minute intervals according to a labeled 11-point scale. Each subject also completed a running test that made possible the assessment of the subject's maximum aerobic capacity (i.e., the person's maximum rate of oxygen absorption). Each subject's walking performance then was scored as a proportion of his maximum capacity.

The physical characteristics of Pattern A and Pattern B subjects (e.g., percentage of body fat) were essentially identical. But Pattern A subjects reached an oxygen absorption rate on the walking treadmill test that averaged 91.4% of their capacities, whereas pattern B subjects averaged only 82.8% of their capacities. Apparently, then, A's worked at levels closer to the limits of their endurance than did B's. Even while doing so, however, A's expressed less fatigue than did B's. As is indicated in Table 3.1, Type A subjects rated their fatigue as significantly lower than did Type B's on each of the last four ratings made prior to termination of the walking test.

As has been suggested, this tendency to suppress fatigue may be interpreted in terms of the achivement orientation of Pattern A. Suppression, or denial, of fatigue has instrumental value: It aids in the struggle for attainment of desired goals. To acknowledge fatigue, to allow it to intrude, might interfere with task mastery, a situation that A's do not easily tolerate.

Subsequent research has pursued the implications of this finding in two quite different ways. One study (Carver, DeGregorio, & Gillis, 1978) was conducted to assess whether this Pattern A characteristic could be observed in a field setting. College football players were rated by their coaches on the degree to which they exerted themselves to their limits during practices and during game situations. Differences between A's and B's appeared in the coaches' ratings for the subset of subjects who were confronted with the greatest challenge—those who were playing while injured. Among these players, Type A's were seen as exerting themselves closer to their limits than Type B's by both the head coach and the assistant coaches. Other researchers (Matthews & Brunson, in press) have attempted to gain additional information as to the mechanism involved in findings such as those from the treadmill study. By using research paradigms from cognitive psychology, they have provided evidence consistent with the position that Type A's actively

TABLE 3.1
Final Four Fatigue Ratings Among Type A's and Type B's
Walking on Treadmill

	Fourth to Last Rating	Third to Last Rating	Second to Last Rating	Last Rating
Type A	5.30	4.10	3.10	2.20
Type B	3.40	2.80	2.20	1.50

Note: Smaller numbers indicate greater fatigue ($n = 10$ per group).
[a](Data from Carver, Coleman, & Glass, 1976. Copyright 1976 by the American Psychological Association. Reprinted by permission.)

suppress their awareness of potentially distracting stmuli. It thus seems likely that Type A's are not simply making a public denial of their fatigue. Instead, they apparently are preventing many of the internal fatigue cues from reaching consciousness.

Another important component of Pattern A is a sense of time urgency. Type A's become impatient with delay, and they report that a time interval of 1 minute elapses reliably sooner than do Type B's (Burnam et al., 1975). This sense of impatience has important behavioral consequences. For example, Type A's do more poorly than Type B's on a task that requires a delayed response (Glass, Snyder, & Hollis, 1974). Because this task provides "differential reinforcement of low rates of responding," it is typically abbreviated as *DRL*. On the DRL task, the subject must wait for a fixed time interval before responding; a premature response resets the timer, and the subject does not obtain reinforcement. The DRL task is quite difficult and can be mastered only with considerable patience. Glass et al. (1974) found the reinforcement scores of Type A subjects to be significantly lower on this task than those of Type B's. As one might expect, Type A's performed more poorly because they were unable to wait long enough after receiving reinforcement before responding again. Behavioral observations also confirmed that A's openly displayed impatience with delayed responding. Approximately 48% of the A's, but only 12% of the B's, displayed tense and hyperactive movements during their DRL sessions.

Lengthy intervals between trials on other kinds of tasks—for example, reaction-time procedures—might also be expected to arouse impatience in A's, with resultant restless behavior and distraction. Should such activity divert attention away from the task at hand, it would cause the Type A to respond more slowly than the Type B when the cue for response eventually appeared. To test this reasoning, A's and B's were subjected to a complex reaction-time task in which intertrial intervals were either short (1.5 seconds) or relatively long (random intervals ranging from 4 to 9 seconds). Analysis of subjects' latency scores revealed that B's were faster than A's when intertrial intervals were long, whereas A's were slightly faster than B's when intervals were short. In sum, Type A's reacted more slowly when conditions placed a premium on patience than when such delays were not imposed. By contrast, Type B's showed similar reaction times irrespective of the length of the intervals between trials.

The third major facet of Pattern A is hostility and aggressiveness. Carver and Glass (1978) have conducted two experiments to examine this behavioral tendency. The first study tested the idea that Type A's would react with enhanced aggressiveness toward another person who denigrated their efforts to perform a difficult task, to a greater degree than would Type B's. Accordingly, some subjects in this study were harassed by a confederate while attempting to solve a very difficult puzzle ("instigation" condition). An

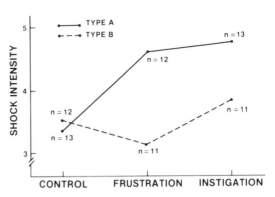

FIG. 3.1. Mean shock intensities among Type A's and Type B's after pretreatment with a control procedure, a task frustration, or an instigation (frustration plus interpersonal harassment). (From Carver & Glass, 1978. Copyright 1978 by the American Psychological Association. Reprinted by permission.)

opportunity was later given to subjects to administer electric shocks to the harassing individual (cf. Buss, 1961). Subjects in a control condition participated only in the shock phase of the study. In comparison to the control treatment, the instigation procedure aroused substantial aggression, but this was largely attributable to the high levels of shock delivered by Type A subjects. That is, instigated A's delivered stronger shocks than did their control group counterparts, but instigated B's did not shock at reliably higher levels than did control group B's.

Subsequent research (Carver & Glass, 1978, Study 2) replicated this finding and also provided additional information regarding antecedents of differences in aggression between A's and B's. This second experiment included a "frustration" condition, in which subjects failed at the puzzle but were not harrassed by the confederate. Analysis of shock means from this study revealed that the most reliable difference between Pattern A and Pattern B individuals occurred in the frustration condition (see Fig 3.1). Indeed, Type A's were very nearly as aggressive after having been frustrated as they were when exposed to the full instigation procedure. Type B's, in contrast, responded to the frustration with a (nonsignificant) decrease in aggression. Thus elicitation of aggression from the Type A apparently does not require an interpersonal provocation; a task frustration by itself is sufficent to evoke that response. Type B's, however, seem to be indifferent to frustration.

ENVIRONMENTAL CHALLENGE, STRESS, AND PATTERN A CHARACTERISTICS

The research on Pattern A described in the foregoing sections provides systematic documentation for the three behavioral components of Pattern A. In so doing, the research also provides evidence for the construct validity of the measures that were used to classify subjects as A's or B's. But these results may also be examined from a more conceptual perspective. We believe that such a conceptual analysis provides insight both into the motivational dynamics of Pattern A and into the relationship between this behavior pattern and psychological stress. This perspective may have some important implications, in that consideration of these issues may suggest mechanisms by which Pattern A adversely affects the cardiovascular system.

If one examines the construct validation studies as a group, one may discern a commonality among the many specific empirical findings. Type A's work hard to succeed, suppress subjective states (e.g., fatigue) that might interfere with their task performances, conduct their activities at a rapid pace, and express hostility after being frustrated or harassed in their efforts at task completion. It can be argued that at the crux of all these behavioral effects is an attempt by the Type A to assert and maintain control over environmental challenges and demands. Moreover, it also seems likely that meeting these demands involves at least minimal stress, in that most environmental challenges imply the threat of potential failure. Taking all this reasoning together, the coronary-prone behavior pattern thus might be described as being a characteristic style of responding to environmental stressors that threaten the individual's sense of control. The Type A is engaged in a continual struggle to maintain control, whereas the Type B, relatively free of such concerns, shows an absence of Pattern A behavioral traits.

The concept of control (cf. Glass & Singer, 1972) may be defined in terms of perceptions of contingencies. If a person perceives a contingency between his or her behavior and an outcome (i.e., believes that his or her behavior determines that outcome), the outcome is defined as controllable. By contrast, if a person believes that his or her actions do not influence an outcome, the outcome is uncontrollable. Stressors can be either controllable or uncontrollable. A controllable stressor is a potentially harmful stimulus that can be avoided by appropriate instrumental responses. An uncontrollable stressor is a harmful stimulus that the person can neither escape nor avoid.

Responses to Uncontrollable Stressors

The Type A's initial response to an uncontrollable stressor may be termed *hyper-responsiveness;* it reflects increased effort to assert control over the stressor. In comparison to B's, A's display increased motivation—at least initially—to master stressful situations that they perceive as being potentially uncontrollable. An important question would seem to be whether this heightened motivation generalizes across tasks. If so, after brief exposure to an uncontrollable stressor (for example, a few trials of inescapable noise stimulation), the Type A would be expected to exert greater efforts than the

Type B to master a subsequent task of a different type in an attempt to reestablish a sense of control.

If Type A's motivation were enhanced by exposure to a stressor, the result thus might be performance facilitation. For example, consider the reaction-time study described earlier, in which there were long intertrial intervals. Pattern A subjects, it will be recalled, exhibited longer response latencies than Pattern B subjects, presumably because of their inability to sustain the patience needed to remain alert during the relatively long waiting period. If exposure to uncontrollable stress were to enhance the motivation of A's, one might expect shorter response latencies among A's if the long-interval reaction-time task were administered after exposure to inescapable noise. That is, after being threatened with loss of control, A's might be expected to make special efforts to contain their impatience in order to perform well, thereby reasserting control. The result should be relatively faster responses among A's following the uncontrollable stressor. One would expect Type B's, by contrast, to show less improvement after an experience with uncontrollability, because B's are assumed to be less responsive to the threat to environmental control.

This reasoning was tested in the following manner. Twenty Type A's and 20 Type B's were exposed, in a pretreatment, to 12 bursts of 100-decibel noise.[2] Half the A's and half the B's in the study were able to escape from each of the noise bursts by appropriate lever-pressing responses (escape condition). The other half of the subjects were unable to terminate the sound (no-escape condition). Immediately following the noise pretreatment was the test phase, consisting of a reaction-time task with long intertrial intervals. The major dependent measure was subjects' response latencies, averaged across trials.

The escape versus no-escape pretreatment was successful in inducing differential perceptions of lack of control, as assessed by self-reports. Analysis of response-latency data (see Fig. 3.2) yielded a reliable interaction between behavior pattern and type of pretreatment. Recall that Type A's are normally slower than B's on this particular task. The interpolation of an escapable pretreatment was not expected to alter this difference, and it did not. But the threat inherent in exposure to uncontrollable noise apparently motivated Type A subjects in the no-escape condition to try harder. Thus they reacted more rapidly to the signal light despite the lengthy waiting period. Type B's, in contrast, may have experienced a decrement in motivation. Their reaction-time performance was impaired by experience with uncontrollability.

---

[2]This amount of stimulation was selected as constituting a brief exposure to an uncontrollable stressor, because research discussed later indicated that more prolonged exposure (e.g., 35 noise bursts) produces learned helplessness rather than facilitation effects (see also Hiroto, 1974).

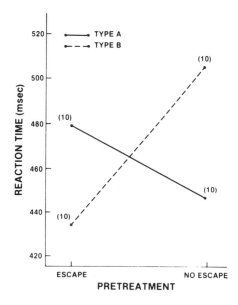

FIG. 3.2.   Mean reaction times of Type A's and Type B's after pretreatment with escapable or inescapable noise (group sizes in parentheses). (From Glass, 1977.)

These results were conceptually replicated in an experiment that induced perceived lack of control by giving subjects random positive and negative feedback (i.e., "correct" or "incorrect" evaluations) for their attempts to solve two cognitive tasks (see Hiroto & Seligman, 1975; Seligman, 1975). Perceptions of controllability were induced among other subjects by responding with "correct" when their answers were correct and "incorrect" when their answers were wrong. The effects of these two pretreatments were measured by means of a subsequent DRL task. Recall that Type A's generally do more poorly on DRL than Type B's. But if an uncontrollable pretreatment enhances Type A's motivation to succeed, one might expect A's to exhibit better performances than B's after such a pretreatment.

As is readily apparent from Fig. 3.3, the data from this study formed a pattern that is remarkably similar to the pattern from the previous study (Fig. 3.2). The only difference is that a delayed response is correct here, whereas a fast response was correct in the first study. This replication shows, then, that the performance of A's was enhanced after exposure to uncontrollable stress, even though such enhancement required them to suppress their customary impatience with a DRL task.

Taken together, the findings of these two studies support the inference that had been made from the validity studies—that Pattern A behavior emerges in the presence of perceived threats to environmental control. The enhanced performances of Type A's presumably reflect attempts to reassert and maintain control after its loss has been threatened. It thus would appear reasonable to conclude that Type A behavior represents a strategy for coping

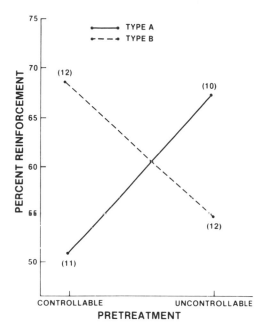

FIG. 3.3. Percent reinforcement for Type A's and Type B's over the DRL session after pretreatment with controllable (soluble) or uncontrollable (insoluble) problems (group sizes in parentheses). (From Glass, 1977.)

with potentially uncontrollable stress. This interpretation has received additional support from studies using other techniques to induce threat to control, including partial reinforcement procedures that are perceived as differing in controllability (see Glass, 1977).

Responses to Prolonged Exposure to Uncontrollable Stressors

Enhanced efforts at asserting control over an uncontrollable stressor are, of course, ineffective in the long run. Extended exposure to the stressor must eventually lead to the perception that no relationship exists between responses and outcomes. The behavioral result of such perceptions is termed *hypo-responsiveness* (cf. Wortman & Brehm, 1975). This is a giving-up response, which has also been discussed as *learned helplessness* (Seligman, 1975). Although all persons may experience helplessness under these circumstances, it is the Type A's who may show the greatest hypo-responsiveness, because of their tendency to experience loss of control as highly threatening.

The first test of this hypothesis (Krantz, Glass, & Snyder, 1974) made use of Seligman's (1975) learned-helplessness paradigm. Subjects were exposed to a pretreatment in which either loud (105-decibel) or moderate (78-decibel) noise was administered, thus varying the degree of stress experienced. Thirty-five, rather than 12, noise bursts were given to each subject. Half the cases within each stress-level condition were unable to escape from the noise, whereas the other half could terminate the noise by manipulating rotary switches. In the test phase of the study, subjects were administered the same intensity noise as had been given in the first part of the experiment. In contrast to pretreatment, however, all subjects could now escape or even avoid the noise by making appropriate responses with a shuttle-box lever.

The primary dependent variable of this study was the number of trials that subjects took to achieve a criterion of three consecutive escape and/or avoidance responses (see Table 3.2). Analysis of this measure indicated that Type A's in the no-escape–high-stress condition took significantly more trials to learn the escape response than did A's given the escapable high-stress pretreatment. Type B's in the escape and no-escape groups did not differ from each other under high-stress conditions. Just the opposite pattern occurred in conditions of moderate stress. Type B's who had been given the no-escape pretreatment took more trials to reach criterion than did B's given the escapable pretreatment, whereas there was no difference between A's in the escape and no-escape groups.

The latter results were somewhat surprising. The intitial prediction had been only that behavior pattern would interact with the pretreatment manipulation of controllability. However, the results suggested a more complex relationship, in which stress level somehow mediates the reactions of A's and B's to prolonged exposure to uncontrollable stressors. An obvious possibility that might help to explain this finding is that A's might have experienced more arousal than B's. However, the A–B variable failed to show any reliable association with either electrodermal or self-report measures of arousal that were collected during and immediately after the pretreatment phase of the study. It is always possible, of course, that differences were

TABLE 3.2
Mean Number of Trials to Criterion for Escape
and/or Avoidance Learning

	Escape	No Escape
High Stress, Pattern A	6.3 ($n = 9$)	12.7 ($n = 9$)
High Stress, Pattern B	7.2 ($n = 6$)	8.7 ($n = 6$)
Moderate Stress, Pattern A	7.7 ($n = 7$)	8.5 ($n = 6$)
Moderate Stress, Pattern B	9.0 ($n = 8$)	20.0 ($n = 9$)

Note: Comparisons between cell means were conducted using the error-mean-square from a three-way analysis of variance. These comparisons revealed a number of significant differences ($p < .05$ or better), including those between the following cell means: (1) 12.7 and 6.3; (2) 20.1 and 9.0; (3) 20.1 and 8.7; (4) 20.1 and 8.5. The differences between (1) 12.7 and 8.5, (2) 9.0 and 7.2, and (3) 7.7 and 6.3 were not statistically significant ($ps > .20$).

present but went undetected because of inadequate sampling of physiological channels. However, the physiological results from this experiment did not indicate that an arousal-based explanation of the learned-helplessness results was particularly viable. Therefore, a cognitive interpretation was developed and explored in subsequent research.

This interpretation was as follows. If Type A's are more concerned than Type B's about preserving control over events, A's might be expected to distort or deny cues that signify that control has been lost—to the degree that such cues do not compel recognition. If Type A's can thereby minimize their awareness of the fact that they are unable to control the situation, they may not encode the fact of uncontrollability effectively. For this reason, they may fail to display learned helplessness in the subsequent task. This may have been what occurred in the Krantz et al. (1974) research among Type A's who received only moderately loud inescapable noise. If, on the other hand, the absence of control is highly salient—as should have been the case when the inescapable noise was loud enough to be aversive—A's should experience more difficulty in ignoring lack of control. Perhaps A's then even exert increased efforts at locating control-relevant cues. Finding such cues should lead only to stronger certainty that nothing can be done to gain control. These unfavorable expectations may then transfer from the pretreatment to the test phase of the paradigm, where they are reflected as impaired learning of escape and avoidance responses.

This line of reasoning (see also Schachter & Rodin, 1974) appears to fit the pattern of findings obtained by Krantz et al. (1974). But it is a post hoc interpretation and therefore requires independent verification. Accordingly, a second study was conducted (see Glass, 1977), which used a different manipulation of salience and a manipulation of uncontrollability based on noncontingency of reinforcements for performance on cognitive tasks (see the foregoing).

In this study, subjects were exposed to four, rather than two, cognitive problems for which they received feedback of "correct" and "incorrect." Salience was manipulated by varying the prominence of this reinforcement. That is, some subjects were asked to keep detailed records of whether their responses were correct or incorrect. This made it relatively simple for the subjects to see if there was a relationship between their answers and the reinforcements they received during the session. The effects of these manipulations were assessed with an anagrams task, which had been used in previous learned-helplessness research (Hiroto & Seligman, 1975) The major dependent measure was the number of trials that it took the subject to achieve a criterion of three consecutive anagram solutions in less than 15 seconds each (for a more complete account, see Glass, 1977, Chap. 8).

This study yielded results that were very similar to those of Krantz et al. (1974). Type A's in this second study showed greater helplessness (i.e., more trials required to reach the criterion) after uncontrollable than controllable pretreatment but only if the cues signifying lack of control had been made salient. When these cues were low in salience, Type A's showed minimal evidence of helplessness. Unlike the previous study, however, Type B's in the low-salience–uncontrollable condition took only marginally more trials to reach the criterion than did B's in the controllable condition.

In sum, although brief exposure to uncontrollable stressors causes Type A's to exhibit enhanced efforts to control their environment, prolonged exposure to the same kind of uncontrollable stress causes them to display a pronounced giving-up response. However, this vulnerability of A's to learned helplessness must be qualified by the fact that it appears to occur only when the cues signifying absence of control are highly salient.

CONTROL, HELPLESSNESS, AND HEART DISEASE

The helplessness results already reported take on added significance when viewed in the light of recent work on the relationship between stress in an individual's life and the occurrence of disease. Early researchers in this area suggested that accumulated life events—whether positive or negative—had an impact on the incidence of disease. The important factor, it was believed, was the total amount of change that was experienced within a given time period (e.g., Holmes & Rahe, 1967). More recent studies indicate, however, that events must be negative in order to potentiate illness (e.g., Dohrenwend & Dohrenwend, 1974). Indeed, some evidence even suggests that it is the sense of uncontrollability and helplessness induced by certain types of negative life changes that is critical in facilitating disease onset (cf. Paykel, 1974).

Events such as the death of a loved one, or a sudden financial setback, are not easily influenced by our own actions. Such losses often lead to helplessness, depression, and a tendency to give up efforts to cope with environmental demands (Seligman, 1975). It has been proposed (e.g., Engel, 1968; Schmale, 1972) that this kind of helplessness-inducing event has a role in the pathogenesis of a variety of physical diseases, ranging from the common cold to cancer. It has also been shown (Greene, Goldstein, & Moss, 1972) that sudden death is abnormally frequent among men who (according to reports of next of kin) had been depressed for a period of a week to several months prior to death. These data are certainly not conclusive, but they do suggest the possibility that helplessness-inducing life events may be precursors to coronary heart disease, as well as other diseases. Because so many disorders have been linked to uncontrollable life stressors, however, consideration must be given to what other factor might interact with helplessness to result specifically in coronary disease. A reasonable possibility for investigation would seem to be that the Type A behavior pattern is a predisposing condition that mediates the relationship between stress-induced helplessness and cardiovascular pathology. The laboratory studies described earlier indicate that extended experience with salient, uncontrollable stressors results in giving-up behavioral responses among Type A's. By extrapolation, it might be argued that the interaction of Pattern A and helplessness-inducing life events serves as a precursor to clinical coronary disease.

The best test of this hypothesis would require a prospective study. Any support gained from retrospective research might conceivably reflect a tendency for coronary cases to rationalize their illness in terms of hurrying and hard work and/or the stress of uncontrollable life events. Unfortunately, practical considerations have so far made it impossible for us to do longitudinal research on this question. One exploratory retrospective study has been conducted, however. In this project, hospitalized coronary patients and noncoronary controls were compared to each other in terms of their A–B scores and their recall of life events prior to disease onset. A 1-year period of life events was selected for assessment, because previous research suggested this period as most relevant to clinical coronary disease (Theorell & Rahe, 1975).

Three samples were examined in this study: 45 patients in the coronary care unit of the Veterans Administration Hospital in Houston, Texas; 77 patients in the general medical and psychiatric wards of the same hospital (the hospitalized control group); and 50 building maintenance employees from the University of Texas at Austin campus (the healthy or nonhospitalized control group). All participants were males, aged 35 to 55, and the groups were frequency matched in terms of social class, race, and religion.

Each subject completed the Jenkins Activity Survey and a modified version of the Schedule of Recent Experience, an instrument used in previous research on stressful life change (e.g., Holmes & Rahe, 1967). This measure asked the respondent to enumerate the occurrences of each of 47 life events during the 1-year period prior to hospitalization or, in the case of the healthy controls, prior to the time the questionnaire was completed. Before the study was conducted, a 10-item loss index was developed using selected items from the set of 47 events. These items were agreed upon by three members of the research staff as reflecting stressful events over which minimal control could be exerted. Examples are "death of a close family member," "being fired," and "large decline in financial status." A 7-item negative events index was constructed at the same time. These items were designed to reflect life events that would be experienced as stressful but not necessarily as uncontrollable or helplessness inducing. Items in this index included "detention in jail" and "large increase in number of arguments with spouse."

The data from this study formed quite an interesting pattern. Analysis of loss-index responses determined that a reliably higher percentage of each patient group (coronaries and hospitalized noncoronaries) than healthy controls reported having experienced at least one major loss in the previous year. By contrast, percentages for the negative events index did not differ among subject samples. Finally, coronary patients had significantly higher Pattern A scores than did either the hospitalized or nonhospitalized controls.

These data suggest that helplessness-inducing life events—not just negative events—discriminate persons with illness from those without disease. Moreover, the relative presence of Pattern A characteristics seems to discriminate persons with coronary heart disease from those with other diseases. These findings are consistent with the reasoning already presented— that an excess of life events involving loss of environmental control, when experienced by persons possessing the Type A behavioral style, may be specifically associated with coronary disease. Prospective research obviously is needed, however, to corroborate these findings.

A TENTATIVE MODEL
OF BIOBEHAVIORAL INTERACTION

The long-range goal of our research is to ascertain how Pattern A and uncontrollable stress interact with each other to influence the development of coronary disease. Attaining this goal will require systematic examination of physiological and biochemical processes, for such processes must mediate the impact of behavioral events on cardiovascular pathology. The research necessary to establish these links is only in its early stages. Nevertheless, it is possible even at this date to specify some of the possible mediating physiological mechanisms.

As was discussed earlier in this chapter, there is evidence that elevated levels of adrenaline and noradrenaline may potentiate the development of coronary disease. Because these two catecholamines are intimately related to autonomic nervous system discharge, it is not surprising that stress influences their relative presence in the blood. It should also be noted that active coping with a stressor may lead to a specific increase in noradrenaline, whereas adrenaline levels remain relatively unchanged (e.g., Elmadjian, 1963; Funkenstein, King, & Drolette, 1957; Weiss, Stone & Harrell, 1970). According to other research, although adrenaline levels sometimes rise intially in response to stressful stimulation, they decline as the person's feelings of being able to master the disturbing stimuli increase (Frankenhaeuser, 1971). Recent studies have also shown that severe depletion of brain norepinephrine in rats is associated with helplessness and giving-up responses (e.g., Weiss, Glazer, & Pohorecky, 1976).

An integration may be possible between these biochemical processes and the behavioral findings already reported. When a person perceives a threat to his or her sense of control, that individual struggles behaviorally to reestablish and maintain control. During this period of active coping, one might expect concomitant elevations in circulating noradrenaline. As the realization develops that control has been lost, however, the person gives up and becomes passive behaviorally. During this period, noradrenaline levels may be declining, perhaps even to levels below the normal baseline.

This behavioral sequence—efforts to exert control, followed by giving up—doubtlessly occurs over and over during the course of a lifetime. It is entirely possible that the more frequently this cycle occurs, the more one's coronary arteries are affected by atherosclerotic processes. This extrapolation derives in part from data cited earlier that suggest that excessive elevations of catecholamines over time may serve as an intermediary process whereby stress leads to coronary pathology (see, e.g., Raab et al., 1964; Rosenman & Friedman, 1974). The extrapolation also derives from more speculative notions implicating the rise and fall of catecholamines and rapid shifts between sympathetic and parasympathetic activity in the etiology of coronary disease and sudden death (Engel, 1970; Richter, 1957). Research indicating that patients with coronary heart disease show substantially impaired parasympathetic regulation of heart rate (Eckberg, Drabinsky, & Braunwald, 1971) may also be relevant here.

The implications of Pattern A for this general picture are as follows. As was noted earlier, Type A's seem to show enhanced platelet aggregation in response to noradrenaline, compared to Type B's (Simpson et al., 1974). Moreover, at least three studies have indicated that A's display elevated noradrenaline reactions to stressful stimulation, whereas B's fail to show this responsiveness (Friedman et al., 1975; Friedman, St. George, Byers, & Rosenman, 1960; Simpson et al., 1974). Given these findings, it seems reasonable that the atherogenetic processes already described for people in general are particularly applicable to Type A's. In other words, persons possessing Pattern A characteristics may experience the alternation of active coping efforts and giving up with greater frequency and intensity than persons with fewer of these characteristics. Recall that A's vigorously engage in efforts to master their environments; and remember that many human struggles end in failure and helplessness. To the extent that a cycle of hyper-reactivity and hypo-reactivity has an impact on coronary disease, the fact that Type A's are especially susceptible to the disease might be accounted for by the cumulative effects of the excessive rise and fall of catecholamines released by the repetitive interplay of Pattern A and uncontrollable stress.

These speculations obviously do not represent the entire story. But they do offer a heuristic guide to future thinking and research. Coronary disease clearly must be regarded as having a multifaceted etiology. Traditional risk factors (e.g., elevated serum cholesterol) must, of course, be part of any complete analysis of the pathogenesis of the disease. However, a thorough knowledge of how psychological and physiological variables interact to contribute to coronary disease will add an important dimension to our understanding of its etiology and development.

IMPLICATIONS FOR INTERVENTION

We have spent most of this chapter discussing stress, Pattern A behavior, and how these two variables relate to cardiovascular pathology. We should, however, also give some consideration to the implications of the foregoing material for the development of strategies for treating and perhaps even preventing coronary disease. That is, just as treatment programs can be designed to alter the patient's dietary and smoking habits, perhaps steps can be taken to alter the behavioral experiences that may be contributing to the development of cardiovascular pathology. Elimination of uncontrollable aversive events from one's life—though perhaps desirable in principle—is obviously unattainable. More relevant to present concerns is the possibility of altering how the person attempts to deal with such threats to his or her sense of control over the environment. The Pattern A response to such stressors may initially be adaptive in that it rapidly mobilizes resources for coping. In the long run, however, the risk to health that is embodied in these responses may outweigh their initial advantage.

How easily the Type A individual can alter his or her characteristic style of responding to stressors is a matter of some debate. It seems likely that Pattern A response tendencies are learned relatively early in life (cf. Matthews, 1977), and probably they can become pervasive in the individual's moment-to-moment activity by the time intervention is attempted. Despite these potential difficulties, a variety of intervention strategies have been proposed as applicable to the problem. Some of these focus on alteration of Pattern A characteristics by psychopharmacological means. For example, it has been proposed (Sigg, 1974) that administration of sedative-type drugs might reduce the emotional and muscular tension that is characteristic of the Type A. The same author suggests that beta-adrenergic blocking agents (e.g., propranolol) may be useful in altering ways of coping with psychosocial stressors.

Many nondrug approaches to altering Pattern A characteristics have been suggested as well. Most of these approaches derive fairly directly from one or another traditional technique of psychotherapy. For example, several programs (Rosenman & Friedman, 1977; Roskies, Spevack, Surkis, Cohen, & Gilman, 1978) have made use of a psychoanalytic approach to understanding and changing Pattern A behavior. The rationale for such programs is largely based on the clinical impression that Type A characteristics arise in a family constellation consisting of a demanding and aggressive mother and a psychologically passive father. The aim of this type of therapy program is to provide for patients a corrective emotional experience and a heightened awareness of the dynamics that may underlie their need for control and mastery (cf. Roskies, in press). The implicit assumption behind this approach is that if the persons involved come to recognize why they have these needs, the needs themselves will diminish. The results of such programs have been mixed. Rosenman and Friedman (1977) report that such therapy experiences did not by themselves result in diminished Pattern A behavior over the long term. Roskies et al. (1978), on the other hand, are more optimistic, though at the same time acknowledging that their own findings are somewhat ambiguous.

Whereas the psychoanalytic approach to Pattern A focuses on altering the person's need for mastery, other psychotherapeutic approaches leave that need untouched and focus instead on the behavioral consequences of that need. More specifically, many training programs have utilized a wide variety of techniques to enable persons to lower their levels of emotional and physiological arousal consciously, when they perceive themselves to be in stressful circumstances. These techniques range from deep muscle relaxation, which is taught as part of systematic desensitization, to yoga, meditation, "secularized" meditation, biofeedback, stress inoculation, and self-instructions (see, e.g., Benson, Marzetta, & Rosner, 1974; Goldfried, 1977; Meichenbaum, 1977; Suinn, 1975; Suinn & Richardson, 1971; White & Fadiman, 1976). These approaches emphasize the fact that they are active strategies for coping with the stressors. They are, however, strategies that are less harmful and more adaptive than the strategies used by the patients prior to therapy. There is a marked conceptual contrast between systematic relaxation training and the superficially similar advice to "relax, slow down, take it easy—it doesn't matter if you don't get it all done." Such advice is often given to persons with Pattern A characteristics. It is well-meaning advice, but it is ultimately self-defeating in that it induces its own sense of helplessness and passivity. Systematic techniques for reducing one's arousal states, on the other hand, combine two important characteristics. They enable the person to reduce the physiological arousal to which they are being subjected. Yet they also incorporate the assumption that, far from causing the person to give up or hide from the stressor, the techniques are providing a tool by which the person can be effective in controlling the stressors that confront him or her.

Evaluation of the successfulness of these various strategies for altering Pattern A behavior is a difficult and complex process (cf. Chesney, 1978). Moreover, it is a process that is now only in its initial stages. Some of the evidence collected thus far is quite encouraging, but nearly all the evidence is methodologically inadequate to allow firm conclusions to be drawn. Most of the data, for example, represent short-term rather than long-term follow-ups of the individuals who have been treated. Many studies have relied on self-reports of behavior and feelings rather than on objective behavioral observations. And in some cases there are highly plausible alternative interpretations for the obtained findings. Moreover, evaluation of clinical intervention strategies has thus far been aimed only at determining the degree to which Pattern A behaviors are diminished as a function of the intervention. There still remains the important question of whether or not these changes in behavior will substantially alter the person's subsequent risk of cardiovascular disease.

ACKNOWLEDGMENTS

The research reported in this chapter was made possible by grants to David C. Glass from the National Science Foundation and the Hogg Foundation for Mental Health. A modified version of the chapter appeared in the *American Scientist*, March–April 1977.

REFERENCES

Ardlie, N. G., Glew, G., & Schwartz, C. J. Influence of catecholamines on nucleotide-induced platelet aggregation. *Nature*, 1966, *212*, 415–417.

Balke, B. Optimale Koerperliche Leistungsfaehigkeisihre Messung und Veraenderung infrolage Arabeitsermuedung. *Arbeitsphysiologie*, 1954, *15*, 311–323.

Balke, B., Grillo, G. P., Konecci, E. G., & Luft, U. C. Work capacity after blood donation. *Journal of Applied Physiology*, 1954, *7*, 231–238.

Benson, H., Marzetta, B. R., & Rosner, B. A. Decreased blood pressure associated with the regular elicitation of relaxation response: A study of hypertensive subjects. In R. S. Eliot (Ed.), *Stress and the heart*. Mount Kisco, N.Y.: Futura, 1974.

Blumenthal, J. A., Williams, R. B., Kong, Y., Thompson, L. W., Jenkins, C. D., & Rosenman, R. H. *Coronary-prone behavior and angiographically documented coronary disease*. Paper delivered to the Annual Meeting of the American Psychosomatic Society, March 21, 1975, New Orleans, La.

Brand, R. J., Rosenman, R. H., Sholtz, R. I., & Friedman, M. Multivariate prediction of coronary heart disease in the Western Collaborative Group Study compared to the findings of the Framingham Study. *Circulation*, 1976, *53*, 348–355.

Burnam, M. A., Pennebaker, J. W., & Glass, D. C. Time consciousness, achievement striving, and the Type A coronary-prone behavior pattern. *Journal of Abnormal Psychology*, 1975, *84*, 76–79.

Buss, A. H. *The psychology of aggression*. New York: Wiley, 1961.

Carver, C. S., Coleman, A. E., & Glass, D. C. The coronary-prone behavior pattern and the suppression of fatigue on a treadmill test. *Journal of Personality and Social Psychology*, 1976, *33*, 460–466.

Carver, C. S., DeGregorio, E., & Gillis, R. *Challenge and Type A behavior among intercollegiate football players*. Unpublished manuscript, 1978.

Carver, C. S., & Glass, D. C. Coronary-prone behavior pattern and interpersonal aggression. *Journal of Personality and Social Psychology*, 1978, *36*, 361–366.

Chesney, M. A. *Coronary-prone behavior and coronary heart disease: Intervention strategies.* Paper presented at the annual meeting of the American Psychological Association, Toronto, 1978.

Dawber, T. R., & Kannel, W. B. Susceptibility to coronary heart disease. *Modern Concepts in Cardiovascular Disease,* 1961, *30,* 671–676.

Dembroski, T. M., MacDougall, J. M., & Lushene, R. Interpersonal interaction and cardiovascular response in Type A subjects and coronary patients. *Journal of Human Stress,* in press.

Dembroski, T. M., MacDougall, J. M., & Shields, J. L. Physiological reactions to social challenge in persons evidencing the Type A coronary-prone behavior pattern. *Journal of Human Stress,* 1977, *3,* 2–10.

Dembroski, T. M., MacDougall, J. M., Shields, J. L., Petitto, J., & Lushene, R. Components of the Type A coronary-prone behavior pattern and cardiovascular responses to psychomotor performance challenge. *Journal of Behavioral Medicine,* 1978, *1,* 159–176.

Dohrenwend, B. S., & Dohrenwend, B. P. *Stressful life events: Their nature and effects.* New York: Wiley, 1974.

Duguid, J. B. Thrombosis as a factor in the pathogenesis of coronary atherosclerosis. *Journal of Pathology and Bacteriology,* 1946, *58,* 207–212.

Eckberg, D. L., Drabinsky, M., & Braunwald, E. Defective cardiac parasympathetic control in patients with heart disease. *New England Journal of Medicine,* 1971, *285,* 877–883.

Eliot, R. S. (Ed.) *Stress and the heart.* Mount Kisco, N.Y.: Futura, 1974.

Elmadjian, F. Excretion and metabolism of epinephrine and norepinephrine in various emotional states. *Proceedings 5th Pan American Congress of Endocrinology,* November 1963, 341–370.

Engel, G. L. A life setting conducive to illness: The giving-up–given-up complex. *Annals of Internal Medicine,* 1968, *69,* 293–300.

Engel, G. L. Sudden death and the "medical model" in psychiatry. *Canadian Psychiatric Association Journal,* 1970, *15,* 527–538.

Frankenhaeuser, M. Behavior and circulating catecholamines. *Brain Research,* 1971, *31,* 241–262.

Friedberg, C. K. *Diseases of the heart* (3rd ed.). Philadelphia: Saunders, 1966.

Friedman, M. *Pathogenesis of coronary artery disease.* New York: McGraw-Hill, 1969.

Friedman, M., Byers, S. O., Diamant, J., & Rosenman, R. H. Plasma catecholamine response of coronary-prone subjects (Type A) to a specific challenge. *Metabolism,* 1975, *24,* 205–210.

Friedman, M., & Rosenman, R. H. Association of specific overt behavior pattern with blood and cardiovascular findings. *Journal of the American Medical Association,* 1959, *169,* 1286–1296.

Friedman, M., Rosenman, R. H., & Carroll, V. Changes in the serum cholesterol and blood-clotting time in men subjected to cyclic variation of occupational stress. *Circulation,* 1958, *17,* 853–861.

Friedman, M., St. George, S., Byers, S. O., & Rosenman, R. H. Excretion of catecholamines, 17-ketosteroids, 17-hydroxycorticoids, and 5-hydroxyindole in men exhibiting a particular behavior pattern associated with high incidence of clinical coronary disease. *Journal of Clinical Investigation,* 1960, *39,* 758.

Funkenstein, D. H., King, S. H., & Drolette, M. E. *Mastery of stress.* Cambridge, Mass.: Harvard University Press, 1957.

Glass, D. C. *Behavior patterns, stress, and coronary disease.* Hillsdale, N.J.: Lawrence Erlbaum Associates, 1977.

Glass, D. C., & Singer, J. E. *Urban stress: Experiments on noise and social stressors.* New York: Academic Press, 1972.

Glass, D. C., Snyder, M. L., & Hollis, J. F. Time urgency and the Type A coronary-prone behavior pattern. *Journal of Applied Social Psychology,* 1974, *4,* 125–140.

Goldfried, M. R. The use of relaxation and cognitive relabeling as coping skills. In R. B. Stuart (Ed.), *Behavioral self-management: Strategies, techniques, and outcome.* New York: Brunner/Mazel, 1977.

Greene, W. A., Goldstein, S., & Moss, A. J. Psychosocial aspects of sudden death: A preliminary report. *Archives of Internal Medicine,* 1972, *129,* 725-731.

Hiroto, D. S. Locus of control and learned helplessness. *Journal of Experimental Psychology,* 1974, *102,* 187-193.

Hiroto, D. S., & Seligman, M. E. P. Generality of learned helplessness in man. *Journal of Personality and Social Psychology,* 1975, *31,* 311-327.

Holmes, T. H., & Rahe, R. H. The social readjustment rating scale. *Journal of Psychosomatic Research,* 1967, *11,* 213-218.

House, J. S. Occupational stress as a precursor to coronary disease. In W. D. Gentry & R. B. Williams, Jr. (Eds.), *Psychological aspects of myocardial infarction and coronary care.* St. Louis, Mo.: C. V. Mosby, 1975.

Jenkins, C. D. Psychologic and social precursors of coronary disease. *New England Journal of Medicine,* 1971, *284,* 244-255; 307-317.

Jenkins, C. D. Recent evidence supporting psychological and social risk factors for coronary disease. *New England Journal of Medicine,* 1976, *294,* 987-994; 1033-1038.

Jenkins, C. D., Rosenman, R. H., & Friedman, M. Replicability of rating the coronary-prone behavior pattern. *British Journal of Preventive and Social Medicine,* 1968, *22,* 16-22.

Jenkins, C. D., Rosenman, R. H., & Zyzanski, S. J. *The Jenkins Activity Survey for Health Prediction (Form B).* Boston: Authors, 1972.

Jenkins, C. D., Zyzanski, S. J., & Rosenman, R. H. Risk of new myocardial infarction in middle-aged men with manifest coronary heart disease. *Circulation,* 1976, *53,* 342-347.

Krantz, D. S., Glass, D. C., & Snyder, M. L. Helplessness, stress level, and the coronary-prone behavior pattern. *Journal of Experimental Social Psychology,* 1974, *19,* 284-300.

Lazarus, R. S. *Psychological stress and the coping process.* New York: McGraw-Hill, 1966.

Manuck, S. B., Craft, S., & Gold, K. J. Coronary-prone behavior pattern and cardiovascular response. *Psychophysiology,* 1978, *15,* 403-411.

Manuck, S. B., & Garland, F. N. Coronary-prone behavior pattern, task incentive, and cardiovascular response. *Psychophysiology,* in press.

Mason, J. W. Organization of psychoendocrine mechanisms: A review and reconsideration of research. In N. W. Greenfield & R. A. Sternbach (Eds.), *Handbook of psychophysiology.* New York: Holt, Rinehart, & Winston, 1972.

Matthews, K. A. Assessment and developmental antecedents of Pattern A behavior in children. In T. Dembroski (Ed.), *Proceedings of the forum on coronary-prone behavior.* Washington, D.C.: Department of HEW Publication No. (NIH) 78-1451, 1977.

Matthews, K. A., & Brunson, B. I. Allocation of attention and the Type A coronary-prone behavior pattern. *Journal of Personality and Social Psychology,* in press.

Meichenbaum, D. *Cognitive behavior modification: An integrative approach.* New York: Plenum, 1977.

Parkes, C. M., Benjamin, B., & Fitzgerald, R. G. Broken heart: A statistical study of increased mortality among widowers. *British Medical Journal,* 1969, *1,* 740-743.

Paykel, E. S. Life stress and psychiatric disorder: Applications of the clinical approach. In B. S. Dohrenwend & B. P. Dohrenwend (Eds.), *Stressful life events: Their nature and effects.* New York: Wiley, 1974.

Raab, W., Chaplin, J. P., & Bajusz, E. Myocardial necroses produced in domesticated rats and in wild rats by sensory and emotional stresses. *Proceedings of the Society of Experimental Biology and Medicine,* 1964, *116,* 665-669.

Raab, W., Stark, E., MacMillan, W. H., & Gigee, W. R. Sympathetic origin and antiadrenergic prevention of stress-induced myocardial lesions. *American Journal of Cardiology,* 1961, *8,* 203-211.

Richter, C. P. On the phenomenon of sudden death in animals and man. *Psychosomatic Medicine*, 1957, *19*, 191–198.

Rosenman, R. H., Brand, R. J., Jenkins, C. D., Friedman, M., Straus, R., & Wurm, M. Coronary heart disease in the Western Collaborative Group Study: Final follow-up experience of 8 1/2 years. *Journal of the American Medical Association*, 1975, *233*, 872–877.

Rosenman, R. H., & Friedman, M. Neurogenic factors in pathogenesis of coronary heart disease. *Medical Clinics of North America*, 1974, *58*, 269–279.

Rosenman, R. H., & Friedman, M. Modifying Type A behavior pattern. *Journal of Psychosomatic Research*, 1977, *21*, 323–333.

Roskies, E. Considerations in developing a treatment program for the coronary-prone (Type A) behavior pattern. In P. Davidson (Ed.,) *Behavioral medicine: Changing health life styles.* New York: Brunner/Mazel, in press.

Roskies, E., Spevack, M., Surkis, A., Cohen, C., & Gilman, S. Changing the coronary-prone (Type A) behavior pattern in a non-clinical population. *Journal of Behavioral Medicine*, 1978, *1*, 201–216.

Schachter, S., & Rodin, J. *Obese humans and rats.* Hillsdale, N.J.: Lawrence Erlbaum Associates, 1974.

Schmale, A. H. Giving up as a final common pathway to changes in health. *Advances in Psychosomatic Medicine*, 1972, *8*, 18–38.

Schucker, B., & Jacobs, D. R., Jr. Assessment of behavioral risk for coronary disease by voice characteristics. *Psychosomatic Medicine*, 1977, *39*, 219–228.

Seligman, M. E. P. *Helplessness: On depression, development, and death.* San Francisco: Freeman, 1975.

Shekelle, R. B., Schoenberger, J. A., & Stamler, J. Correlates of the JAS Type A behavior pattern score. *Journal of Chronic Diseases*, 1976, *29*, 381–394.

Sigg, E. B. The pharmacological approaches to cardiac stress. In R. S. Eliot (Ed.), *Stress and the heart.* New York: Futura, 1974.

Simpson, M. T., Olewine, D. A., Jenkins, C. D., Ramsey, F. H., Zyzanski, S. J., Thomas, G., & Hames, C. G. Exercise-induced catecholamines and platelet aggregation in the coronary-prone behavior pattern. *Psychosomatic Medicine*, 1974, *36*, 476–487.

Suinn, R. M. The cardiac stress management program for Type A patients. *Cardiac Rehabilitation*, 1975, *5*, 13–15.

Suinn, R. M., & Richardson, F. Anxiety management training: A nonspecific behavior therapy program for anxiety control. *Behavior Therapy*, 1971, *2*, 498–510.

Theorell, T. Life events before and after the onset of a premature myocardial infarction. In B. S. Dohrenwend & B. P. Dohrenwend (Eds.), *Stressful life events: Their nature and effects.* New York: Wiley, 1974.

Theorell, T., & Rahe, R. H. Life change events, ballistocardiography, and coronary death. *Journal of Human Stress*, 1975, *1*, 18–24.

Weiss, J. M., Glazer, H. I., & Pohorecky, L. A. Coping behavior and neurochemical changes in rats: An alternative explanation for the original "learned helplessness" experiments. In G. Serban & A. King (Eds.), *Animal models in human psychobiology.* New York: Plenum, 1976.

Weiss, J. M., Stone, E. A., & Harrell, N. Coping behavior and brain norepinephrine level in rats. *Journal of Comparative and Physiological Psychology*, 1970, *72*, 153–160.

White, J., & Fadiman, J. (Eds.). *Relax.* New York: Confucian Press, 1976.

Wortman, C. B., & Brehm, J. W. Responses to uncontrollable outcomes: An integration of reactance theory and the learned helplessness model. In L. Berkowitz (Ed.), *Advances in experimental social psychology* (Vol. 8). New York: Academic Press, 1975.

Zyzanski, S. J., Jenkins, C. D., Ryan, T. J., Flessas, A., & Everist, M. Psychological correlates of coronary angiographic findings. *Archives of Internal Medicine*, 1976, *136*, 1234–1237.

4 Destruction and Perceived Control

Vernon L. Allen
David B. Greenberger
University of Wisconsin

The present paper explores the relation between sense of personal control and behavior directed toward effecting a modification in the physical environment. One particular type of change in the physical environment is emphasized—destruction. Perceived control is viewed both as an antecedent and consequence of destruction. We propose that a lowered level of perceived control (efficacy or competence) will, under certain conditions, stimulate attempts to modify aspects of the physical environment through the act of destruction. Further, it is proposed that the act of destroying an object or portion of the physical environment will influence a person's perception of control.

The present paper is divided into three major sections. The first section presents some of the existing evidence concerning the techniques that persons employ to alter their physical environment and discusses the possibility that perceived control plays an important role in this type of behavior. The second section outlines a proposed conceptual framework for understanding the connection between destruction, perceived control, and other critical related concepts. Finally, the third section reports three new experiments designed to test some of the proposed links between destruction and control.

MODIFYING THE PHYSICAL ENVIRONMENT

Several related concepts have been employed by investigators to indicate the extent to which a person believes that he or she can produce effective changes in the environment. Concepts such as internal–external control (Rotter,

1966), competence (White, 1959), self-efficacy (Bandura, 1977), powerlessness or alienation (Seeman, 1959), and learned helplessness (Seligman, 1975) seem to share a common conceptual basis, in spite of certain obvious differences in emphasis. We use the term *perceived control* when discussing the phenomena covered by these terms. Perceived control of the environment is an extremely general concept; it can refer to the influence that a person exerts in the physical, social, or cognitive world. Perhaps one of the most direct ways in which an individual gains a sense of control is by manipulating aspects of the natural or man-made physical environment (Piaget, 1952; White, 1959).

In the case of the built environment, an individual can experience an increase in sense of control by altering, modifying, or transforming it in some manner. Making such modifications at the discretion of the occupant has been called *personalization* (Becker, 1977). Reported changes have ranged from making structural alterations to the exterior or interior of a building (Boudon, 1969) to changing decorations inside the dwelling. One of the explanations that has been offered for the personalization of one's dwelling is that it contributes to a sense of competence and mastery (Becker, 1977). (It should be mentioned here that graffiti are also a variant of personalization but a form of personalization that is socially disapproved.) In short, then, one method of modifying the physical environment entails making socially approved changes in one's own living space; these changes are usually made in a manner that is consistent with one's values, individuality, and self-concept.

A second way of exerting an influence upon the physical environment is by modifying it more drastically by an act of destruction. According to several accounts, it appears that perceived control is often implicated in acts of destruction in factories and institutions. A study of industrial sabotage by Taylor and Walton (1971) concluded that one of the primary causes of the destruction was an assertion of control by the workers. Many of the men stated explicitly in interviews that they had smashed things in order to increase control—or in their words, "to show them who was in charge." It has been said that Luddite behavior should be recognized as collective bargaining by riot. In the same vein, the following assertion was made by Debord (cited in Ward, 1973) in connection with a discussion of the Watts riots: "The man who destroys commodities shows his human superiority over commodities [p. 285]."

Destruction of windows, furniture, and equipment is not uncommon in institutions (e.g., children's residential institutions, mental hospitals, prisons) and public housing (Yancey, 1972) as well as in the public schools (Wenk & Harlow, 1978). All these cases seem to be characterized by the individual's having low control over the social and physical environment. Furthermore, acts of vandalism are most often perpetrated by persons who are striving to achieve an increase in sense of personal control but who are still quite powerless—that is, adolescent or near-adolescent boys (Martin, 1961). We recently conducted interviews with a sample of 120 young men 18 to 20 years of age. Each respondent was asked to relate in detail recent incidents in which he had broken or destroyed something and to describe the circumstances under which it had occurred. One series of open-ended questions concerned the motivation for destruction. Reports from a number of responses indicated that a sense of control or mastery was an important factor. For example, one person felt that he had "accomplished something by the breaking." Similarly, a person who had smashed a locker in his high school recalled passing it for the next three years and each time thinking proudly, "there's my little destruction to this brand new school."

Property destruction is a primitive but very effective method by which an individual can be successful in changing the physical environment in a direct fashion; as a consequence of the destruction, the person is likely to experience an increment in perceived control. Of course, the physical environment has the particular advantage of being readily available and highly salient as a target of destruction. We hypothesize that destruction of the physical environment should mitigate an individual's perception of low control. Likewise, it is predicted that persons who are low in perceived control will express a greater preference for engaging in destruction if given the opportunity. These ideas are discussed more fully in the next section.

THEORETICAL FRAMEWORK

In a well-known paper, White (1959) criticized existing drive theories and reviewed evidence from several areas of theory and research that appeared to converge on the concept called competence drive. He argued that individuals have a need to manipulate and control their surroundings—to produce an effective change in the environment. [Bandura's (1977) term *self-efficacy expectations* can be used if one wishes to avoid the residual meaning attached to "need" theories.] We shall restrict the domain of the present discussion of control to the manipulation of the physical environment only.

Let us assume a level of expected or perceived control (or self-efficacy) that is sufficient for the individual to possess some expectations about ability to influence outcomes—that is, a level of control greater than would be present in a state of learned helplessness. If this general level of perceived control undergoes a temporary (or longer term) negative discrepancy from adaptation level, it is proposed that efforts will be made on the part of the individual to restore control.

A decrement in perceived control may arise from a number of sources. Objective experiences such as failure are among the major causes of a decrease in control. Beliefs or perceptions about level of control may also change, however, without having any objective basis in experience. In quite a different way, engaging in social comparison with another person or reference group may raise one's desired level of control, so that a discrepancy is seen to exist with one's present level of control. It is suggest that when the person perceives a lessening of personal control (self-efficacy) for any reason whatsoever, efforts will be undertaken to restore control by acting upon the environment in some way. As Wortman and Brehm (1975) suggest, if failure or loss of control persists for a long period of time without some success in restoration, instrumental efforts will finally cease, and the individual may enter a helplessness state.

We suggest that before passing into a state of helplessness, an individual will make efforts to modify the physical environment if attempts to affect the social environment are not available or have not been successful. This modification of the environment may take a benign and socially approved form such as personalization or other physical changes; at other times, more drastic changes may occur, such as intentionally breaking or destroying an object. The effect of these changes may be to provide the person with an increased sense of competence or success. Merely demonstrating to one's self some degree of success in creating a change in the physical environment might provide the perception of a contingent relation between one's behavior and outcomes, and thereby prevent a sense of helplessness.

Some evidence can be adduced in support of the argument advanced here. Research on reactance theory (Brehm, 1966; Wicklund, 1974) has demonstrated that a person will attempt to regain freedom if someone else has prevented a response from occurring. As Wortman and Brehm (1975) point out, such a decrease in freedom of action is likely to result in the expression of hostility along with efforts to restore control. Control can be readily increased by altering some relevant aspect of the social environment; if another person or group is responsible for lowering one's perceived control, then acting against this target is probably highest on the response hierarchy. Likewise, physical objects may be selected for destruction if breaking them enables a person to attain a desired goal. An example would be the destruction of a fence in order to permit the successful attainment of a desired object.

Situations exist, however, in which a person is unable to produce the desired effect on another person or on the physical environment in a direct and instrumental fashion. In such instances we suggest that behavior may be directed toward the physical environment even if it is not directly instrumental in reaching a goal; that is, displaced destruction will occur. For example, a teacher may prevent a student from leaving the classroom, contrary to the student's wishes. Later the student throws a rock through a window of the school. Although the student's lack of control in the classroom has not been improved, the sense of loss of control is somewhat ameliorated by having been successful in breaking the window.

Relevant to the possibility that behavior will be directd toward the physical environment more generally is research indicating that aggression may be displaced toward another target in the event of unavailability of the original source of frustration. In one of the few recent studies conducted with humans, Fenigstein and Buss (1974) showed that subjects chose to aggress toward targets on the basis of the level of intensity of anger whether or not the target was associated with the anger. Although frustration is not synonymous with decreased control, this research suggests that substitutability of targets may be a more plausible and more general phenomenon than has been assumed. It appears that the desire to inflict harm may generalize from the source of frustration to other persons. Similarly, it is reasonable to expect that the desire to increase control may be displaced from the original cause of the decreased control to other aspects of the physical environment. The physical environment is a particularly propitious target for substitution responses associated with attempts to increase control, as we discuss more fully later.

The particular processes that are related to or that mediate the relation between control and destruction should be discussed briefly at this time. First, it can be argued that control is highly correlated with one's affective state; that is, a change in mood is associated with a corresponding change in perceived control. Existing research on control suggests that affect may play a critical role. Several studies utilized success or failure on a task as a way of creating high or low levels of control (e.g., Jenkins & Ward, 1965). It is possible that the critical factor influencing control in this situation (at least in part) is not success per se but the positive affect (good mood) associated with the success. Positive affect responses may create a penumbra of pleasure in the individual, and a sense of personal control may be included. It is probable that positive affect and high control have been frequently associated in an individual's past experience. Therefore, when a person experiences positive affect, it is likely that he or she will also perceive greater personal control than when in a negative mood.

The foregoing speculations suggest that the manipulation of mood may be sufficient to alter perceived control. Several observers have noted that participants often consider destruction (Piaget, 1952) and vandalism (Martin, 1961; Zimbardo, 1970) to be "fun." Systematic research by Allen and Greenberger (1978) has shown that destruction is an enjoyable experience— even when a person simply views the destruction instead of actually participating. Conversely, then, it follows that a direct relation should exist between affect and control: An increase in positive affect should promote a greater sense of control. Therefore, it can be predicted that a person who experiences low control will choose to destroy an object that will produce the greatest degree of positive affect or enjoyment (e.g., more complex stimuli).

A second concept is important because of its close relation to the sense of control—social identity (Ziller, 1973). Social identity is the social aspect of the self and consists of all the cognitive residues or consequences of inferences made about behavior by one's self and by others (Sarbin & Allen, 1968). It is a vast simplification to treat specific beliefs such as sense of control as if they existed in isolation, independent of other components of the individual's cognitive-social system. The construct of social identity plays an important unifying role for the individual in providing guidelines for behavior as well as in establishing standards against which to evaluate behavior. Sense of control is one of the central dimensions of one's social identity; therefore a change in perceived control will reverberate more broadly across other dimensions of social identity. The impact of a change in control on social identity may be manifested by affective consequences and revealed by change in mood and activity level. Space does not permit discussing the role of social identity in any detail, but clearly it is important in many acts of destruction. In this connection, one observer commented that in the civil conflict in Lebanon, the purpose of much of the destruction seemed to be for "the existential expression of the moment" (Geyer, 1978).

Before ending this section, a few comments should be made about the physical environment. As we suggested earlier, there are several reasons for believing that modifications to the physical environment may be a highly effective means of enhancing one's sense of control. The physical environment possesses certain characteristics that make destruction a particularly attractive means of effecting changes in the external world.

First of all, the probability is usually high that an individual will be successful. For example, if a person wants to break a window, success is almost assured if a stone is thrown in the proper direction and with sufficient velocity. Making a change in the environment—and particularly destruction—illustrates vividly to the individual that one does possess considerable power and that the appearance and meaning of the physical environment are vulnerable to change. Further, in addition to being very dramatic, the process of destruction provides clear and immediate feedback concerning one's impact. Sometimes particular objects will be selected in order to increase the difficulty of the breaking (i.e., to decrease the probability of success). An increase in difficulty means that the perceived sense of control is undoubtedly higher when the object is broken successfully. Whether a person chooses to break an object of high or low difficulty depends on situational factors as well as personality characteristics such as achievement motivation.

Second, destruction may be an especially impressive way of restoring a sense of control because it produces a high level of arousal. Because destruction of other persons' property is frequently carried out in a stealthy manner, it is likely that the person will experience fear, nervousness, and apprehension. It is possible that misattribution will occur in connection with this arousal (Nisbett & Valins, 1972) and that instead of being interpreted as nervousness, it will be viewed as excitement and accordingly experienced as a pleasant sensation. As Berlyne (1971) and others have shown, an increase in arousal from adaptation level will create a positive hedonic experience.

Third, it is important not to overlook the role of one's peers as a factor contributing to feelings of control brought about by destruction of the physical environment. Several authors (Cohen, 1973; Madison, 1970; Martin, 1961) have reported that one type of destruction—vandalism—typically occurs in a group context. Other persons who witness one's success at manipulating the environment serve an important function in helping to validate the social reality of one's successful attempt to alter the physical world. A group may also influence the selection of more risky targets for destruction (Dion, Baron, & Miller, 1970), which would contribute to an increase in level of arousal. One other social aspect of destruction should be noted. After the destructive act, observation of one's handiwork by other persons increases its importance. Moreover, because others are affected (usually inconvenienced) by one's destructive behavior, the person can clearly see that a small act of destruction has a strong impact on the behavior of a large number of people.

Fourth, the ease with which physical objects or structures (e.g., school, church, business) lend themselves to being viewed in a symbolic way makes destruction in many instances a very meaningful act.

Finally, destruction of selected aspects of the physical environment is usually considerably safer than acting negatively in a direct way toward another person, simply because the physical environment does not retaliate! So it may be the wiser course to pursue. In sum, destruction of the physical environment provides an important and very accessible means by which an individual is able to enhance a sense of control.

EMPIRICAL STUDIES

Experiment 1: Affect and Destruction

The first test of the theory was designed to evaluate the effect of mood and destruction on self-attribution of control. Three hypotheses are tested. First, it is expected that a general affective state will influence one's sense of control. Perceived control is expected to change directly as a function of affect; the more positive the mood, the greater the perception of control. In the present study differential mood is created experimentally. It is predicted that subjects who experience positive affect should perceive themselves as being more successful.

The second hypothesis is that differential mood will influence the person's perception of perceived control concerning a standard change made in the physical environment. In the study the subjects were given some degree of control over the physical environment; the amount of control was either high, low, or ambiguous. Persons may vary in the perception of the degree to which their own behavior actually controlled a standard outcome in the environment. We predict that the nature of a person's affective state at the time of engaging in an action will influence the attribution about the degree of personal control over the outcome. Other research has investigated attribution of control in the face of ambiguous outcomes (e.g., Langer, 1975).

The third hypothesis is that simply the act of breaking an object should increase a person's perceived control; that is, subjects should feel more successful after having broken an object than before. This increase in control should occur for subjects in both affect conditions. The amount of change should be greater in the negative affect condition, however, due to a possible ceiling effect in the positive condition.

We are positing that relations exist among affect, feeling of success, and perceived control. Data obtained from the present study will enable us to assign a causal status to affective state (mood), but the particular causal direction of the relation between feelings of success and perceived control will remain ambiguous. Three causal sequences can be suggested as follows:

1. Affect → Feeling of Success → Perceived Control
2. Affect → Perceived Control → Feeling of Success

3. Affect $<$ Feeling of Success / Perceived Control

The relation depicted as the last sequence (3) seems to us to be the most plausible, but results will not afford an unequivocal choice among the three possibilities.

In the present experiment subjects were instructed to break a tower constructed of small wooden blocks. Specifically, the subjects actually broke the tower by releasing a ball that rolled into the structure. Objectively, the amount of control that subjects possessed over the outcome was very small in an absolute sense. That is, subjects exerted only a minimal amount of effort in releasing the ball: They could not guide the direction of the ball, and they had no control over the manner in which the tower actually broke.

Method

Design.   The experiment was a 2 × 3 fully crossed design. Each subject was initially assigned to one of two mood conditions: positive or negative.

Afterwards, each subject participated in one of three conditions. In one condition, subjects were immediatly asked to complete a mood questionnaire, and subsequently they broke a block structure composed of wooden blocks. Finally, they responded to a set of items on a questionnaire similar to the mood questionnaire. A second condition was identical to the first except that subjects did not receive the initial mood qustionnaire. Instead, they rested for the period of time taken by subjects in Condition 1 to fill out the questionnaire. Subjects in Condition 2 did receive the second mood questionnaire. The third condition (control) was similar to the first condition except that subjects did not break the block structure. Instead, they merely rested for the equivalent period of time. Subjects in Condition 3 did complete the two mood questionnaires (excluding items referring to the breaking).[1]

Subjects. The subjects were 96 male and female students enrolled in introductory psychology classes at a large state university; they received course credit for participation. Subjects were assigned randomly to one of the six experimental conditions, with an equal ratio of males to females in each condition.

Manipulation of Affect. The subjects' mood was manipulated by the use of a technique developed by Velten (1968). This procedure requires subjects to read a sentence appearing on each of 50 cards. The sentences are intended to create one of two mood states—elation or depression. All the statements differ. Sentences in the elation condition emphasize how well and energetic the person feels, and sentences in the depression condition deal with negative aspects of life (i.e., feeling depressed and tired).

In a pretest it was determined that reading the cards aloud with appropriate intonation was more effective in establishing mood than the usual procedure of silent reading. Accordingly, subjects were instructed to read each card aloud with an expression appropriate for the meaning of the sentence. It was stated (falsely) by the experimenter that giving the appropriate expression was important, because a paralinguistic recognition task would follow the reading of the cards. The experimenter left the room during the mood-induction period in order to minimize any potential embarrassment subjects

---

[1]Conditions 2 and 3 provide controls for the data obtained in Condition 1. Condition 3 is a control for the possibility that the retest data might simply represent a regression to the mean. Condition 2 controls for the possibility that the initial questionnaire might interact with the experimental manipulation and with the second questionnaire. Analysis of the data did not show a significant regression effect on responses to the second questionnaire in Condition 3. Also, there was no difference between Conditions 1 and 2 on responses to the second questionnaire.

might feel. Monitoring of the room indicated that all the subjects did read the cards aloud with appropriate expressions as instructed.

Dependent Measures.   Two questionnaires were administered to subjects, one immediately after the mood induction and the other immediately after the breaking had taken place. The first questionnaire was given only to subjects in Conditions 1 and 3 and consisted of items referring to the subjects' mood. The items were verbally anchored, bipolar scales, and subjects indicated their mood at the moment by making a mark through a 15-cm scale. Several filler items were included in order to prevent subjects from being aware of the goals of the study.

Subjects in Conditions 1 and 2 completed a second questionnaire after breaking the blocks. This questionnaire differed slightly from the first one and included questions dealing with subjects' perceived control over the outcome of the breaking and their reactions to the breaking (e.g., enjoyment, beauty). Subjects again responded by making a mark through a 15-cm, verbally anchored, bipolar scale. After completing these items, the subjects then responded to the same mood items that had appeared in the first questionnaire. On the second questionnaire, subjects in Condition 3 (who did not engage in breaking) received only the items pertaining to mood.

Destruction.   An effort was made to ensure that the block tower used for destruction always broke in a standard manner and that subjects expended the same (minimal) effort in all cases. The technique not only assured that the tower would break in an almost identical manner on each occasion, but it also provided subjects with the opportunity to observe their accomplishment immediately.

A tower was constructed from small wooden blocks. The tower was composed of 12 square rings of wooden blocks placed on top of each other to a height of 72 cm. Each ring consisted of eight blocks (two on each of the four sides); each block measured 4.5 × 6 × 3.5 cm. The appearance of the towers was identical for all subjects.

The method for breaking the tower utilized an inclined ramp (2.8 m long) that was elevated at one end (2.4 m), with the other end resting on the floor. The angle of the incline was 35 degrees. The lower end was placed adjacent to the tower of blocks. Subjects were instructed to place a volleyball at the top of the ramp and simply to release it—permitting the ball to roll down the ramp. The velocity of the ball was always sufficient to break the tower. After each breaking, the tower was reconstructed before the next subject appeared.

It should be noted that this procedure enabled subjects to feel that the outcome was caused by them. At the same time, control over the outcome was sufficiently ambiguous to provide for the possibility of a considerable degree of variation in responses across experimental conditions.

Results

To determine whether the procedure for inducing mood had been successful, an analysis of variance was conducted for scores on the enthusiastic–depressed scale for subjects in the two conditions that received the first questionnaire. A significant difference was found between the two mood-induction conditions, $F(1,52) = 35.20$, $p < .01$. As expected, subjects in the elation condition indicated more positive affect than subjects in the depressed condition ($M = 12.32$ vs. 7.48, respectively).

Mood and Perceived Success. It was hypothesized that affect would influence subjects' feeling of success. Results showed that the two mood states did create a significant difference in the subjects' scores on the success/failure dimension, $F(1,52) = 24.72$, $p < .01$. Subjects in the elation condition felt more successful (11.88) than subjects in the depressed condition (7.36). It should be emphasized that the feeling of success was measured immediately after the manipulation of mood state and before the breaking of the blocks had taken place.

Destruction and Perceived Success. Subjects in one of the conditions responded to mood items on the questionnaire prior to and after breaking the block tower. Responses of these subjects can be used to determine whether the experience of destruction affected their feelings of success. It was hypothesized that the simple act of breaking an object would increase feelings of success for subjects in the depressed mood state. Relevant data are presented in Fig. 4.1. As can be seen, feeling of success was greater after the break than before. A planned comparison was performed on the repeated measures data for subjects who were depressed and who later engaged in the breaking. A significant difference in felt success was found from the pre- to the posttest, $F(1,19) = 4.68$, $p < .05$. The means were in the predicted direction: There was an increase in felt success of subjects after having engaged in the breaking. A similar analysis of data did not reveal a significant change from pre- to posttest for depressed subjects who did not break the block tower, indicating that the results cannot be explained as being simply a regression to the mean.

Destruction and Control. It was hypothesized that merely being in an elated or depressed state would influence the person's sense of control over an outcome held constant across conditions. On the second questionnaire, the following item was included for subjects who broke the blocks: "How much control did you have over the outcome of the break?" Results showed a significant difference between the two mood states on perceived control, $F(1,76) = 7.52$, $p < .01$. Subjects who were in the elation condition felt

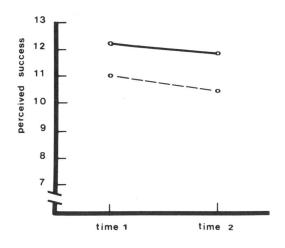

ELATED

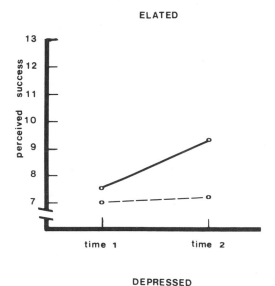

DEPRESSED

o— — —o no break
o————o subject breaks

FIG. 4.1. Perceived success as a function of mood and destruction.

more control than did subjects in the depressed condition (M = 10.75 vs. 8.75, respectively). Therefore, mood was sufficient to influence sense of control in this somewhat ambiguous situation. The significant difference between the two mood conditions in perceived control was obtained in spite of the fact that the act of destruction augmented the sense of control across all conditions, as reported earlier. Remember, too, that all subjects used precisely the same technique to break the tower and the outcome was always almost identical. Any minor differences across occasions could only have occurred by chance and could not be associated in any systematic way with experimental conditions.

Discussion

Results of Experiment 1 demonstrated: (1) a relation between affect and perceived success; (2) a relation between affect and perceived control; and (3) an effect of destruction on perceived control. Therefore, it seems that differential mood alone is sufficient to influence feelings of success and control. Given the rather weak manipulation of mood produced in an experimental situation, the changes in perceptions and attributions about self (success and control) are very noteworthy. As we suggested earlier, a close association exists in one's past experience between certain objective occurrences (such as success and control) and concomitant and subsequent affective states. This close association may increase the likelihood that an affective state will lead an individual to make attributions and evaluations about self in a way consistent with the existing mood.

An important finding of the present study was that destruction had a significant impact on perceived success and control. Elsewhere we have reported research indicating that destruction can be an enjoyable experience (Allen & Greenberger, 1978). Thus, it was expected that the enjoyment produced by an act of destruction would be sufficient to produce an increase in perceived success and control. It should be noted that, as we predicted, the increase in sense of success and control after engaging in destruction occurred for those subjects who were in the depressed condition. The pleasantness of the experience of destruction may have contributed significantly to the increase in subjects' sense of control and success. But as we pointed out earlier, there are other important elements involved in destruction that make it a particularly effective means of increasing perceived control and success.

Experiment 2: Control and Destruction

Experiment 1 demonstrated that breaking an object increases the feeling of success and control concerning the specific act in question. In the present experiment, these results are extended by directly manipulating subjects' initial general sense of control by feedback about performance on a task.

We have posited that if a person's state of control is reduced, he or she may be motivated to increase control by attempting to change some aspect of the physical environment. This behavior might be directed toward the specific cause of the decreased control; but it was argued further that the behavior may be directed to some aspect of the environment not at all associated with the original loss of control. It is hypothesized in the present study that a sense of control will be increased by allowing an individual to manipulate some aspect of the physical environment (i.e., destruction). The effect of destruction should occur primarily with subjects who have experienced a decrease in control. Subjects who perceive high control (success) should show little change in sense of control as a consequence of engaging in destruction.

A second factor was also examined in the present study—vicarious versus direct destruction. Perhaps a person need not actively participate in breaking an object for destructive behavior to alter feelings of control. Merely observing the destruction might be sufficient. In other words, an increase in control might be gained by vicarious means. If this is the case, it might help explain why people are eager to observe a variety of types of destruction (e.g., motion pictures and demolition derbies).

On the other hand, although mere observation of destruction should increase arousal, observation alone may not produce perceived control in the individual. To examine vicarious destruction in the present study, the subjects in one condition were responsible for performing the destruction personally but in another condition they watched while the experimenter did the breaking. (In a third condition destruction did not occur at all.) It is hypothesized that enjoyment of destruction and change in control will be more strongly affected when the individual personally performs the destruction than when he or she simply watches the same destruction being performed by the experimenter.

Method

Design.   The experiment was a 2 × 3 between-subjects design. Subjects either succeeded or failed on a word association task. After working on this task and being informed that they had been successful or unsuccessful, subjects were randomly assigned to one of three conditions. In one condition the subject was allowed to break a tower constructed from wooden blocks. Then dependent measures were obtained by a questionnaire. In a second condition the experimenter broke the tower while the subject watched, and the subject received the same questionnaire. In the third condition (control) the subject remained alone for the same period of time that elapsed in the two breaking conditions. These subjects also completed the questionnaire containing the dependent measures.

Subjects.   Subjects were 102 undergraduates who were enrolled in introductory psychology classes at a large state university. They received course credit for participating in research. Subjects in the success condition received extra credit for their performance on the task in addition to the standard credit received by all subjects.

Experimental Manipulation. All subjects were made to feel initially that they had succeeded or failed on a word association task. The experimenter presented a series of target words, and subjects were instructed to respond with the single word that they believed most other persons associated with the target word. The task presumably assessed the subjects' ability to identify how other persons think. The experimenter supposedly had a list of the most frequently cited associations for each target word, which was used to determine immediately the correctness of each subject's response.

A total of 100 target words was presented. Subjects were told that most other subjects had received a score of about 50 correct out of the 100. Knowledge of others' performance was intended to establish a peer standard for the subjects' evaluation of their performance. Subjects were also told that if they were correct on at least 65 of the 100 trials, they would be rewarded with extra credit in addition to the credit normally received for participation. Not only did this incentive provide a very specific performance standard it also increased the importance of succeeding on the task.

Subjects were given predetermined feedback (aloud) about correctness of each response on each trial. The experimenter delivered this feedback from an adjacent room by using an intercom. After all 100 items had been presented, the experimenter reported the total score that the subject presumably had earned. Subjects who were assigned to the success condition received a score of 74% correct, and subjects assigned to the failure condition were given a score of only 26% correct.

Results

Manipulation Check. Because subjects in the control condition did not see the block tower breaking, their responses were used as the baseline for determining the effectiveness of the success/failure manipulation. One item asked subjects how successful or unsuccessful they felt. A significant difference was found between the responses of subjects in the success and failure conditions, $t(32) = 2.75, p < .05$. Subjects in the success condition felt more successful than subjects in the failure condition (10.81 vs. 8.04, respectively). Subjects who had succeeded on the task were expected to show a greater perception of general control. One item asked: "In general, how much control do you feel you have over the events in your life?" The success/failure manipulation was effective in creating differential feelings of control, $t(32) = 2.42, p < .05$. Subjects who succeeded on the task reported greater control over their lives than subjects who had failed on the task ($M = 11.18$ vs. 9.38).

Feelings of Control.   The principal hypothesis of this study is that simply engaging in an act of destruction will lead to greater feelings of personal control. Subjects who had failed on the word association task experienced a decrement in control; therefore, they were expected to show much greater feelings of control after having broken the tower than the subjects who also experienced failure but did not engage in breaking the tower. Little change in control was expected for persons who had been successful on the task.

Results supported the hypothesis. The analysis of variance revealed a significant interaction between the experimentally induced success/failure factor and the break/no-break factor, $F(2,96) = 4.59$, $p < .05$. Data for the failure condition is examined first. As can be seen in Fig. 4.2, subjects who experienced failure and later broke the block tower expressed a higher level of

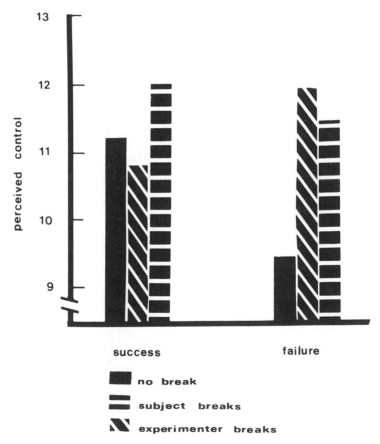

FIG. 4.2.   The effect of destruction on perceived control under conditions of success and failure.

general control than the subjects who failed but did not engage in breaking (11.98 vs. 9.38, respectively). Interestingly, results for subjects who merely watched the experimenter break the blocks fell somewhat between the means of the other two conditions (11.49). These subjects, too, indicated significantly more control than did subjects who engaged in no destruction, $t(32) = 3.04$, $p < .05$. These results indicate that being a nonparticipating witness to an act of destruction does have some effect upon perception of control, though not quite as much as when one actually engages in the act personally. It is possible that there would have been a much greater difference in perceived control between the participating and observing conditions with a more dramatic type of destruction (e.g., breaking a large piece of glass) than with the simple destruction used in the present experiment. Now turning to the success condition, it can be seen from Fig. 4.2 that subjects showed little change across the three conditions. The mean score for perceived control was 10.82 for subjects who broke the structure themselves, 12.06 for those who saw the experimenter break it, and 11.18 for subjects who did not see it break at all.

Discussion

In the present experiment the person's sense of control was manipulated directly. Subjects were either successful or unsuccessful in performing an important task and thus had demonstrated to themselves that they were capable or not capable of controlling an outcome. Subjects who were successful on the task showed little change in perceived control as a consequence of later engaging in the breaking of the block structure. By contrast, subjects who had failed on the task exhibited a dramatic increase in sense of control after they had broken the structure, the mean level of their control being almost identical to that of subjects who experienced success on the task.

These results indicate that when faced with a decrement in control as a result of failure, a person may increase the felt control by destroying an object. Engaging in destruction cannot alter the fact that one was unsuccessful on the task, but it does seem to influence general control. Destruction may provide information indicating not only that the environment can be controlled but also that one is still capable of exercising some control personally.

It would seem reasonable to expect that observing an act of destruction by another person might have little influence on self-attribution of control. This expectation was not supported by the data. In the case of subjects who had previously experienced failure, merely observing the destruction produced by the experimenter resulted in an increase in self-control. (It should be remembered that the dependent measure refers to a generalized sense of control rather than to control over the specific act of destruction.) If we assume that the observation of destruction increased positive affect, then the present finding is consistent with the results obtained in Experiment 1 that demonstrated a relation between positive affect and sense of control.

Experiment 3: Control, Complexity, and Affect

The present study investigates the effect on enjoyment of a subject's objective control over the outcome of destruction and of the degree of complexity of the destruction. Experiment 2 examined the effect of destruction on a general sense of control that had been previously decreased by behavior on a task (success/failure) that was unrelated to the destruction. In the present study the subject's objective control of the breaking and the outcome of the breaking were experimentally manipulated. The subjects experienced either high, medium, or low control over the destruction. It is hypothesized that a person's having objective control over an act of destruction will be directly related to enjoyment of the outcome. Greater control of outcome should create more involvement and hence greater arousal, which in turn should produce positive affect or enjoyment.

The effect on enjoyment of the complexity of outcome of a destructive act was also investigated. Allen and Greenberger (1978) reported that persons prefer to destroy objects that break in more complex ways and that enjoyment is also greater when observing more complex processes of destruction. It is hypothesized that subjects' enjoyment will be greater when an object breaks in a more complex as compared to a simpler manner.

Method

Subjects.   Subjects in the experiment were 120 students enrolled in introductory psychology classes in a large state university. All subjects received course credit for their participation in the experiment.

Design.   The study was a 2 × 3 between-subjects design. The two factors were complexity of the breaking (complex/simple) and level of subjects' perceived control over the breaking (low/moderate/high). Complexity of outcome was manipulated by varying the size of the blocks used in the structures. One structure was composed of 24 large blocks (4 × 9 × 10 cm) and broke in a rather simple way; the other structure was made from 96 small blocks (4 × 5 × 4.5 cm) and broke in a much more complex and interesting way. Otherwise, the dimensions of the two structures were identical (22.5 × 22.5 × 80 cm). The difference in the size of the blocks in the two structures was very apparent to subjects.

The subjects' control over the outcome was varied across three experimental conditions. In one condition the experimenter broke the structure (low control); in a second condition subjects broke the structure by using the technique already described (moderate control); and in a third condition the subjects assembled the apparatus and then broke the blocks (high control). The high-control condition should be described in more detail. Subjects were told they could assemble the apparatus for breaking the structure in any way that they preferred. The ramp was lying on the floor, and the chairs used to raise one end of it were placed to one side. The experimenter asked if the subject would arrange the apparatus in a certain manner, because only a few more subjects were needed to complete one cell in the experiment. It was emphasized to subjects that they were perfectly free to arrange the breaking apparatus in any way they preferred but that their agreement with the experimenter's request would be appreciated. All subjects did agree. The apparatus was then arranged in the standard manner used to produce the breaking in the other two conditions. Therefore, the nature of the breaking was held constant across all conditions.

Dependent Measures. The questionnaire used in Experiment 1 was administered to subjects. Since all subjects either witnessed or engaged in the destruction, the questionnaire contained mood items as well as items referring to the breaking itself. Subjects completed this questionnaire after the structure was broken.

Results

Manipulation Check. Subjects indicated the degree of control they felt about the change occurring as a result of destruction of the structure. An analysis of variance revealed a significant main effect for the perceived control factor, $F(2,114) = 26.35$, $p < .01$. As expected, subjects in the low-control condition (who watched the experimenter produce the breaking) reported a very low level of control ($M = 2.23$). In two conditions the subjects actually broke the structures themselves; here, the reported level of control was much higher. Yet the perceived control was very similar in the two participation conditions: The mean was 9.01 when subjects did the breaking and 8.44 when they did the breaking and also assembled the apparatus. The condition that was intended to produce the highest sense of control obviously did not. Perhaps the high level of control we expected did not occur because the subject's apparent freedom to produce the break in any way was subsequently withdrawn by the experimenter, who asked that the subject do it in a certain way. Thus, the experimental manipulation created one very low and two moderately high levels of control instead of three distinct levels. Nevertheless, all three conditions are included in the statistical analyses.

Affective Reactions. A 2 × 3 analysis of variance was performed on data from a scale measuring enjoyment of the breaking and from a more general mood scale. For enjoyment of the breaking, the main effect for control of outcome failed to reach statistical significance, $F(2,114) = 2.15, p < .12$. The main effect for complexity of the breaking was significant, $F(1,114) = 10.06$, $p < .01$. Although the result for control of outcome was not statistically significant, the trend was in the predicted direction: Subjects expressed greater enjoyment of the breaking when they had greater control over the outcome. Thus, mean enjoyment of the destruction was lowest when the experimenter performed the breaking (6.91), highest when the subject produced the breaking (8.53), and intermediate when the subject both assembled the apparatus and did the breaking (8.35).

Turning to enjoyment of the breaking as a function of complexity of the structure, the results supported our prediction. Subjects expressed more enjoyment in connection with the breaking of the structure that was composed of small as compared to large blocks ($M = 9.03$ vs. 6.82, respectively). This finding is particularly impressive because a between-subjects design was used, so the subjects' responses were based on absolute rather than relative judgments.

A second dependent measure of affect consisted of a general mood scale (happy–sad). Results for the analysis of variance showed a main effect for control of outcome, $F(2,114) = 9.42, p < .01$. The result for complexity of the break did not reach an acceptable level of significance, $F(1,114) = 2.71$, $p < .10$. Means for the control factor indicated that subjects who broke the blocks were happiest ($M = 11.75$); those who broke blocks and also assembled the apparatus were least happy ($M = 9.91$); and subjects who watched the experimenter perform the break were intermediate ($M = 8.98$). Inspection of the data for the complexity factor indicated that the failure to reach significance was due primarily to the condition in which the experimenter did the breaking. Means for the other two conditions were quite strongly in the expected direction (more positive affect for the more complex break).

Perceived Success. A 2 × 3 analysis of variance was performed on data from a question measuring the subjects' general level of felt success. Significant main effects were found both for control over outcome, $F(2,114) = 10.42, p < .01$, and for complexity of the break, $F(1,114) = 5.05$, $p < .05$. Means are shown in Fig. 4.3. Results for the control factor were consistent with data for affective reactions already reported. That is, highest feelings of success ($M = 11.92$) were reported by subjects who felt most control (subjects did the breaking); least success ($M = 8.26$) was reported by subjects who watched the experimenter perform the breaking; and the mean

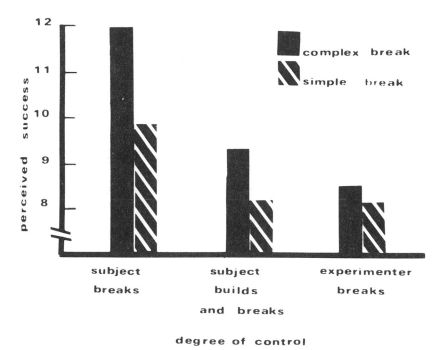

FIG. 4.3.   Felt success as a function of control over outcome and complexity
of break.

was intermediate (M = 8.77) for subjects who assembled the apparatus and
did the breaking. Results for the complexity variable were in the predicted
direction: Subjects who broke the small-block structure felt more successful
(M = 9.88) than subjects who broke the large-block (less complex) structure
(M = 8.75). It should be noted that the smallest difference as a function of
complexity occurred in the condition of lowest control (experimenter
breaking).

Discussion

The present experiment manipulated two factors: (1) the subject's level of
objective control over breaking, and (2) the complexity of the process of
destruction. Objective control did influence the level of general affect, with
greater control resulting in higher positive affect. Objective level of control of
the destruction also influenced the subjects' general level of perceived success.
Notice that success was measured by a general mood item embedded among
many other items, and the item did not refer to success on the specific task. A

manipulation check for the control variable obtained prior to the breaking resulted in rank ordering the experimental conditions on control in a way slightly different from expected. It is interesting to note that the rank order of means for perceived success was precisely parallel to subjects' rank order for perceived control on the manipulation check in the three experimental conditions. Specific control, then, does seem to have an influence upon the general level of perceived success.

In the present study subjects felt more successful when actively participating in destruction than when merely observing. In contrast, results of Experiment 2 revealed no differential impact on perceived control as a function of participating in versus observing destructive. How can we explain these apparently incongruous results? First, it should be noted that different (though related) dependent measures were used in Experiments 2 (perceived success) and 3 (perceived control). A better comparison could be obtained by observing results for the same measure in both studies. Fortunately, data on perceived success were collected (but not reported) in Experiment 2. Inspection of results in Experiment 2 for perceived success also revealed no difference between the participation and observation conditions. Thus, there was disagreement between Experiments 2 and 3 even when using the same dependent measure. A very important difference exists between the two experiments that may explain the discrepancy in results: Subjects in Experiment 2 experienced success or failure on a task prior to destruction. Therefore, it is possible that the high level of arousal produced by success or failure eliminated the differential impact of participation versus observation that would normally be produced under neutral arousal conditions. Since different levels of arousal have not been created in a single experiment, this speculation remains to be tested in future research.

The results for complexity have very interesting implications. Complexity was defined operationally as the size (and number) of blocks composing a structure (tower). The structure built from many small blocks definitely broke in a more complex way than the one built with larger (and fewer) blocks. Consistent with earlier findings (Allen & Greenberger, 1978), subjects expressed more enjoyment when the process of destruction was more complex. More important for the present research was the relation between complexity and felt success: Felt success was higher for subjects who observed the more complex, as compared to the simpler, process of destruction. This result indicates that the particular nature of destruction—in this case, the aesthetic quality—may influence felt success (and, by extension, control). Hence, variation in the aesthetic quality of the process of destruction may result in different self-attributions about competence and control. This relationship between control and beauty of destruction suggests a highly unusual method for increasing control!

CONCLUSIONS AND IMPLICATIONS

We have adopted a very modest and limited goal in this paper: to provide relevant theory and data in support of the contention that modification of the physical environment—in the form of destruction—is related in important ways to the sense of personal control. Results of three related experiments converge to support this general conclusion. Three major sets of findings from these experiments should be emphasized. First, the experiments indicated that destruction increases a person's feeling of perceived control and success. Furthermore, the greatest change in perceived control occurred for persons who were placed in a state of low general control (failure) prior to the destruction. Thus, by engaging in destruction of some aspect of the physical environment subsequent to a reduction in control, a person is able to enhance the sense of control. Second, the studies demonstrated that preexisting affective states and certain processes involved in the destruction itself can influence perceived control. Positive affect prior to the destruction contributed to the level of control produced by destruction. And when the destruction occurred in a more complex manner, the resulting feeling of success was greater. Finally, the degree of a person's objective control over an act of destruction seems to influence the feeling of success. In sum, the studies have investigated control both as a dependent and as an independent variable.

It is obvious that many of the issues and theoretical assumptions alluded to in an earlier section have not been subjected to empirical examination. It has been a basic assumption that persons actively seek out opportunities to engage in behavior (such as destruction) that will serve to reestablish a previously existing level of control. Thus, an individual seeks to maintain or increase the stable level of control or competence, and a loss of that control will act as a motivating force. A very important problem in this regard is the relation between strength of motivation to regain a loss in control and a person's prior (stable) level of control. It would seem reasonable to hypothesize that a direct relation exists between level of control and strength of the responses directed toward restoring control when a noticeable decrement has occurred. This is, the motivation to restore control should be even stronger for persons having a stable high, rather than low, level of control.

We speculated earlier that destruction may be used as a technique for increasing control when other avenues of action are either not available or have been tried and found to be unsuccessful. An implication of this line of thinking is that persons who suffer from a chronically low level of control might be especially predisposed, because of their past experience, to engage in destruction of the physical environment. A low permanent level of control is more likely to be characteristic of certain portions of the population than others (e.g., residents of ghettos or low-income housing projects and other persons of low socioeconomic status). Consistent with this reasoning, a high rate of vandalism is common in low-income housing projects. One consequence of repeatedly engaging in destruction may be that it comes to be increasingly enjoyable due to certain reinforcing qualities intrinsic to such behavior. Thus, some persons may engage frequently in destruction because of the resulting feelings of success and positive affect and—most important— the boost it gives to one's sense of control.

It should be remembered that the destruction engaged in by subjects in our research was approved by the experimenter. It seems reasonable to expect that socially disapproved destruction would exert an even stronger impact on perceived control. Several reasons can be cited for maintaining that illegal property destruction such as vandalism is probably a very effective way of increasing one's sense of control: Such destruction is accompanied by a high level of arousal; often it possesses symbolic significance; frequently it is committed in a group; and usually it influences other people's behavior. Nevertheless, if central characteristics of self are incongruent with this type of destructive behavior, a strong increase in sense of control may not ensue. That is, the increase in sense of control usually produced by destruction may be inhibited or weakened by the operation of other aspects of the person's self-system. Hence, an important task for future research is to integrate destruction and sense of control with broader aspects of personality structure and dynamics.

Many other important questions remain to be clarified by future research. Do persons attempt to increase their sense of control by engaging in attempts to modify the physical environment only after having attempted to change some aspect of the nonphysical environment? What techniques are available for increasing a sense of control by changing the physical environment, and when is one technique used instead of another (e.g., personalization versus destruction)? And a crucial question concerns the nature of the processes determining one's choice among potential targets in the physical environment. The research reported in the present paper was not designed to answer questions such as these, of course. At this point, we have made only a small beginning on one aspect of a more general but very important psychological problem: specifying the nature of the reciprocal influence between certain cognitive processes and transformation of stimuli in the physical environment.

REFERENCES

Allen, V. L., & Greenberger, D. B. An aesthetic theory of vandalism. *Crime & Delinquency,* 1978, *24,* 309–321.
Bandura, A. Self-efficacy: Toward a unifying theory of behavioral change. *Psychological Review,* 1977, *84,* 191–215.

Becker, F. D. *Housing messages.* Stroudsburg, Pa.: Dowden, Hutchinson & Ross, 1977.

Berlyne, D. E. *Aesthetics and psychobiology.* New York: Appelton-Century-Crofts, 1971.

Boudon, P. *Lived-in architecture.* Cambridge: MIT Press, 1969.

Brehm, J. W. *A theory of psychological reactance.* New York: Academic Press, 1966.

Cohen, S. Property destruction: Motives and meanings. In C. Ward (Ed.), *Vandalism.* New York: Van Nostrand, 1973.

Debord, G. *The decline and fall of the spectacular commodity economy.* New York: Situationist International, 1967.

Dion, K. L., Baron, R. S., & Miller, N. Why do groups make riskier decisions than individuals? In L. Berkowitz (Ed.), *Advances in experimental social psychology* (Vol. 5). New York: Academic Press, 1970.

Fenigstein, A., & Buss, A. Association and affect as determinants of displaced aggression. *Journal of Research in Personality,* 1974, *7,* 306–313.

Geyer, G. A. Beirut . . . *Chicago Sun-Times,* November 3, 1978.

Jenkins, H. M., & Ward, W. C. Judgment of contingency between responses and outcomes. *Psychological Monographs,* 1965, *79*(Whole No. 594).

Langer, E. The illusion of control. *Journal of Personality and Social Psychology,* 1975, *32,* 311–328.

Madison, A. *Vandalism: The not-so-senseless crime.* New York: Seabury Press, 1970.

Martin, J. M. *Juvenile vandalism: A study of its nature and prevention.* Springfield, Ill.: Charles C. Thomas, 1961.

Nisbett, R. E., & Valins, S. Perceiving the causes of one's own behavior. In E. E. Jones, D. Kanouse, H. H. Kelley, R. E. Nisbett, S. Valins, & B. Weiner (Eds.), *Attribution: Perceiving the causes of behavior.* Morristown, N.J. General Learning Press, 1972.

Piaget, J. [*The origins of intelligence in children*] (M. Cook, trans.). New York: International University Press, 1952.

Rotter, J. B. Generalized expectancies for internal versus external control of reinforcement. *Psychological Monographs,* 1966, *80*(1, Whole No. 609).

Sarbin, T. R., & Allen, V. L. Role theory. In G. Lindzey & E. Aronson (Eds.), *The handbook of social psychology* (2nd ed.) (Vol. 1). Reading, Mass.: Addison-Wesley, 1968.

Seeman, M. On the meaning of alienation. *American Sociological Review,* 1959, *24,* 783–791.

Seligman, M. E. P. *Helplessness.* San Francisco: Freeman, 1975.

Taylor, L., & Walton, P. Industrial sabotage: Motives and meanings. In S. Cohen (Ed.), *Images of deviance.* London: Penguin Books, 1971.

Velten, E. A laboratory task for induction of mood states. *Behavioral Research and Therapy,* 1968, *6,* 473–482.

Ward, C. (Ed.) *Vandalism.* New York: Van Nostrand, 1973.

Wenk, E., & Harlow, N. (Eds.). *School crime and disruption.* Davis, Calif.: Responsible Action, 1978.

White, R. W. Motivation reconsidered: The concept of competence. *Psychological Review,* 1959, *66,* 297–333.

Wicklund, R. *Freedom and reactance.* Hillsdale, N.J.: Lawrence Erlbaum Associates, 1974.

Wortman, C. B., & Brehm, J. W. Responses to uncontrollable outcomes: An integration of reactance theory and the learned helplessness model. In L. Berkowitz (Ed.), *Advances in experimental social psychology* (Vol. 8). New York: Academic Press, 1975.

Yancey, W. L. Architecture, interaction, and social control: The case of a large-scale housing project. In J. F. Wohlwill & D. H. Carson (Eds.), *Environment and the social sciences: Perspectives and applications.* Washington, D.C.: American Psychological Association, 1972.

Ziller, R. C. *The social self.* New York: Pergamon Press, 1973.

Zimbardo, P. G. The human choice: Individuation, reason and order vs. deindividuation, impulse and chaos. In W. J. Arnold & D. Levine (Eds.), *Nebraska Symposium on Motivation* (Vol. 17). Lincoln, Neb.: University of Nebraska Press, 1970.

5 Judgment of Contingency: Errors and Their Implications[1]

Lyn Y. Abramson
State University of New York at Stony Brook

Lauren B. Alloy
University of Pennsylvania

Learning about relationships or contingencies between events is an important part of people's knowledge of the world. The degree to which one event predicts another or one response controls an outcome provides an individual with information necessary for adaptive behavior. A number of psychologists have suggested that in attempting to predict and control events in the world, people act as "naive scientists" (e.g., Heider, 1958; Kelley, 1967; Weiner, 1974). This view emphasizes a rational basis for people's decisions and behavior. In contrast, a number of investigations recently have begun to discover systematic errors or irrationalities in people's cognitions or beliefs about relationships between events (e.g., Alloy & Abramson, in press; Jenkins & Ward, 1965; Langer, 1975). Can these two opposing views be reconciled?

In this chapter we review basic laboratory research about people's accuracy in detecting relationships between events and relationships between their responses and outcomes. We attempt to extract a common theme or themes that unify the instances in which people misjudge relationships in the world. Finally, we discuss the real-world implications of this research for people's adaptive behavior.

Before reviewing the empirical work on people's detection of environmental relationships or contingencies, it is useful to define the concept of contingency itself. *Contingency* is a general term and refers to the degree of relationship between any two events. When the two events of interest are both stimuli, the relationship between them is best construed as one of

---

[1]The order of authors' names is random.

predictability. The first stimulus event provides either some or no information about the occurrence of the second. Alternatively, when the two events in a relationship consist of an individual's responses and some outcome, the relationship may be described as one of controllability. The response exerts either some or no control over the outcome. An example highlights the distinction between prediction and control. Scores on the Scholastic Aptitude Test (SAT) predict grades in college, whereas the response of studying controls college grades [see Jenkins & Ward (1965) and Seligman (1975) for a discussion of predictability and controllability]. It is worth noting that in statistics, the phi coefficient (ϕ) commonly is used to quantify the degree of contingency or relationship between two events. However, as we see later, investigators have differed somewhat in their operationalizations of the concept of contingency.

EMPIRICAL WORK ON
THE JUDGMENT OF CONTINGENCY

Studies in Human Learning

During the 1960s a number of investigators in the operant tradition became interested in "superstitious" responding in humans. In these studies, human subjects behaved as if their responses controlled outcomes, although, objectively speaking, no relationship existed between their responses and outcomes. For example, Bruner and Revusky (1961) exposed high school students to operant conditioning procedures in the laboratory. In this study the students were seated in front of a keyboard with four telegraph keys and were instructed to press the keys in such a way as to maximize delivery of rewards. A reward consisted of the onset of a bell and a light and the accumulation of a nickel. In reality, reward could be obtained only when subjects responded with a specified interresponse time on the third telegraph key from the left. The other three keys were nonfunctional, and pressing them was noncontingently related to the delivery of rewards. The experiment consisted of three phases. In the first phase, students' operant levels of key pressing were assessed, and no responses were rewarded. The second phase was the crucial part of the experiment. During this phase, subjects were rewarded each time they pressed the third telegraph key from the left provided consecutive presses on this key were separated by greater than 8.2 seconds but less than 10.25 seconds. Finally, during the extinction phase, no key presses were rewarded. The results were clear-cut. During the second phase of the experiment, all students performed systematic patterns of responding involving at least one of the nonfunctional keys. Such complex patterns were not observed during the baseline or extinction phases. Moreover, when interviewed after the experiment, all students expressed the opinion that these patterns of responding were necessary to produce reward. No student asserted that delivery of rewards depended on the passage of time.

Similar to Bruner and Revusky (1961), Catania and Cutts (1963) found that human subjects developed complex patterns of responses involving both a button contingently related to rewards as well as a button noncontingently related to rewards. These investigators presented college undergraduates with two response buttons and instructed them to maximize rewards (onset of a green light) by pressing one, but not both, of the buttons each time a yellow light flashed. The yellow light flashed 100 times a minute. The experimental situation was designed so that presses on one button were rewarded on a variable-interval schedule (30 seconds), whereas presses on the other button were never rewarded. Catania and Cutts hypothesized that temporal contiguity between responses on the nonfunctional button and reward was responsible for the development and maintenance of superstitious responding. They tested this hypothesis by imposing a delay between any presses on the nonfunctional button and the availability of reward on the functional button. For all subjects, the introduction of the delay was followed by an abrupt cessation of responding on the nonfunctional button if the delay had a large effect on the frequency of reward. It is worth pointing out that subjects who experienced a delay from the beginning of the experiment did develop complex superstitious responses, although less frequently than subjects with no delay.

Whereas Catania and Cutts (1963) emphasized the role of temporal contiguity in superstitious responding, Wright (1962) found that frequency of reward also contributed to the consistency of responding maintained by noncontingent reward. Wright presented college undergraduates with 16 unmarked, identical buttons arranged in a circle and instructed the subjects to operate the buttons one at a time so as to maximize the number of rewards (onset of a buzzer). Subjects were told that one or more correct selections or sequences of buttons would be rewarded. In fact, rewards were noncontingently related to subjects' button presses and were presented according to a preprogrammed schedule. Those subjects who received high probabiities of noncontingent reward showed a greater tendency to use repeatedly the same button or interbutton interval than subjects who received low probabilities of reward. Thus, the consistency of superstitious patterns of responding appears to be related to the overall frequency or probability of occurrence of noncontingent rewards.

A general theme runs through these studies. People often act as if outcomes are dependent on their responses when they are not. Perhaps people do not have a concept of contingency that enables them to distinguish cases in which their responses do control outcomes from cases in which their responses do not control outcomes. Jenkins and Ward (1965) systematically investigated people's knowledge about relationships between responses and outcomes by examining verbalized judgments of contingency.

In three experiments, Jenkins and Ward (1965) presented subjects with a series of contingency problems in an instrumental learning situation. For each problem subjects were given trials on which a choice between two responses was followed by one of two possible outcomes. The contingency problems differed in the objective degree of contingency as well as in the overall frequency with which the outcome of interest occurred. At the end of each problem, subjects were asked to rate, on a 0-to-100 scale, the degree of control (contingency) their response choices had exerted over the outcomes. Jenkins and Ward defined the objective degree of contingency between response and outcome as the differential probability of an outcome given the occurrence of one response versus the probability of that outcome given the occurrence of another response. When there is no difference between these conditional probabilities, the outcome is said to be uncontrollable. The results from Jenkins and Ward's study indicated that humans' judgments of contingencies were quite inaccurate. Specifically, in all problems, regardless of the actual degree of contingency, subjects' ratings of degree of control correlated highly with the frequency of reward and were completely unrelated to the actual degree of control.

Jenkins and Ward found that erroneous judgments of contingency persisted despite remedial efforts. One remedial strategy consisted of presenting subjects with exemplars of contingent or noncontingent response–outcome sequences and informing them of the objective degree of contingency in these problems. A second strategy involved reducing subjects' active involvement in the task by allowing them simply to watch a display of the responses and outcomes generated by an active subject. Neither of these strategies was effective in enhancing the accuracy of subjects' judgments of control. Based on these results, Jenkins and Ward concluded that people do not have a concept of contingency that enables them to assess response–outcome relationships accurately.

More recently, Alloy and Abramson (in press) questioned the generality of Jenkins and Ward's conclusion about people's lack of a concept of contingency. Alloy and Abramson (in press) found that under some laboratory conditions but not all (see following), subjects were able to judge accurately the degree of contingency between their responses and outcomes. [For a discussion of potential factors leading to inaccurate judgments of control in Jenkins and Ward's (1965) study, see Alloy and Abramson (in press).]

To this point we have reviewed studies of people's behavior and beliefs concerning the relationship between their responses and outcomes—that is, controllability. We now turn to studies in the human learning tradition that examine people's behavior and beliefs concerning the relationship between two stimulus events—that is, predictability.

Hake and Hyman (1953) presented subjects with a random series containing two kinds of stimuli. One stimulus was a vertical column of four lights, whereas the other was a horizontal row of four lights. On each trial after a warning light came on, subjects were required to predict which of the two possible stimuli would appear on that trial. Subjects were given no information about the rules by which the series was constructed. Similar to subjects in many of the controllability studies already cited, Hake and Hyman's subjects responded as though the series were not random. Instead, their predictions suggested that they believed that future behavior of the series could be predicted from past or present subsequences in the series.

Do subjects every accurately assess the degree of relationship between events? Ward and Jenkins (1965) asked three groups of subjects to judge the degree of relationship between cloud seeding and rainfall. The information "seed" or "no seed" followed by "rain" or "no rain" was presented in one of three different ways. One group of subjects received this information presented in a serial fashion (i.e., trial by trial); a second group received the information in an organized numerical summary; and a third group received the information serially followed by an organized summary. The only group successfully judging the degree of relationship between cloud seeding and rain was the second group, which received the information only in the organized summary form. Interestingly, when information was presented over time, as is often the case in real life, subjects were inaccurate. In particular, inaccurate subjects often relied on the frequency of confirming cases in arriving at their judgments of the degree of relationship between cloud seeding and rainfall. In the context of Ward and Jenkins' experiment, confirming cases were defined as the sum of the number of instances in which seeding and rain occured *plus* the number of instances in which no seeding and no rain occurred. Ward and Jenkins believed that the inaccuracy of subjects' judgments with a serial presentation of information was not due to an inability to sum information over trials. Pilot work indicated that subjects were able to reproduce with considerable accuracy the frequencies of the four possible sets of events: seed–rain, seed–no rain, no seed–rain, no seed–no rain.

Taken together, studies on human contingency learning suggest that people often err in detecting relationships between their responses and outcomes and/or between events. It is interesting, however, that under some conditions, people accurately assess these relationships.

Studies in Social Psychology

Social psychologists also have been intrigued by people's erroneous beliefs about control. Langer (1975) has investigated the effects of introducing elements characteristic of skill situations into objectively uncontrollable or chance situations on producing the "illusion of control." Langer defined an illusion of control as an expectancy of personal success probability inappropriately higher than the objective probability would warrant. Langer found that introducing such elements as competition, choice, or practice into an objectively uncontrollable situation inappropriately increased subjects' expectancies of success on the task.

Langer emphasized the role of motivation in producing illusions of control. She argued that people may believe they have control in objectively uncontrollable situations because they are motivated to achieve personal competency or mastery over their environment. A number of studies have shown that when people believe they have control over an aversive event, even if this belief is false, the aversiveness of that event is reduced (Corah & Boffa, 1970; Geer, Davison, & Gatchel, 1970; Hokanson, DeGood, Forrest, & Brittain, 1971; Pervin, 1963; Stotland & Blumenthal, 1964). Accordingly, Langer has speculated that another reason why people may show illusions of control is that there is a motivation to avoid the negative consequences that often accompany a belief in no control. In addition to motivational factors, Langer also suggests that cognitive factors play a role in producing the illusion of control. She maintained that people often attribute positive outcomes to the action that preceded them because, in reality, most positive outcomes are caused by the immediately preceding action.

Langer and Roth (1975) studied the illusion of control as a function of patterns of success and failure on a coin-tossing task. They found that subjects who exerienced early successes and late failures rated themselves as significantly better at predicting coin tosses than subjects who experienced early failures and late successes or a random sequence of successes and failures on the task. In addition, subjects with early successes and late failures had higher expectations of future successes than the other subjects. Langer and Roth noted that although group differences on expectancies were small in magnitude, the fact that coin tossing is an obviously chance task emphasizes the robustness of the illusion-of-control phenomenon.

Although Langer (1975) and Langer and Roth (1975) have demonstrated the interesting finding that people overestimate their probability of success on chance tasks, it is not clear that such overestimation represents an illusion of control. The problem here is that expectancy of success may not be an adequate index of belief in control. For example, in betting situations in which the odds are very good, people may believe they have no control over the outcome yet have a high expectancy of success. Thus, Langer and Langer and Roth may not be studying exactly the same phenomenon as investigators in the human learning tradition.

Similar to Langer (1975), Wortman (1975) asked whether or not factors other than the objective degree of control influenced people's feelings of control in chance situations. Wortman showed subjects two prizes and told them they would get to win one by a chance drawing. Two marbles of different colors were placed in a can and mixed up. Subjects who knew which marble stood for which prize beforehand and who picked one of the two marbles themselves believed they had more control over obtaining the preferred prize than subjects who knew what each marble stood for but were not allowed to pick the marble themselves and than subjects who were allowed to pick their own marble but did not know what the marbles stood for. Thus Wortman argued that foreknowledge of a chance outcome and "causing" that outcome are important determinants of perceived control. The results of the social psychological studies parallel those of the human learning studies: people show systematic errors in judging relationships between events and between responses and outcomes.

Studies in Clinical Diagnosis

A number of theorists (e.g., Chapman & Chapman, 1967; Meehl, 1960) have commented on the puzzling tendency of practicing clinical psychologists to agree in their clinical observations that various symptoms or behavioral characteristics of psychiatric patients are correlated with scores on conventional psychodiagnostic tests despite research evidence to the contrary. For example, clinicians frequently report that paranoid individuals show elaborations of the eye on the Draw-a-Person (DAP) test, even though four separate studies have failed to confirm such a relationship (Fisher & Fisher, 1950; Holzberg & Wexler, 1950; Reznikoff & Nicholas, 1958; Ribler, 1957). These errors in psychodiagnosis are pertinent to the present discussion because they are another instance of prediction gone awry.

Chapman and Chapman (1967) and Starr and Katkin (1969) have conducted experiments designed to determine the sources of such "illusory correlation." Chapman and Chapman, in a series of six experiments, asked whether naive college undergraduates would "rediscover" the same erroneous correlations between patients' symptoms and drawings from the DAP. Students were presented with a series of DAP drawings randomly paired with contrived symptom statements of the alleged patients who drew the pictures. So, similar to the clinic, there was no objective relationship between type of psychiatric symptoms on one hand and drawing on the other. Rather than perceiving the lack of relationship between symptoms and drawings, students saw the same positive correlations between symptoms and drawings as do clinicians. Offering students a prize of $20 for accuracy or providing them with extra time to examine the stimulus materials did not remediate substantially their errors. In a final remedial strategy, Chapman and Chapman allowed students to become maximally familiar with the stimulus materials in addition to offering a $20 prize for accuracy. Students were allowed to shuffle the stimulus materials, rearrange them, compare groups of stimuli, and return to any stimulus as often as they wished. Although this intensive remedial effort increased students' accuracy somewhat, Chapman and Chapman noted that the most striking aspect of the findings was the resistance of the error to the influence of reality.

Chapman and Chapman hypothesized that associative connections between symptom statements and parts of the body emphasized in the drawings were the basis for these illusory correlations. They tested this notion by giving a different sample of subjects a questionnaire constructed for measuring the associative strength between the problem area of each symptom statement and the parts of the body that are referred to in the various drawing characteristics. The results showed that the rated associative strength between body parts and symptoms predicted subjects' ratings of correlation between the two. These results suggest that the higher the associative connection between two events, the more likely it is that people will believe erroneously that one predicts the other.

A study by Starr and Katkin (1969) attested to the robustness of illusory correlation in the diagnostic setting. In this experiment, subjects observed five completed sentences taken from the Sentence Completion Test paired equally frequently with each of five statements purporting to describe the major problem of the patient who had completed the paired sentence. Despite the fact that Starr and Katkin's experiment was designed to reduce the information load on subjects, subjects reported illusory correlations that paralleled relationships generated by a group of experienced clinical psychologists.

The work of Smedslund (1963) shows that illusory correlations about diagnosis are not confined to the psychiatric setting. Smedslund presented student nurses with information about the frequency of various symptoms and medical diagnoses. The results indicated that the judgments of student nurses showed no relation to the actual contingency between symptom and diagnosis. In arriving at their judgments of the relationship between symptom and diagnosis, nurses appeared to rely on the simple frequency with which symptom and diagnosis appeared together (i.e., positive confirming cases only). In summary, in both medical and psychiatric settings, naive observers and experienced clinicians claim to see relationships between events that are unrelated in reality.

Studies in Experimental Psychopathology

The work we have reviewed thus far shows that normal individuals show systematic errors or irrational beliefs about relationships between events in the world and between their responses and outcomes. One might suppose that such irrational beliefs about contingencies would be exaggerated in psychiatric populations of individuals. In fact, a number of clinicians have classified psychopathological individuals on the basis of the nature of alleged distortions about reality. For example, Beck (1967) has characterized the manic individual as suffering from unrealistic beliefs about personal control over environmental events. Drawing on these clinical intuitions, Langer (1975) has speculated that manic or hypomanic individuals may be especially susceptible to the "illusion of control."

The greater part of theorizing and experientation on psychopathological individuals' beliefs about prediction and control has been in the area of depression. Both practicing clinicans and academic psychologists have proposed theories of depression that embody the core concept of helplessness or hopelessness (e.g., Arieti, 1970; Beck, 1967, 1976; Bibring, 1953; Lichtenberg, 1957; Melges & Bowlby, 1969; Seligman, 1975). In this view, the depressive is characterized as one who believes he or she is ineffective and powerless to control outcomes in the world. The learned-helplessness model (Abramson, Seligman, & Teasdale, 1978; Seligman, 1975; Seligman, Klein, & Miller, 1976) is the most explicit statment of a helplessness theory of depression. according to this model, depressed people have generalized expectancies of independence between their responses and outcomes that cause the motivational, cognitive, and emotional symptoms of depression. The motivational symptom consists of retarded initiation of voluntary responses and is reflected in the passivity of the depressed individual. The cognitive symptom has been referred to as a "negative cognitive set" (Beck, 1967) that makes it difficult for the depressed individual to see that personal responses do control environmental outcomes. Finally, the emotional symptom consists of sad affect.

A deduction from the learned-helplessness model is that depressed individuals will have a bias toward seeing noncontingency between responses and outcomes when contingency actually exists (Alloy & Seligman, 1978). In other words, depressives should tend to underestimate the degree of control their responses exert over outcomes. Alloy and Abramson presented depressed and nondepressed college students with one of a series of problems varying in the actual degree of control subjects' responses exerted over outcomes. In each problem students estimated the degree of contingency between their responses (pressing or not pressing a button) and an environmental outcome (onset of a green light). Performance on a behavioral task and estimates of the conditional probability of green-light onset associated with the two response alternatives provided additional measures for assessing beliefs about control.

Surprisingly, depressed students accurately judged the degree of control their responses exerted over outcomes in all conditions of all experiments. Nondepressed students, on the other hand, overestimated the degree of control their responses exerted over outcomes when uncontrollable outcomes were frequent and/or desired and underestimated the degree of control when controllable outcomes were undesired. Nondepressed students also underestimated the degree of control when the passive response of not pressing the button was associated with the higher percentage of reward in a hedonically charged situation. Thus, contrary to the prediction of the learned-helplessness model, depressed students did not misjudge the relationship between their responses and outcomes, whereas nondepressed students often did inaccurately judge these relationships. A further study by Abramson, Alloy, and Rosoff (1978) suggests that even when depressives do underestimate degree of control, it is not because of a cognitive bias to see noncontingency; rather it appears to be a function of a reduced tendency to generate potential controlling responses.

Alloy and Abramson argued that the source of nondepressed students' errors in judging contingency was the organization of response–outcome sequence data and not the perception of these data themselves. Support for this claim comes from the fact that both nondepressed and depressed students accurately judged the conditional probabilities of outcomes given responses. Drawing on work in social psychology (e.g., Streufert & Streufert, 1969; Wortman, Costanzo, & Witt, 1973) and clinical theorizing about depression (e.g., Beck, 1967, 1976; Bibring, 1953; Freud, 1917/1957), Alloy and Abramson suggested that motivational factors may account for the difference between depressed and nondepressed students' judgments of control. According to this motivational account, nondepressed people overestimate their degree of control over desirable outcomes and underestimate their degree of control over undesirable outcomes because they are motivated to maintain or enhance their self-esteem. Depressed people, on the other hand, do not make such errors in judging control because they do not have a specific motivation to preserve self-esteem. Future research is necessary to show whether clinically depressed individuals show similar accuracy in judging the relationship between their responses and outcomes.

At present, the causal direction of the correlation between depression and accuracy in judging contingencies between one's responses and outcomes is not clear. Perhaps the state of depression itself causes people to assess contingencies accurately. According to this view, people would judge contingencies accurately when they are depressed but not when they are not. Alternatively, those people who tend to judge accurately how much control they have over outcomes may be more prone to depression than people who systematically misjudge the efficacy of their responses. According to this interpretation, people who are "realistic" about their impact on environmental events would be at high risk for depression. Currently, we are conducting studies to untangle the directionality of the correlation between depression and accuracy in judging control.

In summary, a number of studies from diverse areas of psychology demonstrate that people often err in judging the degree of contingency between events and between their responses and outcomes. People frequently treat unrelated events as if they are related. That is, they act as though outcomes are dependent on responses when they are not and as though one event can be predicted from another when it cannot. In some situations people's judgments of contingency are wholly unrelated to the objective degree of contingency and, instead, seem to be based on a number of invalid heuristics.

COMMON THEMES IN
ERRONEOUS JUDGMENTS OF CONTINGENCY

Are there common themes unifying the instances in which people misjudge the degree of relationship between environmental events or between their responses and outcomes? Search for common themes is difficult because each investigator has proposed a relatively unique hypothesis to account for people's errors in judging contingencies. A listing of the hypotheses demonstrates their diversity. For example, whereas Catania and Cutts (1963) suggested that temporal contiguity induces overestimations of control, other investigators have emphasized the role of frequency of reward (Alloy & Abramson, in press; Jenkins & Ward, 1965; Wright, 1962) and valence of outcome (Alloy & Abramson, in press) in affecting people's judgments of contingency. People's reliance on the erroneous heuristic of confirming cases in judging contingencies also has been noted (Alloy & Abramson, in press, Jenkins & Ward, 1965; Smedslund, 1963; Ward & Jenkins, 1965). Other experimenters have underscored the importance of the mode (Ward & Jenkins, 1965) and sequence (Langer & Roth, 1975) of presentation of events in contingency learning situations. Investigators interested in illusory correlations in psychodiagnosis stressed the associative strength between stimuli as a factor in people's judgments about the contingency between them (Chapman & Chapman, 1967; Starr & Katkin, 1969). Social psychologists pointed to the introduction into chance situations of elements characteristic of skill situations (Langer, 1975) and foreknowledge of the goal and choice (Wortman, 1975) as determinants of the illusion of control. Moreover, Langer (1975) and Alloy and Abramson (in press) suggested that people's beliefs about control may be motivated. People may show erroneous beliefs about control because they are motivated to maintain self-esteem or to avoid the negative consequences accompanying a belief in no control. Still other investigators have argued that erroneous judgments of contingency result from faulty organization, rather than faulty perception, of stimulus data (Alloy & Abramson, in press, Smedslund, 1963; Ward & Jenkins, 1965). Finally, Alloy and Abramson (in press) argued that individual differences exist in people's susceptibility to erroneous judgments of contingency, with depressed college students less likely to err than nondepressed college students.

Historically, explanation of people's errors often has led to general insights about psychological functioning (e.g., Freud, 1920; Gregory, 1966, 1970). It is important, then, to ask whether or not a unified account of people's errors in judging contingencies can be given. We believe that it is possible to give a more parsimonious account of people's erroneous judgments of contingency than merely to enumerate the experimental factors found to influence these judgments.

An important theme running through the judgment of contingency studies is that people err in judging relationships because of the way they organize incoming information rather than because they misperceive this information. Therefore, an account of people's errors in judging contingency must delineate the conditions in which people use faulty organization in arriving at judgments of contingency and the conditions in which they do not. Two major classes of factors appear to influence people's organization of information relevant to contingency judgments: motivational and cognitive.

A number of theorists have argued that people's perception and cognitions about events are influenced by motivational factors (e.g., Bruner & Postman, 1947; Erdelyi, 1974; Freud, 1920). Although Heider (1958) likened people to naive scientists, he also argued that sometimes people's attributions of causality are subject to motivational biases. We speculate that two different kinds of motivational biases may influence judgments of contingency. First, a large number of studies have documented that people experience less anxiety and depression in response to stressful stimuli when they believe they control these stimuli than when they believe they do not control the stimuli (e.g., Corah & Boffa, 1970; Geer et al., 1970; Hokanson et al., 1971; Seligman, 1975; Stotland & Blumenthal, 1964). Interestingly, even individuals who erroneously believe they have control over aversive outcomes show less stress than individuals who correctly believe they do not control these outcomes. Thus, as Langer (1975) suggested, an extrapolation from these studies is that people may erroneously believe that they have control over an event in order to avoid the negative consequences that accompany a belief in no control. To date, however, no experimenter has demonstrated convincingly that such motivated overestimations of control occur. Current demonstrations of people's overestimations of control are equally well explained by postulating ignorance, as opposed to motivation, on the part of the experimental subjects. More sophisticated research designs are necessary to determine whether people's beliefs about control are motivated by a desire to avoid the aversive consequences of a belief in no control. It should be noted, of course, that this motivational account is not pertinent to cases in which people underestimate their degree of control over outcomes.

A second motivational account of people's faulty organization of information relevant to judgments of control was suggested by Alloy and

Abramson (in press) to account for depressed students' accurate judgments of control. Alloy and Abramson suggested that the pattern of nondepressed students' errors in judging control resembled the "self-serving" attribution bias sometimes found in social psychological studies (e.g., Wortman et al., 1973). The logic of the second motivational account is that people's beliefs about the efficacy of their own responses may be motivated by a desire to maintain or enhance their self-esteem. Such a self-serving motivational account should be entertained in studies in which people erroneously believe they control good, but not bad, outcomes. Similar to the prior motivational account, no existing study clearly demonstrates that people's motivation to maintain or enhance self-esteem influences their beliefs about control. The finding, however, that depressed people do not show the pattern of errors in judged control indicative of a motivation to maintain self-esteem, whereas nondepressed people do, may be revealing. Indeed, the depressive often is characterized by low self-esteem (Beck, 1967, 1976; Bibring, 1953; Freud, 1917/1957), and moreover, Bibring (1953) has argued that depressives are not motivated to regain self-esteem precisely because the mechanism for self-deception has broken down in these individuals. Thus, nondepressed people's tendency to believe they have control when good events occur but not when bad events occur may be motivated.

At present both motivational accounts of faulty organization of information about control should be viewed as very tentative. Both accounts are in need of rigorous experimental tests. Such experimental tests may be forthcoming given current attempts to develop laboratory techniques for assessing the influence of motivational factors on cognition (e.g., Erdelyi, 1974).

At present the contribution of cognitive factors to faulty organization of information pertinent to judging contingencies is more clear-cut than that of motivational factors. Recently, investigators interested in the psychology of prediction have argued that people have intuitive casual theories of events and that these stories guide the use of information for purposes of prediction (e.g., Ajzen, 1977; Tversky & Kahneman, in press). Although such causal theories often lead to reasonable predictions, they sometimes lead to systematic errors. Similarly, we believe that people's intuitive theories about control and prediction sometimes lead them to make erroneous judgments of contingency. Next we spell out the implications of this cognitive view for people's judgments of control. A parallel analysis is possible for people's judgments about the predictive relationship between two events.

According to the present account, people have an intuitive theory or set of expectations about what it means to have control over an outcome. At present it is unclear as to whether or not people can verbalize these intuitive theories; such theories may be tacit. It is likely that this theory is in propositional form and consists of a set of sufficiency conditions about the implications of having control over an outcome. A nonexhaustive list of such conditions includes the following:

1. If I have control, then one response will be more effective in producing the outcome than another.
2. If I have control, then good outcomes or outcomes of interest will occur frequently.
3. If I have control, then elements associated with skill tasks such as practice and competition will be salient.
4. If I have control, then my responses and outcomes will occur in close temporal succession.
5. If I have control, confirming cases will be more frequent than disconfirming cases.

In and of itself, such a propositional theory is rather useful. Although only the first proposition is true by definition (Alloy & Abramson, in press; Jenkins & Ward, 1965; Seligman, 1975), the others probably have an empirical basis. For example, it happens more often than not that if a person has control over an outcome, good outcomes *do* occur frequently. The problem arises when people mistakenly assume that their relatively valid set of sufficiency conditions about control implies a set of necessity conditions about control. That is, we speculate that people reason that because control over an outcome is sufficient for a particular state of affairs, then control over an outcome is necessary for that state of affairs as well. Such reasoning leads to a valid conclusion only for Statement 1; by definition, control is necessary and sufficient for differential efficacy of responses (for discussion of the definition of control, see Alloy & Abramson, in press; Jenkins & Ward, 1965; Seligman, 1975; Ward & Jenkins, 1965). In all other cases, inferring necessity from sufficiency leads to erroneous propositions. For example, from the proposition that having control over an outcome implies a high frequency of good outcomes, people erroneously reason that a high frequency of good outcomes implies control over an outcome. Similar invalid inferences of necessity are likely to be drawn from the other statements of sufficiency. The plausibility of this account is increased by noting that a number of studies of reasoning show that people confuse the concepts of necessity and sufficiency (Wason & Johnson-Laird, 1972). Anyone who has attempted to teach college students the concepts of necessity and sufficiency should not be surprised at people's confusion of the two!

Does the foregoing model fit a large subset of the existing data on people's errors in judging control? It is interesting to recall some of the experimental conditions in which people overestimated the degree of control: temporal contiguity between responses and desired outcomes, high frequency and desirability of reward, large number of confirming cases, introduction of elements characteristic of skill situations into chance situations, and introduction of choice into chance situations. Of course, the factors manipulated in these studies are precisely those that people presumably view as consequences of having control. We speculate that subjects in these studies reasoned backward and inferred that the presence of these factors implied that they had control over outcomes. To use one of the sufficiency conditions as an example, it is as if subjects reasoned as follows: "If I have control, then the outcome I desire will occur frequently; the outcome I desire is occurring frequently; therefore I must have control." [See Ward & Jenkins (1965) and Einhorn & Hogarth (1978) for a similar protrayal of subjects' reasoning.] Although much experimental work is consistent with this cognitive account of errors in the judgment of contingency, further research is necessary to test it directly. In particular, means of assessing people's intuitive theories about contingency must be developed. Moreover, it must be shown that people frequently misuse these theories by inferring necessity from theory-based propositions of sufficiency to arrive at judgments of contingency.

A drawback of the proposed cognitive account of errors in the judgment of contingency is that it does not easily explain why depressed people are more accurate than nondepressed people in judging control. The framework of the cognitive account, however, suggests some possible reasons for depressive accuracy in judging control. First, depressed people may have a less embellished concept of control than do nondepressed people. That is, whereas nondepressed people believe that control is sufficient for differential efficacy of responses, high frequency of desired outcomes, temporal contiguity of response and outcome, etc., depressed people may assimilate only the definitional notion of differential efficacy of responses into the concept of control. Thus, even if depressed people are as "illogical" as nondepressed people in confusing sufficiency and necessity, they will err less frequently in judging control. Second, depressed people may subscribe to the same set of sufficiency propositions about the implications of having control as do nondepressed people but fail to infer necessity from them. Perhaps depressed people simply are more "logical" than nondepressed people when it comes to evaluating the efficacy of their own responses. Finally, depressed people may have additional specific knowledge or beliefs based on prior experience that biases them against accepting the conclusions that result from inferring necessity from sufficiency in such situations.

To summarize, we have suggested that both motivational and cognitive factors contribute to people's faulty organization of information pertinent to judging relationships between events and between responses and outcomes. The operation of one set of factors, say motivational, in no way excludes the operation of the other. Motivational and cognitive factors may work synergistically. For example, people may resort to errors in reasoning such as confusing necessity and sufficiency in order to attain some motivational goal such as enhancement of self-esteem. In this regard Wason and Johnson-Laird (1972) have emphasized the influence of the content about which inferences are made on the reasoning processes itself.

At present we view our account of errors in the judgment of contingency as speculative and emphasize the need for further direct experimental tests. Although tentative, a unified account of people's errors in the judgment of contingency is of considerable heuristic value in that it integrates findings from diverse areas of psychology and suggests directions for future research.

PRACTICAL IMPLICATIONS OF WORK ON ERRORS IN THE JUDGMENT OF CONTINGENCY

What are the practical implications of the numerous studies showing that people frequently err in judging the degree to which one event predicts another and the degree to which a response controls an outcome? At the outset it is useful to distinguish between beliefs that are irrational and beliefs that are maladaptive. The work on judged contingency shows that people often hold irrational beliefs about prediction and control, but the adaptiveness of these beliefs is still at issue. Beliefs may be irrational and yet adaptive. For example, a nonveridical perception of control over an aversive event reduces stress (Geer et al., 1970). Thus, in some situations erroneous beliefs about control and prediction will be maladaptive, whereas in other situations they may be adaptive.

Studies on errors in the judgment of contingency have disturbing implications for the practice of clinical diagnosis. Recall that both naive undergraduates and professionals frequently "saw" a relationship between a particular symptom and a diagnosis when no such relationship actually existed (Chapman & Chapman, 1967; Smedslund, 1963; Starr & Katkin, 1969). Particularly worrisome is the fact that subjects in these studies observed symptoms and diagnoses under conditions much more amenable to accuracy of observation than the conventional clinical situation. Whereas the experimental subjects viewed symptoms and diagnoses in close temporal succession, the observations of clinical practitioners are separated by days. As Ward and Jenkins (1965) have shown, people have difficulty in judging relationships between events presented over time. Errors in psychodiagnosis in the clinic, then, may be greater than those observed in the laboratory (but see Kurtz and Garfield (1978) for a discussion of differences between the clinic and the laboratory that may limit the generalizability of Chapman and Chapman's findings to the clinic). Such errors in psychodiagnosis would have maladaptive consequences for patients. Patients might be given invalid diagnoses and, consequently, invalid treatment.

Because illusory psychodiagostic observations potentially are harmful to patients, it is important to ask whether strategies are availabe that render clinicians less susceptible to these errors. Although experimenters (Chapman & Chapman, 1967; Kurtz & Garfield, 1978) have been relatively unsuccessful in developing remedial techniques for errors in psychodiagnosis, the finding that people accurately judge the relationship between events when pertinent information is presented in summary form rather than over time (Ward & Jenkins, 1965) suggests one possible remedial strategy. Clinicians, particularly beginning clinicians, could be induced to maintain ongoing organized records about the frequency of symptoms and diagnoses. Further research is needed to determine methods for breaking up illusory correlations in the clinic.

Studies on errors in the judgment of control have interesting implications for issues concerning psychological well-being and coping. The work of Richard Lazarus and his colleagues suggests that cognitive distortions about stressful events sometimes have palliative effects (Lazarus, 1966; Lazarus & Launier, in press). Illusions of control probably reduce anxiety and depression (see Geer et al., 1970; Seligman, 1975). Interestingly, in Alloy and Abramson's (in press) study, depressed students were more accurate in judging the efficacy of their responses than were nondepressed students. Perhaps the price paid for such accuracy is low self-esteem and bouts of depression. Thus, errors in judged control may be adaptive for individuals in some situations.

Jenkins and Ward (1965) have asked how peope get along as well as they do in the world even though they often are unable to judge correctly whether some event is controlled by or is not controlled by their responses. If people do not accurately assess the relationship between their actions and outcomes, how is it that they frequently act in a way that allows them to "get what they want"? One possible answer to this question concerns the generalizability of laboratory findings on the judgment of contingency to situations outside the laboratory. Perhaps laboratory and nonlaboratory situations differ sufficiently to make generalizations from one to the other tenuous. Future studies on the judgment of contingency must examine people in their natural environments and determine whether their errors in everyday life resemble their errors in the laboratory.

A second answer to the foregoing question focuses on the nature of the errors people make in judging contingencies. An accurate judgment of the degree of contingency between two events such as a response and an outcome requires two pieces of information—the degree to which the response is sufficient for the outcome and the degree to which the response is necessary for the outcome. By definition, a response exerts complete control over an outcome if it is both necessary and sufficient for that outcome (Alloy & Abramson, in press). As already noted, subjects in judgment of contingency studies frequently inferred erroneously that a response controlled an outcome when it was merely sufficient but not necessary for that outcome. For instance, when good outcomes occurred frequently but independently of subjects' responses, subjects believed they had control over the outcome. Outside the laboratory, people may be more concerned with getting what they want than with discovering the relationship between what they do and what they get. If people are mainly concerned with what they get, then their erroneous judgments of control may not be very maladaptive in some situations. After all, knowledge of which action is sufficient for an outcome is all one needs to know if one is merely interested in getting what one wants in the world.

A final question concerns the tenacity of people's erroneous judgments of contingency. Is it possible to develop methods that correct people's erroneous beliefs about prediction and control? The few therapy studies so far have been relatively unsuccessful in altering these erroneous beliefs (Chapman & Chapman, 1967; Jenkins & Ward, 1965; Kurtz & Garfield, 1978). Work in perception shows that visual illusions often persist even when people have "insight" about the nature of their errors (e.g., Gregory, 1966, 1970). Perhaps the cognitive illusions discussed in this chapter will prove to be equally persistent.

ACKNOWLEDGMENTS

Preparation of this manuscript was supported by U.S. Public Health Service Bimedical Research Support Grant 5 SO7 RR 07067-13 to the State University of New York at Stony Brook and by National Institute of Mental Health Predoctoral Fellowship, MH 07284-01.

REFERENCES

Abramson, L. Y., Alloy, L. B., & Rosoff, R. *The role of complex hypotheses in the judgment of response-outcome contingencies.* Unpublished manuscript, University of Pennsylvania, 1978.

Abramson, L. Y., Seligman, M. E. P., & Teasdale, J. Learned helplessness in humans: Critique and reformulation. *Journal of Abnormal Psychology,* 1978, *87,* 49–74.

Ajzen, I. Intuitive theories of events and the effects of base-rate information on prediction. *Journal of Personality and Social Psychology,* 1977, *35,* 303–314.

Alloy, L. B., & Abramson, L. Y. Judgment of contingency in depressed and nondepressed students: Sadder but wiser? *Journal of Experimental Psychology: General,* in press.

Alloy, L. B., & Seligman, M. E. P. On the cognitive component of learned helplessness and depression. In G. H. Bower (Ed.), *The psychology of learning and motivation* (Vol. 13). New York: Academic Press, 1978.

Arieti, S. Cognition and feeling. In M. B. Arnold (Ed.), *Feelings and emotions.* New York: Academic Press, 1970.

Beck, A. T. *Depression.* Philadelphia: University of Pennsylvania Press, 1967.

Beck, A. T. *Cognitive therapy and emotional disorders.* New York: International Universities Press, 1976.

Bibring, E. The mechanism of depression. In P. Greenacre (Ed.), *Affective disorders.* New York: International Universities Press, 1953.

Bruner, A., & Revusky, S. H. Collateral behavior in humans. *Journal of the Experimental Analysis of Behavior,* 1961, *4,* 349–350.

Bruner, J. S., & Postman, L. Emotional selectivity in perception and reaction. *Journal of Personality,* 1947, *16,* 69–77.

Catania, A. C., & Cutts, D. Experimental control of superstitious responding in humans. *Journal of the Experimental Analysis of Behavior,* 1963, *6,* 203–208.

Chapman, L., & Chapman, J. Genesis of popular but erroneous psychodiagnostic observations. *Journal of Abnormal Psychology,* 1967, *72,* 193–204.

Corah, N. L., & Boffa, J. Perceived control, self-observation, and response to aversive stimulation. *Journal of Personality and Social Psychology,* 1970, *16,* 1–14.

Einhorn, H. J., & Hogarth, R. M. Confidence in judgment: Persistence of the illusion of validity. *Psychological Review,* 1978, *85,* 395–416.

Erdelyi, M. H. A new look at the new look: Perceptual defense and vigilance. *Psychological Review,* 1974, *81,* 1–25.

Fisher, S., & Fisher, R. Test of certain assumptions regarding figure drawing analysis. *Journal of Abnormal and Social Psychology,* 1950, *45,* 727–732.

Freud, S. Mourning and melancholia. In J. Strachey (Ed. and trans.), *The complete psychological works of Sigmund Freud* (Vol. 14). London: Hogarth Press, 1957. (Originally published, 1917.)

Freud, S. *A general introduction to psychoanalysis.* New York: Pocket Books, 1920.

Geer, J. H., Davison, G. C., & Gatchel, R. I. Reduction of stress in humans through nonveridical perceived control of aversive stimulation. *Journal of Personality and Social Psychology,* 1970, *16,* 731–738.

Gregory, R. L. *The psychology of seeing.* New York: McGraw-Hill, 1966.

Gregory, R. L. *The intelligent eye.* New York: McGraw-Hill, 1970.

Hake, H. W., & Hyman, R. Perception of the statistical structure of a random series of binary symbols. *Journal of Experimental Psychology,* 1953, *45,* 64–74.

Heider, F. *The psychology of interpersonal relations.* New York: Wiley, 1958.

Hokanson, J. E., DeGood, D. E., Forrest, M. S., & Brittain, T. M. Availability of avoidance behavior in modulating vascular-stress responses. *Journal of Personality and Social Psychology,* 1971, *19,* 60–68.

Holzberg, J. D., & Wexler, M. The validity of human form drawings as a measure of personality deviation. *Journal of Projective Techniques,* 1950, *14,* 343–361.

Jenkins, H. M., & Ward, W. C. Judgment of contingency between responses and outcomes. *Psychological Monographs,* 1965, *79*(1, Whole No. 594).

Kelley, H. H. Attribution theory in social psychology. In D. Levine (Ed.), *Nebraska Symposium on Motivation* (Vol. 15). Lincoln, Neb.: University of Nebraska Press, 1967.

Kurtz, R. M., & Garfield, S. L. Illusory correlation: A further exploration of Chapman's paradigm. *Journal of Consulting and Clinical Psychology,* 1978, *46,* 1009–1015.

Langer, E. J. The illusion of control. *Journal of Personality and Social Psychology,* 1975, *32,* 311–328.

Langer, E. J., & Roth, J. Heads I win, tails it's chance: The illusion of control as a function of the sequence of outcomes in a purely chance task. *Journal of Personality and Social Psychology,* 1975, *32,* 951–955.

Lazarus, R. S. *Psychological stress and the coping process.* New York: McGraw-Hill, 1966.

Lazarus, R. S., & Launier, R. Stress-related transactions between person and environment. In L. A. Pervin & M. Lewis (Eds.), *Interaction between internal and external determinants of behavior.* New York: Plenum, in press.

Lichtenberg, P. A definition and analysis of depression. *Archives of Neurology and Psychiatry,* 1957, *77,* 516–527.

Meehl, P. E. The cognitive activity of the clinician. *American Psychologist,* 1960, *15,* 19–27.

Melges, F. J., & Bowlby, J. Types of hopelessness in psychopathological process. *Archives of General Psychiatry,* 1969, *20,* 690–699.

Pervin, L. A. The need to predict and control under conditions of threat. *Journal of Personality,* 1963, *31,* 570–587.

Reznikoff, M., & Nicholas, A. L. An evaluation of human figure drawing indicators of paranoid pathology. *Journal of Consulting Psychology,* 1958, *22,* 395–397.

Ribler, R. I. Diagnostic prediction from emphasis on the eye and the ear in human figure drawings. *Journal of Consulting Psychology,* 1957, *21,* 223–225.

Seligman, M. E. P. *Helplessness: On depression, development, and death.* San Francisco: Freeman, 1975.

Seligman, M. E. P., Klein, D. C., & Miller, W. R. Depression. In H. Leitenberg (Ed.), *Handbook of behavior modification and behavior therapy.* Englewood Cliffs, N.J.: Prentice-Hall, 1976.

Smedslund, J. The concept of correlation in adults. *Scandinavian Journal of Psychology,* 1963, *4,* 165–173.

Starr, J. G., & Katkin, E. The clinician as an abberant actuary: Illusory correlation and the Incomplete Sentences Blank. *Journal of Abnormal Psychology,* 1969, *74,* 670–675.

Stotland, E., & Blumenthal, A. The reduction of anxiety as a result of the expectation of making a choice. *Canadian Journal of Psychology,* 1964, *18,* 139–145.

Streufert, S., & Streufert, S.. C. The effects of conceptual structure, failure, and success on attributions of causality and interpersonal attitudes. *Journal of Personality and Social Psychology,* 1969, *11,* 138–147.

Tversky, A., & Kahneman, D. Causal thinking in judgment under uncertainty. In B. Butts & J. Hintikka (Eds.), *Logic, methodology, and philosophy of science.* Dordrecht, Holland: D. Reidel, in press.

Ward, W. C., & Jenkins, H. M. The display of information and the judgment of contingency. *Canadian Journal of Psychology,* 1965,. *19,* 231–241.

Wason, P. C., & Johnson-Laird, P. N. *Psychology of reasoning.* Cambridge, Mass.: Harvard University Press, 1972.

Weiner, B. (Ed.). *Achivement motivation and attribution theory.* Morristown, N.J.: General Learning Press, 1974.

Wortman, C. B. Some determinants of perceived control. *Journal of Personality and Social Psychology,* 1975, *31,* 282–294.

Wortman, C. B., Costanzo, P. R., & Witt, T. R. Effects of anticipated performance on the attributions of causality to self and others. *Journal of Personality and Social Psychology,* 1973, *27,* 372–381.

Wright, J. C. Consistency and complexity of response sequences as a function of schedules of noncontingent reward. *Journal of Experimental Psychology,* 1962, *63,* 601–609.

6 Intrinsic Motivation for Control: Fact or Fiction

Judith Rodin
Karen Rennert
Susan K. Solomon
Yale University

In an era where students and parents are seeking an increased voice in the governance of their schools and where patients are clamoring to become informed consumers of medical care, psychologists have become increasingly interested in understanding the consequences of having more control. In the laboratory, it has been shown that having control makes shocks appear less painful (e.g., Geer, Davison, & Gatchel, 1970), ameliorates the negative aftereffects of noise (Glass & Singer, 1972), and increases the value of items that have been chosen over those that have been assigned (Wortman, 1975). Outside the laboratory, there have been several successful attempts to influence such significant outcomes as health and longevity with manipulations intended to increase real or perceived control (Langer & Rodin, 1976; Rodin & Langer, 1977; Schulz, 1976). These studies show improvement on a variety of measures in ill and aged populations as a function of greater control and responsibility over day-to-day, nonthreatening life events. Such successes support the possibility that control interventions for populations with disturbing, real-life problems such as illness, accidents, or career crises would be beneficial. Before accepting control as a panacea, however, it seems necessary to question some of the basic assumptions that have been made about it and to see whether there should be any limits to the application of the concept. Therefore, in this chapter we examine some of these assumptions with an eye to suggesting how we may define the parameters within which control has positive effects.

HISTORY OF THE CONTROL CONCEPT

Although the history of psychology is rich with theories that have considered the role of control in motivating human behavior (Adler, 1929; Erikson, 1950; Hendrick, 1943; Piaget, 1952; White, 1959), typically these works have not supplied a great deal of empirical evidence for their assertions. Probably the most comprehensive and influential of these conceptualizations was formulated by White (1959). In an attempt to account for behaviors that were inadequately explained by theories of motivation based upon primary drives, White developed the concept of "effectance motivation," "an innate need to manipulate the environment [p. 318]." White suggested that behaviors such as exploring novel objects and places, manipulating and producing changes in one's surroundings, and engaging in general activity all form part of a process whereby one learns to interact effectively with one's environment. He argued that these behaviors are not derived or transformed in some way from the primary drives or instincts but must be conceived to be "motivated in their own right [p. 329]." Further, White maintained that effectance motivation cannot be subsumed under the general category of drive, because it is persistent and does not satiate.

White believed that the most important test of his theory would be the effect that the motive for control has on our understanding of the development of personality, and especially upon such areas as "the self and the vicissitudes of self-esteem [p. 328]." White maintained that "effectance motivation must be conceived to involve satisfaction—a feeling of efficacy— in transactions in which behavior has an exploratory, varying, experimental character and produces changes in the stimulus field [p. 329]." Therefore, engaging in specific acts of manipulating and inducing changes in one's surroundings should benefit self-esteem by increasing this feeling of satisfaction. Thus, implicit in White's conceptualization of control is the idea that exercising control enhances one's self-perception and sense of self-worth.

More recent theories of control have also incorporated a number of the assumptions that are essential to White's formulation. For example, deCharms' theory of personal causation (1968) asserts that people who perceive their behavior as stemming from their own choices will value that behavior and be more task motivated than individuals who see their behavior as stemming from external forces. The theory asserts that general feelings of competence (which should lead to increased self-esteem) result from the perception of personal causation. Bandura's (1977) notion of self-efficacy can also be seen as having commonalities with White. Bandura states that an efficacy expectation is the conviction that one can successfully execute the behavior required to produce desirable outcomes. Although certainly not new, the self-efficacy construct consolidates the view that feelings of control and efficacy, operating through their ability to enhance self-image, mediate important behavior changes.

The ideas presented by White, and reflected in more recent theorists, have also had an impact on much of the research in the field of control. As an example, we may consider Langer's (1975) work on the illusion of control. She concluded, on the basis of several studies of behavior in presumably chance situations, that the motivation to master the environment influences individuals to attribute to themselves greater control over chance events than is objectively warranted. The fact that she assumes this motive to master as a given demonstrates how far the concept has been incorporated into the beliefs of the psychological community. Moreover, she suggests that there is an essential self-perception component to this motivation: "The greatest satisfaction or feeling of competence would result from being able to control the seemingly uncontrollable [p. 323]." Again, this suggests acceptance of White's notion that exerting control is self-esteem enhancing.

In the remainder of this paper, we examine explicitly the two assumptions about control that we have been discussing. Because these assertions have such high face validity, they have not been subjected to empirical confirmation until this point. Certainly it seems entirely plausible that people should be intrinsically motivated by the opportunity to gain such a valuable item as control. Similarly, the belief that enhancement of self-esteem is an important process involved in making control desirable is a reasonable and compelling assumption, both in its parsimony and its exciting implications. By bringing these assumptions into the light and examining them, we can determine just how far to accept them. Delineating the parameters within which they are valid will help us both theoretically—to understand more about how control operates—and practically—to design better intervention strategies using control. The unpublished research detailed in this paper was conducted, except where noted, in the research laboratories of the first author at Yale University by us and other research colleagues as cited.

IS CONTROL MOTIVATING?

In order to investigate the assumption that having control is *intrinsically* motivating in all cases, a study was conducted to test directly the hypothesis that people value control for its own sake (Solomon, 1976). Solomon investigated choice or decision freedom (Steiner, 1970), because this seemed to be the form of control closest to White's description of manipulation of the environment. The subjects were students in a large introductory psychology class who believed that they were to rate one of several novel tastes for a number of trials. There were 10 different experimental conditions. For present purposes we describe only the ones most relevant to the question of intrinsic motivation. Subjects in one condition were told that they could first work on a visual perception task to obtain a choice of the flavors they would be given to taste. In this condition, they were told that all the possible flavors they might be given to choose among were good tasting. Thus, whether or not they were able to make a choice, they were essentially assured of obtaining a reasonably good flavor. Subjects in a second condition were not assured of getting a good outcome. For them, hard work on the visual perception task determined whether they would acquire a good flavor.

Subjects in the latter condition ($\bar{x}$ = 375.05) worked significantly harder to attain control than did those in the former condition ($\bar{x}$ = 297.65), presumably because it would enable them to be assured of getting a good outcome [$F(1,75)$ = 3.43, $p < .05$]. Subjects in the former group were already assured of getting at least a good outcome and were working for a choice among these good outcomes. What is most important is that these subjects worked no harder than subjects in a control group whose performance was not linked to gaining any type of control ($\bar{x}$ = 271.25). Thus, opportunity to manipulate the environment by making choices does not appear to have been motivating in itself as long as a relatively good outcome was already guaranteed.

This finding suggests that the assumption that has been made about the motivating value of control is, at least, too broad. The opportunity to manipulate the environment does not provide sufficient incentive to allow it to serve as a reward in an operant task in all cases. This creates some doubts about White's formulation and the theories and research derived from it. The data suggest that there are conditions under which people do not feel motivated to exert control as well as conditions under which they do. The next task, therefore, was to begin to specify these conditions.

FACTORS THAT INFLUENCE
THE DESIRE TO CONTROL

Information

Perhaps control is only motivating for an individual when he or she has enough information to evaluate the alternatives effectively. A second manipulation in the taste study led some subjects to expect that they would know about the various tastes before making their choice. This prechoice information would be available because they would be given prior tastes of each substance. Others were to make their choices without any prior taste information.

Subjects who expected no prior taste were only weakly motivated to work on a task that would guarantee them the opportunity to choose their taste substance, even though each packet was individually identified with a number corresponding to its supposed "goodness." As the data in Table 6.1 show, those who expected to be allowed to sample the flavors first, and who therefore would have sufficient information to make a reasonable choice, worked significantly harder to obtain the choice than the "no-prior-taste" subjects. This was true whether they believed they were working for the opportunity to choose from among all good flavors or all bad flavors. These data suggest that people may not be motivated to make choices when they perceive that the available information is insufficient. On the other hand, the results indicate that people are motivated to make choices when they believe they have adequate information with which to judge the alternatives.

How does sufficiency of information work to increase the motivating value of control? At least in this instance, it appears that the information increases the individual's belief that he or she can choose the better option, thus making the choice valuable because it raises the chances of receiving a good, or at least a less bad, outcome. This desire to be personally effective in order to insure oneself of good outcomes is of course a desire for control, but it is clearly separable from an *intrinsic need to manipulate* the environment. It is the assumption based on intrinsic need that has thus far been asserted without the support of experimental evidence. We suggest instead that the opportunity for choice becomes valuable to the extent that any factor increases people's perception that the choice they make will increase their chances of getting the best possible outcome. Increased information about the outcomes is an example of one of these factors. Another is whether the individual expects to exert control. Choice that is expected or predictable may be more valuable, because this predictability allows time for the development of coping strategies that raise the perceived likelihood of making the optimal choice. Feedback, by increasing experience with the outcomes of the choice, may have a similar effect.

Before pursuing this line of reasoning, let us consider an alternative mechanism for how information, expectancy, and feedback might affect motivation. Having adequate relevant information leads to greater feelings of

TABLE 6.1
The Effects of Choice and Information
on Mean Number of Words Scanned[a]

	Control	
Outcomes Were	Prior Taste	No Prior Taste
Good	361.24	297.65
Bad	329.17	256.28

[a]Main effect for prior taste manipulation: $F_{(1,73)} = 5.94$, $p < .05$.

control (see Mills & Krantz, in press), and expectancy and feedback presumably have the same effects. Quite possibly, then, it may be that greater perceived control is what is really increasing motivation, rather than the attainment of a good outcome. However, our evidence suggests that increased *feelings* of control alone are insufficient to increase one's motivation for control. Based on the work of Steiner (1970) and Harvey and his colleagues (Harvey & Harris, 1975; Harvey & Johnston, 1973), we know that the perception of control is greater when the difference between the values of the options is smaller. In fact, their work suggests that subjects believe they have the most control when the options are approximately equal in desirability. For example, a choice between a chocolate and vanilla ice cream cone would lead to more perceived control than a choice between a chocolate and a quinine-flavored cone. These choices are analogous to two additional experimental conditions in the taste study described previously—one where subjects were working to choose from among all good flavors and another where the selection was among two good and two poor flavors.

We found that if anything, subjects worked less hard to gain a choice when the options were approximately equal in desirability (all good flavors, $\bar{x}$ = 297.65) than when they were quite different in desirability (among both good and poor flavors, $\bar{x}$ = 330.44). According to Steiner (1970) subjects in the former group should have felt that they had a greater choice than subjects in the latter group. Thus, it appears that subjects in our study were not motivated by an increase in perceived control per se. Rather, they apparently were working to insure a more positive outcome. These data provide inferential support for our earlier assertion that factors such as information do not increase one's motivation for control simply because they lead to increased feelings of control. Instead, it appears that information leads to increased motivation because of its effect on the attainment of a favorable outcome.[1]

Responsibility

Although we are suggesting that control is only sought after when it is seen as a means to some desirable end, we do not intend to imply that people will always be motivated to have outcome control. In addition to believing that having control will increase the probability of obtaining a desired outcome, people must be willing to take the responsibility involved in decision making and exerting outcome control. In many circumstances, this will not be true.

A desire to reduce one's responsibility may, in part, explain why people frequently give up control in situations in which they clearly have the

---

[1]We are not denying, however, that the direct effect of information on increased feelings of control could have some secondary effects on motivation. Believing that events are controllable should increase one's desire to try to exercise that control.

opportunity to exercise control and help determine the outcome. Ferebee (1977) notes the familiar situation of students who go to the movies, rather than study, the night before a big exam. This might be an instance of self-handicapping (Berglas & Jones, 1978), whereby people protect themselves in advance against failure by relinquishing control and thereby reducing their responsibility for the outcome.

This desire to abrogate choice may be heightened to the extent that the choice is important and the consequences of failure large. In the taste study discussed earlier, we compared conditions in which the choice was among all bad flavors to those in which the choice was among good flavors and found that people were not significantly less motivated to work for a choice among bad outcomes. However, due in part to the limitations of laboratory research, these outcomes were relatively trivial. We expect that a difference would emerge if the outcomes were made more crucial, especially because people tend to prefer to take responsibility for positive rather than negative outcomes (Shaw & Skolnick, 1971). These limits must be tested in naturalistic settings, using persons for whom negative outcomes are real and salient.

Conclusions

So far we have looked at the first of White's assumption and found it to be less global than might have been supposed. We conclude that though control may be motivating in many circumstances, this is not the result of an intrinsic need to manipulate the environment per se but rather is a response to believing that such behavior has a greater probability for delivering positive outcomes. However, although people may not be universally willing to work for the opportunity to exert control, there is considerable evidence that once they are actually engaging in control behaviors, they often derive beneficial effects (Langer & Rodin, 1976). Based on White's second assumption, which emphasized the relation between control and self-perception, we asked next whether the benefits of exercising control may result, at least in part, from the positive impact that having control has on self-image. For example, attributions of personal causation increase when people have greater control (Lefcourt, 1973).

THE EFFECTS OF CONTROL ON SELF-ESTEEM

In a first attempt to assess the relationship between control and self-esteem directly, we again operationalized control as choice. In this study conducted by Marsha Levy-Warren (1974), male undergraduates participated in order to fulfill a course requirement. At the beginning of the experimental session, they were told that they would be completing personality tests that had been shown to be good indicators of personality typology. During the experimental session, each subject was given the CPI (Gough, 1957) self-esteem scale and two other personality questionnaires. In order to manipulate choice, half the subjects were told that they would select the three scales on which they wanted to work from nine questionnaires that the experimenter had available. The names of the tests were sufficiently nondescriptive (e.g., Iowa Index of Self-Concept) to allow all subjects actually to be given the same three scales regardless of their stated choices. Further, subjects in this condition were informed that once they had decided which of the scales they wanted to complete, they could look them over and determine the order in which they wanted to complete them.

In contrast, the remainder of the subjects were simply given three personality inventories to complete. Further, subjects in this "no-control" condition were not afforded the option of deciding the order in which to complete the tests.

The results of this study were surprising. Contrary to expectations, subjects who had chosen their tests actually scored significantly lower on the self-esteem scale than did subjects who had not had this opportunity. These data are shown in Table 6.2, where the significant main effect of choice on self-esteem scores is evident. This finding could not be attributed to a failure of the manipulation, because subjects in the choice condition reported feeling significantly more in control than subjects in the no-choice group.

Scott Prussing (1975) replicated this study to rule out the possibility that the results were simply due to the fact that the control manipulation (i.e., letting subjects select the tests to which they wanted to respond) had given subjects the impression that the personality assessment was not terribly important or well standardized. It was hypothesized that if this were true, the "choice" subjects might have felt freer to answer the self-esteem questions honestly, and thus they may only have appeared more self-deprecating. In Prussing's study, an orthogonal manipulation of importance was added to the original design, and the Index of Social Desirability (Crowne & Marlowe, 1964), as well as the CPI, was administered.

Subjects in the high-importance conditions were told that the tests had been well validated and were very accurate in assessing the true personality of

TABLE 6.2
Effects of Choice on Perceived Control and Self-Esteem

	Choice	No Choice	$t_{(45)}$	p
Self-reported feelings of control	4.29	6.43	11.31	$< .01$
CPI scores	51.69	57.33	5.33	$< .05$

Note. Self-report scores range from (1 = totally in control) to (8 = lacking control); higher CPI scores indicate greater self-esteem.

an individual. Those in the low-importance conditions were informed that the measures had been devised by a graduate student and were still in the testing stage. Thus their validity was portrayed as questionable.

Manipulation checks indicated that the manipulations were effective. Subjects reported feeling more personal control in the "control" conditions and reported feeling more nervous and anxious in the high-importance group. The group means are reported in Table 6.3. The personality scale results replicated the Levy-Warren (1974) study. Again self-esteem scores were significantly lower in the choice groups. If subjects felt freer to be honest when the test seemed less important, there should also have been a main effect for importance, with low-importance subjects scoring lower in self-esteem. Instead, the choice × importance interaction was significant, with the choice, high-importance condition actually showing the lowest self-esteem. Further, there were no significant differences among the groups on the social desirability scale. This suggests that the choice and importance manipulations did not differentially influence the need to appear socially desirable.

These data suggest that the lower self-esteem scores of subjects in the choice conditions actually reflected a less positive self-image at that moment. In a pilot study conducted recently, we used a completely different control manipulation and obtained the same results. In this study, the manipulation of control was more analogous to the type of control that people actually exercise in the real world. Subjects were recruited to serve as interviewers. They first underwent a training session that purported to prepare them for this position. After the training, they met "Paul Silver," whom they were to interview. Paul was actually one of four well-rehearsed colleagues of the investigators. All the interviewers (i.e., the actual subjects) had been told that the interview session would be carried out in two parts and that between the sessions, the trainer would take Paul to another room to fill out some questionnaires. The interviewers knew that they would also be asked to complete some questionnaires during this hiatus to provide information about their interaction with Paul up to that point.

During the elaborate training session, the interviewers were given an interview protocol and were asked to follow it exactly in the first part of the interview. The opportunity to exert control in the second part of the sessions was to be based on Paul's behavior during the first part of the interview. If he answered all, or all but one, of the questions put to him from the protocol, interviewers would presumably be able to ask whatever questions they wished during the second half of the interview. If Paul was unable to answer two or more questions, interviewers were led to expect that they would be given another standardized protocol to use during the second half of the experiment. In fact, all of Paul's responses were fixed in advance by the experimenter and varied only in that he failed to answer three questions in half the interviews in order to establish the "no-control" conditions.

TABLE 6.3

Effects of Choice on Perceived Control, Anxiety, Nervousness, and Self-Esteem

	Choice		No Choice		$F_{(1,44)}$	p
	Unimportant	Important	Unimportant	Important		
Self-reported feelings of:						
Control	7.42	7.58	6.50	5.08	6.48[a]	< .05
Nervousness	1.58	2.25	1.42	2.17	4.29[b]	< .05
Anxiety	2.50	3.25	1.67	4.75	8.84[b]	< .01
Social desirability	12.17	11.00	12.58	13.42		ns
CPI	55.25	53.50	58.17	56.10	4.47[a]	< .05
					4.31[c]	< .05

Note. Self-report scores range from (1 = not at all) to (9 = totally); higher CPI scores indicate greater self-esteem.

[a]The significant F comes from a main effect for choice.

[b]The significant F comes from a main effect for importance.

[c]The significant F comes from a choice × importance interaction..

We found, as predicted, that interviewers with the potential opportunity to invent their own questions felt more in control, over both the experiment in general and the person they were interviewing in the experiment. Under these circumstances, interviewer subjects who felt they had more control had lower self-esteem scores. In this experiment self-esteem was measured using the Texas Social Behavior Inventory (Helmreich & Stapp, 1974), which has two forms with high test–retest reliability. Thus, we were able to assess changes in self-esteem from before to after the manipulation of control. From these data and the two earlier studies, it appears that a reduction in self-esteem may be a general consequence of increased perceived control under certain conditions regardless of how control is manipulated.

These findings are in direct contrast to what has generally been assumed about control. Not only does it refute the assumption about self-esteem enhancement; it also presents an empirical case in which control has detrimental effects and thus provides us with a jumping-off point for examining why it usually appears to be so beneficial. As with the assumptions discussed earlier regarding an intrinsic motive for control, it seems likely that the assumption linking control with self-esteem is too broad. Rather, we can specify conditions under which having control will and will not result in decreased self-esteem, and a pattern may be discernible from these conditions.

FACTORS MEDIATING THE RELATIONSHIP BETWEEN CONTROL AND SELF-ESTEEM

Responsibility Revisited

The degree of responsibility that comes with control, an issue previously raised in this paper, may be one condition that affects the relationship between control and self-image. Usually, having control implies increased responsibility. Thus, faced with a choice, people suffer the possibility of incurring a loss in their own self-perception, as well as in the regard of others, for making poor decisions that result in bad outcomes. It should be noted that this cannot simply be explained in terms of dissonance (cf. Festinger, 1957). The drop in self-esteem that we have described derives from the process of exercising control itself; it does not appear limited to the context of choice, and it is not correlated with the degree of differences among the various outcomes. Thus it is quite dissimilar from the experience of dissonance regarding the unchosen alternative.

To consider the role of responsibility, we recently completed a study where students in a psychology class either selected or were assigned to complete one from among four personality tests (Solomon & Rodin, 1978). Some were given a great deal of material implying that the experimenter expected them to make the best decision possible; others were told that the experimenter knew they could not make a very thoughtful choice in the limited amount of time they had but that they should do the best they could. Subjects absolved of responsibility did not show the decrease in self-esteem obtained in the earlier, comparable studies ($\bar{x}$ = 53.67); those in the high responsibility group did ($\bar{x}$ = 46.75).

We are suggesting that having control sometimes makes an individual less able to avoid personal attributions for potentially bad outcomes and thus decreases self-esteem. It follows that reducing perceived responsibility is one way to minimize the negative impact of control on self-esteem. Another is to increase any factor that raises the person's confidence about obtaining good outcomes. If the individual felt more certain that the results of his or her control attempts would be positive, self-esteem might be unaffected or even enhanced. Therefore, in looking for other variables that could affect self-esteem, we might reconsider some of the factors discussed earlier that appear to influence the likelihood of gaining better outcomes and thereby affect one's desire to gain control.

Information Revisited

Feeling well informed makes a person believe that a good choice and favorable outcomes are possible and thus increases the person's willingness to accept the responsibility that goes with increased choice and control. In the two studies in which we directly measured self-esteem, lack of information may have been an important factor in the lowered self-esteem that was evident in the choice conditions, because in both these studies subjects were given only the titles of the personality tests. Thus they had almost no information on which to base a reasoned choice. Exercising control under such conditions appears to lead to feelings of inadequacy and diminished self-confidence. In fact, we might suspect that when a person lacks information, having to choose may have many negative consequences, some of which may be mediated in part by decreased self-esteem. In support of this assertion, we can consider two recent unpublished studies on choice conducted at Cornell University by John Condry (1976).

At the beginning of the experimental session, subjects in Condry's studies were told that they would be working on a task. To vary choice, half the subjects were asked to choose between two tasks, and the other half were told that they would be assigned to a task. Further, before making the choice, half the subjects in each choice condition were given information about the tasks, whereas the rest were not given any information. In each study, all subjects actually performed the same task: In the first study it was a pursuit rotor task, and in the second it was a mechanical drawing task. The studies also differed with regard to the subjects' ages. In the first study the subjects were between 17 and 19 years of age, and in the second they were 8 years old.

In the first study, there was a significant choice × information interaction for subjects' attitude toward the task, with subjects in the choice–no–information condition responding least favorably to the task. In the second study, this choice × information interaction approached significance, with subjects in the choice–no–information condition again being least favorably disposed toward the task.

Regarding the amount of effort expended on the task, in Study 2 there was a significant choice × information interaction. Although the interaction obtained in Study 1 did not attain significance, the pattern of results in both studies was the same. That is, subjects exerted the least effort in the choice–no–information condition.

Thus, in both studies, subjects worked the least hard and felt least good about the task when they were given control but no information. On the basis of these findings, Condry concluded that "giving a person a choice when his understanding of the situation is such that a meaningful choice is impossible may prove more destructive and negative than having no choice at all [p. 17]." Although Condry did not actually measure self-esteem, he discussed his data with the suggestion that the results were mediated by changes in subjects' levels of self-confidence. That is, asking subjects to make a choice without giving them any relevant information on which to base that choice may make them feel inadequate.

We should add, as we did when discussing motivation for control, that increased information is not the only variable that may mitigate against such negative responses. For example, variables that allow the development of coping strategies, such as expecting to exercise control, should operate similarly by increasing the perception that the person can use the control in the best way possible.

At this point, it might be well to summarize the points we have been making. Assumptions about how control operates have been more plentiful than has empirical evidence to back them. Two major assumptions have been that control is intrinsically motivating and that having a choice tends to enhance self-esteem. The evidence reviewed suggests that we cannot accept these assumptions as they stand. Our research implies that control is desirable and has positive effects to the extent that it provides an opportunity to achieve optimal outcomes, especially if we construe outcomes broadly to include such things as the social and personal consequences to the individual of making poor choices. The important points are that there does not appear to be an innate need or drive to manipulate the environment and that exercising control does not necessarily have positive effects on self-perception, which is clearly the implication one would derive from White (1959). In addition there are apparently circumstances where exercising choice can temporarily decrease one's feelings of self-worth.

STRESS

Clearly, we are not unique in suggesting that control can sometimes be burdensome. Fromm (1941), for example, suggests that freedom may often be something to be avoided. The notion that control can be burdensome since it entails personal responsibility has also been implied by Steiner (1970), who argues that control can sometimes be stress inducing. We might especially note Averill's (1973) review, in which he discussed in detail the complex relationship between stress and control, attempting to specify conditions in which control is stress inducing rather than reducing. It is interesting that although Averill is aware of the complexity of the relationship between control and stress, he appears to accept some of the other commonly held assumptions about control that have concerned us in this chapter. Thus, he asserts that although control may sometimes be stress inducing, "the desire for personal control may be a deep-seated motivational variable, whether phylogenetically or ontogenetically based [p. 290]." We would argue that determining when control is motivating is as complex as determining when it is stress reducing. Both depend on a number of situational variables, including those we have discussed in this chapter.

We suspect a great overlap exists between the factors involved in motivation for control and self-esteem enhancement, and those that mediate the relationship between stress and control. For example, adequate information would presumably reduce stress by increasing the likelihood that the individual has engaged in the most reasonable or appropriate behaviors; expectancy and predictability may reduce stress by providing the opportunity to select and prepare coping strategies; and decreased responsibility can reduce stress because it lessens the consequences (for one's self-esteem and in terms of the regard of others) of making a poor choice. The data presented from the Prussing experiment, which showed that making a choice under conditions of high importance led to the lowest self-esteem, are consistent with this interpretation, as this condition was shown by subjects' self-reports to be the most stressful one.

It is too early to hypothesize a causal relationship between motivation for control, self-esteem, and stress. For example, we have not yet determined whether being required to make a choice under certain conditions is stressful and monitoring this stress leads to a decrease in self-esteem, or whether monitoring the negative affective state manifested in a lowering of self-esteem leads to increased stress. Perhaps the variables work in parallel. The potential for futher research in this area is intriguing.

IMPLICATIONS FOR
REAL-WORLD INTERVENTIONS

To end this chapter, it seems important to return to the point we made initially concerning the relevance of the control construct for interventions in real-world settings. We can now suggest that it is crucial to understand the full implications of any control manipulations we might wish to introduce before applying them in these settings. For example, consider applied studies in medical settings. Several have tested the effects of giving patients a great deal of preparatory information including precise descriptions about medical procedures and normal reactions to them (Johnson, 1975; Langer, Janis, & Wolfer, 1975). It was found that information increased expectancies about likely sensations and decreased expectancies about unlikely ones. Under these circumstances, patients felt more eager to become involved in decisions regarding their own treatment. Thus, they appear to be motivated to have control when they feel fully informed and the options are clear and understandable. However, the conclusions reached in this paper should not be taken to imply that more information is always better and that all types of information will have beneficial effects. It is entirely possible to supply essentially useless information or too much information. Consider the case in which a doctor, in good faith, provides a great deal of information to a patient who must make some decisions about his health care but uses terms that are too technical for the patient to comprehend. This information is useless in helping the patient feel that he will select correctly. Furthermore, the fact that he is presumed to be in possession of information may increase his feelings of responsibility for the outcome. The patient in this situation may well be worse off than if he had been told nothing.

Another set of findings from studies in medical settings bears on the issues discussed in this paper. These experiments suggest that people who feel responsibility for poor decisions appear to suffer a loss in self-esteem. For example, people who blame themselves for diseases such as cancer or for serious accidents may suffer debilitating feelings of inferiority and loss of their sense of self-worth (Abrams & Finesinger, 1953; Bulman & Wortman, 1977). When their children are ill, a high proportion of mothers—40% is the figure reported in a study of 800 mothers by Korsch, Gozzi, and Francis (1968)—feel guilty about their children's illness and blame themselves. Feeling that they were in control and responsible for what happened, these individuals now feel lower self-esteem, and subsequently all share an apparent unwillingness to take control over health-promoting behavior. Interestingly, some data suggest that one way to reduce the burden of responsibility and guilt in these instances is through direct self-esteem enhancement (Janis, in press; Janis & Rodin, 1979). In a study of mothers in a rheumatic fever prophylaxis program, for example, decisions to follow medical recommendations for their children were found to be twice as high among mothers who thought their pediatricians had high favorable regard for them (Elling, Whittemore, & Green, 1960). Removing debilitating feelings of responsibility for unavoidable events, in this case by enhancing their self-perceptions, appears to increase mothers' willingness to exert some control over events that are controllable, such as medical regimens and treatment. This is desirable whenever exercising control would lead to better health outcomes.

If our research tell us anything, it is that we must beware of applying indiscriminately control manipulations based on laboratory findings or theories that appear to have face validity. We must question the assumptions we are making about these manipulations and be sure that we understand their ramifications. Given this caveat, we can expect to apply fruitfully our understanding of control to solving problems arising in many domains of society.

ACKNOWLEDGMENT

The research reported here was supported by National Science Foundation Grant BNS76-81126 to the first author.

REFERENCES

Abrams, R., & Finesinger, J. Guilt reactions in patients with cancer. *Cancer,* 1953, *6,* 474–482.
Adler, A. *The science of living.* New York: Greenberg, 1929.
Averill, J. R. Personal control over aversive stimuli and its relationship to stress. *Psychological Bulletin,* 1973, *80,* 286–303.
Bandura, A. Self-efficacy: Toward a unifying theory of behavioral change. *Psychological Review,* 1977, *84,* 191–215.
Berglas, S., & Jones, E. E. Drug choice as a self-handicapping strategy in response to noncontingent success. *Journal of Personality and Social Psychology,* 1978, *36,* 405–417.
Bulman, R. J., & Wortman, C. B. Attribution of blame and coping in the real world: Severe accident victims react to their lot. *Journal of Personality and Social Psychology,* 1977, *35,* 351–363.
deCharms, R. *Personal causation: The internal affective determinants of behavior.* New York: Academic Press, 1968.
Condry, J. *The effects of choice and information on effort and liking for a task.* Unpublished manuscript, Cornell University, 1976.
Crowne, D., & Marlowe, D. *The approval motive.* New York: Wiley, 1964.

Elling, R., Whittemore, R., & Green, M. Patient participation in a pediatric program. *Journal of Health and Human Behavior*, 1960, *1*, 183–191.

Erikson, E. H. *Childhood and society*. New York: Norton, 1950.

Ferebee, N. *Motivation for control*. Unpublished doctoral dissertation, Duke University, 1977.

Festinger, L. *A theory of cognitive dissonance*. Stanford, Calif.: Stanford University Press, 1957.

Fromm, E. *Escape from freedom*. New York: Holt, Rinehart & Winston, 1941.

Geer, J. H., Davison, G. C., & Gatchel, R. I. Reduction of stress in humans through nonveridical perceived control of aversive stimulation. *Journal of Personality and Social Psychology*, 1970, *16*, 731–738.

Glass, D. C., & Singer, J. L. *Urban stress*. New York: Academic Press, 1972.

Gough, H. G. *Manual for the California Psychological Inventory*. Palo Alto, Calif.: Consulting Psychologists Press, 1957.

Harvey, J. H., & Harris, B. Determinants of perceived choice and the relationship between perceived choice and expectancy about feelings of internal control. *Journal of Personality and Social Psychology*, 1975, *31*, 101–106.

Harvey, J. H., & Johnston, S. Determinants of the perception of choice. *Journal of Experimental Social Psychology*, 1973, *9*, 164–179.

Helmreich, R., & Stapp, J. Short forms of the Texas Social Behavior Inventory (TSBI), an objective measure of self-esteem. *Bulletin of the Psychonomic Society*, 1974, *4*(5A), 473–475.

Hendrick, I. The discussion of the instinct to master. *Psychoanalytic Quarterly*, 1943, *12*, 561–565.

Janis, I. L. (Ed.). *Counseling on personal decisions: Theory and research on short-term helping relationships*. New Haven, Conn.: Yale University Press, in press.

Janis, I. L., & Rodin, J. Attribution, control and decision making: Social psychology and health care. In G. Stone, F. Cohen, & N. A. Adler (Eds.), *Health psychology*. San Francisco: Jossey-Bass, 1979.

Johnson, J. Stress reduction through sensation information. In I. Sarason & C. Spielberger (Eds.), *Stress and anxiety* (Vol. 2). New York: Wiley, 1975.

Korsch, B. M., Gozzi, E. K., & Francis, V. Gaps in doctor–patient communication. I. Doctor–patient interaction and patient satisfaction. *Pediatrics*, 1968, *42*, 855–871.

Langer, E. J. The illusion of control. *Journal of Personality and Social Psychology*, 1975, *32*, 311–328.

Langer, E., Janis, I., & Wolfer, J. Reduction of psychological stress in surgical patients. *Journal of Experimental Social Psychology*, 1975, *11*, 155–165.

Langer, E. J., & Rodin, J. The effects of choice and enhanced personal reponsibility for the aged: A field experiment in an institutional setting. *Journal of Personality and Social Psychology*, 1976, *34*, 191–198.

Lefcourt, H. M. The function of the illusion of control and freedom. *American Psychologist*, 1973, *28*, 417–425.

Levy-Warren, M. *Effects of perceived control on expression of self-perception*. Unpublished masters thesis, Yale University, 1974.

Mills, R. T., & Krantz, D. S. Information, choice and reactions to stress: A field experiment in a bloodbank with laboratory analogue. *Journal of Personality and Social Psychology*, in press.

Piaget, J. [*The origins of intelligence in children*] (M. Cook, trans.). New York: International University Press, 1952.

Prussing, S. *The effects on self-esteem of choices made in situations of differing importance*. Unpublished master's thesis, Yale University, 1975.

Rodin, J., & Langer, E. Long-term effect of a control-relevant intervention. *Journal of Personality and Social Psychology*, 1977, *35*, 897–902.

Schulz, R. Effects of control and predictability on the physical and psychological well-being of the institutionalized aged. *Journal of Personality and Social Psychology*, 1976, *33*, 563–573.

Shaw, J. I., & Skolnick, P. Attributions of responsibility for a happy accident. *Journal of Personality and Social Psychology,* 1971, *18,* 380–383.

Solomon, S. K. *Control-seeking behavior: Are people motivated to attain control?* Unpublished manuscript, Yale University, 1976.

Solomon, S. K., & Rodin, J. *Who's responsible for this? An investigation into the relationship between control, self-esteem and responsibility.* Unpublished manuscript, Yale University, 1978.

Steiner, I. D. Perceived freedom. In L. Berkowitz (Ed.), *Advances in experimental social psychology* (Vol. 5). New York: Academic Press, 1970.

White, R. W. Motivation reconsidered: The concept of competence. *Psychological Review,* 1959, *66,* 297–323.

Wortman, C. B. Some determinants of perceived control. *Journal of Personality and Social Psychology,* 1975, *31,* 282–294.

7

Depression Maintenance and Interpersonal Control

Dan Coates
University of Wisconsin

Camille B. Wortman
University of Michigan

In this chapter, we consider how members of the social environment are likely to respond to someone who is hurt or depressed, and how these social responses can contribute to the maintenance of depression. There is a great deal of evidence to suggest that others try to control the depressed person's feelings and behaviors in a number of ways, often with very good intentions of helping the afflicted individual to cope more successfully. Ironically, there is good reason to believe that these attempts to control and eliminate the depression may actually serve to complicate and worsen the depressed person's condition. After a brief overview of research on depression and social interaction, we present a theoretical model that describes this pathogenic interactional sequence.

Most depression theorists have given considerable attention to the question of what factors may prompt the onset of this condition. The activation of inherent negative beliefs about the self, current experience, and the future (Beck, 1967, 1974); uncontrollable outcomes (Seligman, 1975); a lack of response-contingent positive reinforcement (Lewinsohn, 1974a); inadequate or insufficient reinforcers (Lazarus, 1972); a reduction in reinforcer effectiveness (Costello, 1972); important or significant loss (Klinger, 1977); and physiological malfunction (Akiskal & McKinney, 1975) have all been proposed as triggering depression. Generally, less attention has been given to the issue of how depression may be maintained once it has begun, although it may be at least as important to know why people stay depressed as it is to know why they become depressed in the first place. Some investigators have maintained that depressive episodes can be beneficial.

Schmale (1973) argues that the apathy and inactivity associated with depression are comparable to hibernation and fulfill similar functions. When faced with profound loss or a scarcity of reinforcements, it may be quite valuable to reduce activity in order to conserve what resources are available. Wortman and Dintzer (1978) have suggested that the negative affect associated with depression can serve to motivate people to reevaluate their goals in a more healthy, constructive way. Finally, Klinger (1977) has taken the position that depression is a normal response to loss and further, that most depressed individuals recover in time.

These arguments for the value or normalcy of depression would seem most appropriate when the depression is of relatively short duration. The longer the apathy, inactivity, and dysphoria persist, the more disrupted the functioning of the depressed person becomes. As Klinger (1977) indicates, continual depression "would leave the organism incapacitated [p. 176]." Though periods of depression may serve certain positive functions for the individual, persistent depression is harmful and debilitating. The question of how a depressive episode becomes a more chronic or recurring condition is therefore an issue that deserves careful consideration.

Research with animals suggests that the availability of social interaction can have an important influence on how serious or long lasting a depression will become. For example, it has been shown that animals who endure stressful conditions in social isolation are more likely to develop depressionlike symptoms, and to exhibit them longer, than those who have the company of conspecifics. Kaufman (1973) separated juvenile pigtail macaques and juvenile bonnet macaques from their mothers. He found that the pigtails became severely depressed whereas the bonnets did not. Kaufman attributed this finding to the behavior of the remaining adults: The pigtails rejected the orphans, but the bonnet adults were quick to interact with them. More recently, Ellison (1977) injected groups of rats to deplete them of either norepinephrine or serotonin. Low levels of these neuronal transmitters have been implicated as underlying depression. The injected animals did display certain depressive symptoms and were then placed either in isolation cages or back into the rat colony. Although both groups eventually recovered, the rats allowed interaction with others recovered more steadily and quickly.

In the case of humans, the role of social interaction in depression maintenance appears to be more complicated. On one hand, there is some evidence that having others available can minimize the negative impact of stressful events. For example, Clayton, Halikas, and Maurice (1972) found that widowed adults were less likely to become depressed if they had close relationships with their children. Similarly, Bornstein, Clayton, Halikas, Maurice, and Robins (1973) have shown that the majority of bereaved individuals who were still significantly depressed 13 months after the death of their spouses lived apart from, as opposed to with, other family members. In a study to assess the frequency of depression among members of the population at large, Brown,

Bhrolchain, and Harris (1975) found depression to be highly prevalent among London housewives. Many of these women reported that they had recently experienced some upsetting event. However, among women who had ecnountered such difficulties but who also reported an intimate relationship with another person, depression was virtually nonexistent. On the other hand, there is also some indication that close interaction with others increases the likelihood of serious, prolonged depression. Both Overall (1971) and Robertson (1974) conducted surveys on the marital status of patients with psychiatric symptoms and found that married women were such more likely to be depressed than were single women. Shepherd, Cooper, Brown, and Kalton (1966) argue that marital discord is the primary cause for the development and maintenance of many psychiatric illnesses, including depression. Thus, for humans, social interaction apparently has the potential to serve very therapeutic functions, but it may also have pathogenic impact.

Several explanations have been proposed to account for what goes wrong in social relationships so that they increase rather than lessen depression. Some theorists, such as Burgess (1969), argue that others are too kind to the depressed, maintaining this condition by reinforcing symptomatic behaviors such as weeping and withdrawing with support and concern. Others, like Coyne (1976b), indicate that people maintain depression through ambivalent, discrepant responses that confuse the afflicted individual and prevent him or her from adjusting personal behaviors in a more positive direction. Finally, some authors, such as Salzman (1975), have argued that others come to behave quite negatively toward the depressed, maintaining this condition with their expressions of hostility and rejection. We propose that members of the social environment may well use all of these strategies, from kindness and concern to angry retaliation. They do so, in our judgment, in an effort to control the depressed person's feelings and behaviors. We present the following theoretical model indicating why individuals attempt to control others' depressive affect, how their control strategies change over time, and how these control attempts can exacerbate the very problems they are designed to alleviate.

We begin with an individual who, for any number of possible reasons, is experiencing fairly intense feelings that he or she has defined as negative and disturbing. Others' initial responses to such an individual are likely to be quite kind and intended to be helpful. They will try to control and reduce the depressed's negative feelings by distracting them from their troubles and encouraging them to cheer up. These initial control attempts, however, only leave the depressed individuals feeling worse, quite possibly because they lead them to doubt the appropriateness of their feelings and reactions. As the depressed continue to display their misery and intense need, others feel bewildered, frustrated, and annoyed with them. Despite these unfavorable reactions, people continue to try to control the depressed person by keeping up a positive, supportive front and by avoiding any direct expression of their negative feelings. However, discrepancies between their reassuring verbal statements and their nonverbal behaviors, as well as temporal discrepancies in their responses, lead the depressed to doubt the sincerity of others' positive reactions. As a result, the depressed continue to display their symptoms in an effort to clarify others' reactions and to elicit more convincing support. This adds further to the frustration and aggravation of the social environment, so that people escalate their control attempts, showing more obvious negative reactions to the depressed person's behaviors and making more insistent demands for the depressed to improve. These reactions further exacerbate depressive symptoms, first of all by leading the afflicted individual to attribute any improvement in his or her behavior to others' demands for it rather than to a reduction in depression. Simultaneously, the depressed are left feeling that they must hide their true feelings and reactions from others, which seriously undermines their self-esteem and substantially contributes to their feelings of loneliness and isolation.

In the remainder of this chapter, we describe in detail the development and impact of this pathogenic interactional sequence. We conclude by discussing some interventions that may help to prevent such destructive interaction or to alleviate its negative effects.

INITIAL CONTROL ATTEMPTS

Several observers agree that, at least intially, others typically respond to the depressed with sympathy, concern, and a genuine interest in helping them to feel better. Burgess (1969) maintains that others treat the depressed with special care and consideration in an effort to alleviate their negative feelings. Lewinsohn (1974a, 1974b) similarly suggests that early responses to the depressed person are dominated by expressions of concern and attempts to be helpful. Both Coyne (1976b) and Hinchliffe, Hooper, and Roberts (1978) point out that depressive symptoms such as weeping and moping are strong signals of a deep underlying misery, and that the most immediate reaction of the social environment is often some effort to reduce that misery. These well-intentioned attempts to control the depressed person's feelings can take several specific forms.

One way in which others may try to help is by distracting the depressed from their problems and avoiding any discussion of negative or upsetting topics. As Cadden (1964) points out, "It hardly seems like a kindness to remind people of their troubles, to speak of danger, to dwell on grief and sorrow [p. 291]." In an experiment by Coates, Wortman, and Abbey (in press), subjects saw a rape victim's expressions of negative affect as indicative of maladjustment, suggesting that people would discourage such expressions in trying to help the victim to adapt. Caplan and his colleagues have conducted a number of studies investigating how people adjust to crises such as the premature birth of a child or contracting tuberculosis (Caplan, 1959, 1960, 1964; Parad & Caplan, 1960). These researchers report that friends and relatives of the afflicted individual, out of altruistic motives, often enter into a conspiracy of silence and minimize any references to the crisis or its impact. Wortman and Dunkel-Schetter (1979) point out that cancer patients often find that others are reluctant to discuss the disease or its attendant problems and that they become quite adept at avoiding such topics or changing the subject when they come up. Widows and widowers report very similar experiences in their social interactions (Glick, Weiss, & Parkes, 1974; Schulz, 1978). Caplan (1964) has indicated that even health professionals, such as doctors and nurses, often feel it is best for patients to forget about their problems and try to spare the patient from any reminders of them. In a study of nurses' reactions to dying patients, Kastenbaum and Aisenberg (1972) found that 82% of the nurses and orderlies reported that they avoided discussing the patients' fears, doubts, and problems with them. If patients tried to initiate such conversations, these researchers write, "The clear tendency was to 'turn off' the patient as quickly and deftly as possible [p. 222]."

Along with avoiding any discussions that could increase distress, others are likely to make efforts to cheer up the depressed person. Grinker (1964) has suggested that members of the social environment are often quite diligent in their attempts to cheer the depressed and bolster their confidence. Coyne (1976b) similarly notes that at first, people meet the expressed pain and fears of the depressed with direct reassurances. Others may argue that things are not so bleak as they appear or that the depressed person is more capable of dealing with the stress than he or she believes. Coyne (1976b) provides this quote from an experimental subject's conversation with a depressed person: "You certainly seem to have had a lot of problems, but problems are what allow us to grow, and so you'll have lots of opportunity to grow in the future [p. 39]." Watzlawick, Weakland, and Fisch (1974) also maintain that others try to get the depressed person to look on the bright side and stop dwelling on his or her difficulties.

Unfortunately, available evidence suggests that these initial attempts to control the depressed person's feelings will probably not have the desired effects. Although most people apparently believe that it is best to avoid upsetting the depressed with discussions of their problems and misery, many therapists agree that individuals are more likely to recover successfully from stressful events when they can communicate their difficulties and negative affect openly and comfortably to others (see Coates, Wortman, & Abbey [in press] for a review of this work). Caplan's research (e.g., Caplan, 1964) lends empirical support to this argument, showing that those individuals who developed the most serious pathological reactions to crises were likely to have been surrounded by others who tried to maintain a positive atmosphere and avoid any negatively toned conversations.

Direct attempts to cheer the depressed are apparently no more successful in helping the depressed to feel better. Based on his clinical observations, Grinker (1964) has noted that meeting the expressed fears of the depressed with reassurances leaves them feeling more frustrated and upset. Schwartz (1964) writes, "It is well known clinically that one can make a depressed person more depressed by telling him that he is more capable than he feels he is [p. 701]." Watzlawick, Weakland, and Fisch (1974) provide this commentary on the impact of others' cheerfulness:

> What could seem more reasonable to relatives and friends than to try to cheer up a depressed person? But in all likelihood the depressed person not only does not benefit from this, but sinks deeper into gloom. This then prompts the others to increase their efforts to make him see the silver lining in every cloud. Guided by "reason" and "common sense" they are unable to see (and the patient is unable to say) that what their help amounts to is a demand that the patient have certain feelings (joy, optimism, etc.) and not others (sadness, pessimism, etc.). As a result, what for the patient might originally only have been a temporary sadness now becomes infused with feelings of failure, badness, and ingratitude toward those who love him so much and are trying so hard to help him. This then is the depression—not the original sadness [p. 34].

Watzlawick et al. offer an intriguing explanation for why others' initial attempts to distract and cheer up the depressed often leave them feeling worse. By discouraging negative feelings and encouraging more positive ones, members of the social environment provide the depressed person with a standard of how she or he ought to feel. The depressed find it impossible to meet this standard and so see themselves as more incompetent and inept than ever. This situation may contribute to more than the depressed's sense of failure, though. Others' initial reactions and the standard of correctness that they imply could play a very important role in leading the depressed to doubt the state of their own sanity.

EVALUATIONS OF ONE'S OWN BEHAVIOR: JUST SAD OR MENTALLY ILL?

Several social scientists have argued that a critical step in the process of becoming mentally ill is the definition of an individual's feeings or behaviors as sufficiently deviant and inappropriate to warrant special intervention (Goffman, 1959; Mechanic, 1962; Scheff, 1966, 1974). These authors concentrate on factors that lead other people to define someone's actions and expressions as deviant and indicative of mental illness. For the most part, they maintain that individuals come to define themselves as mentally ill as a result of being labelled as such by their social groups. Some of these writers (Goffman, 1959; Mechanic, 1962) have explicitly pointed out that people sometimes define their own feelings and behaviors as seriously inappropriate, even without pejorative labels from members of their social environment. However, they give virtually no attention to how this self-definition process may occur.

The definition of feelings as deviant or inappropriate may be especially important in the development of serious depression. Savage, Leighton, and Leighton (1965) reviewed psychiatric diagnostic manuals in part to determine how severe clinical depression could be distinguished from more usual feelings of sadness and apathy. They conclude: "As a pathological reaction it [depression] is characterized by excessiveness and inappropriateness for the situation and the standards of the culture [p. 49]." The extent to which the afflicted individual sees his or her feelings as appropriate, then, may play a central role in determining whether the depression will be accepted as a normal reaction or a more disturbing pathological response.

Doubtlessly, the process of determining whether one's feelings are deviant is a very complex and multifaceted one. It would seem that a necessary first step in this process would be to find some standard of appropriateness with which to compare our reactions (Mechanic, 1962). We cannot determine whether our feelings are correct unless we know what is the correct way to feel. What standards of appropriateness are available to someone who is feeling depressed?

Objective criteria for distinguishing whether the depression is normal or pathological are likely to be very difficult to find. Even among clinicians, there is little agreement as to how depressive illness should be measured or diagnosed (Weckowicz, Yonge, Cropley, & Muir, 1971). Some authors maintain that serious depression differs from more usual negative feelings and reactions only in its severity and intensity. Others argue that the difference lies in the nature and type of symptoms as well as in their severity (for reviews, see Kendell, 1977; van Praag, 1977). Lewinsohn (1974b) points out that the concept of depression is "ubiquitous and . . . poorly defined [p.1]," often used without adequate distinction to refer to both "a normal feeling state" and a "disease." Kendell (1977) has noted that "what constitutes depressive illness is itself subject to dispute and disagreement: The boundaries between depression and sadness . . . are all arbitrary and ill-defined [p. 5]." Therefore, it is unlikely that the depressed will be able to judge the appropriateness of their feelings and reactions by comparing them to some objective standard.

Schachter (1959) proposed that in the absence of objective criteria, people turn to others in a similar situation to find a standard for determining the appropriateness of their responses. In a series of experiments, Schachter (1959) repeatedly found that subjects who expected to be shocked preferred to wait with others who shared their painful fate rather than waiting by themselves or with someone who was not to be shocked. Schachter hypothesized that people under stress seek out similarly afflicted others in part to interpret and define the ambiguous internal states they are experiencing but also to determine how appropriate these feelings and reactions are. Schachter suggested that through mutual influence, similarly afflicted others develop a consensus as to what the appropriate response is. This consensus provides the individual with a standard for deciding the normalcy and correctness of his or her feelings. Research since Schachter's work has continued to demonstrate that people generally prefer to be with similarly afflicted others when they anticipate frightening outcomes (Becker, 1967; Darley & Aronson, 1966; Miller & Zimbardo, 1966; Zimbardo & Formica, 1963) and also that people are open to influence from such similar others in their judgments of what are appropriate responses (Darley, 1966; Misovich, Colby, & Welch, 1973).

Unfortunately, people who are suffering serious distress may not always be able to discover how others in a similar situation are responding. Clinicians and researchers have suggested that people sometimes suffer from endogenous depression, or depression that occurs in the absence of any apparent incident or event precipitating these feelings (Kendell, 1977; Mendelson, 1974; Rosenthal & Klerman, 1966). Though such individuals may be particularly concerned about the appropriateness of their inexplicable negative reactions, the lack of clarity as to what is prompting their feelings makes it nearly impossible to find others who share the problem. When the cause of the depression is more evident (e.g., the death of a loved one; diagnosis of a serious illness), there simply may not be others available in the social network who have had this experience. Even where some serious problem does bring afflicted individuals into mutual contact, as in a hospital or other treatment settings, there may be a number of barriers preventing more than superficial exchange and discussion among them (Wortman & Dunkel-Schetter, 1979). Thus, people who are seriously upset may often lack the opportunity to evaluate the appropriateness of their feelings by comparing and discussing them with similarly afflicted others.

The only standard that the depressed may have available, then, is the one provided by nonafflicted others in the social environment. When these others discourage the depressed from expressing or dwelling on negative feelings, when they encourage them to see their situation as less bleak or themselves as more capable of dealing with it, they imply that the depressed should not feel as bad as they do. As a result, the depressed may question how normal and correct their reactions are and begin to doubt how well they are coping with their problems. They are confronted with the possibility that their feelings are not appropriate and may be indicative of a more serious disturbance.

These doubts may be heightened by the rather bizarre but common effects that extreme stress or loss can have. For example, several investigators have noted a tendency among the bereaved to see or hear their dead spouses. Depending on the individual study, estimates of the number of bereaved people who experience such hallucinations have ranged from 50% to 90% (Glick, Weiss, & Parkes, 1974; Marris, 1958; Rees, 1971; Yamamoto, Okonogi, Iwasaki, & Yoshimura, 1969) Patients with amputations or mastectomies often have "phantom limb" or "phantom breast" experiences, in which they feel pain or other sensations in the removed bodily part (Jarvis, 1967; Weinstein, Yetter, & Sersen, 1970). Rape victims are sometimes engulfed by sudden, inexplicable panic days or weeks after the sexual assault has occurred (Fox & Scherl, 1972). Although all these experiences are fairly common among people who have endured such stressful outcomes, those who are not aware of this may well find such phenomena extremely disturbing and suggestive of mental illness.

In the early stages of the depression, others are not likely to offer any direct resolution for the depressed's doubts about the appropriateness of their feelings and reactions. Members of the social environment do not typically tell the afflicted individual that it is correct and normal to feel depressed, although some therapists recommend such a tack (Raskin & Klein, 1976). At the same time, research reviewed by Gove (1970) indicates that family members and close associates, at least at first, are very reluctant to label an intimate as mentally ill, even when the intimate's behavior is quite unusual. Thus the depressed are likely to remain uncertain about the appropriateness of their reactions and may continue to display and discuss them in part to resolve this uncertainty.

Even though others' initial attempts to distract and cheer the depressed do not usually prove very comforting, they nonetheless communicate concern and caring for the depressed person. Some authors (e.g., Burgess, 1969) suggest that the afflicted individual continues to act depressed precisely because he or she receives support from others for doing so. This may be part of the reason for the depressed's continued symptomatic behaviors, but some of these expressions and actions seem to be aimed more at eliciting others' confirmation that they are indeed facing serious difficulties and that their negative feelings are appropriate responses. For example, after listening to the tape-recorded conversations of depressed people, Coyne (1976a) concluded that they tended to engage in inappropriate self-disclosure, revealing intimate details of very personal problems and feelings to total strangers. Similarly, Mayo (1968) found that a group of hospitalized neurotic women, some of whom had been diagnosed as depressed, reported disclosing more intimate and personal details of their problems and feelings to spouses and other close friends than such people disclosed to them. Such intimate disclosure may be intended to gain not only support but also clarifying feedback. Unfortunately, others are likely to respond to the depressed's continued display and discussion of their negative feelings and difficulties in a way that leaves the depressed even more doubtful about both the appropriateness of their own reactions and the sincerity of others' support.

TRANSITIONAL CONTROL ATTEMPTS: THE EROSION OF SOCIAL SUPPORT

Although people may feel strongly compelled to help someone who is depressed, there is also good reason to believe they will find depressive displays aversive and annoying. Subjects in an experiment by Gergen and Wishnov (1965) found interacting with a sad partner much more unpleasant than contact with a happy one. Coates, Wortman, and Abbey (in press) report that a rape victim who expressed relatively mild negative affect was rated as less likable by observers than a victim who was more positive. Social interaction with the clinically depressed, perhaps because of their pain and sadness, appears to be a particularly noxious experience. Coyne (1976a) conducted a study in which participants held brief telephone conversations with either depressed patients, non-depressed patients, or nonpatients. Those who spoke with a depressed person reported feeling more unhappy, anxious, and hostile afterward. Subjects also rated the depressed people as less attractive and indicated less interest in further contact with them. Hammen and Peters (1978) conducted a similar study in which college students talked with others who role-played a depressed or nondepressed person. Once again, subjects reported more personal discomfort after interacting with depressed others and rated them as much less attractive.

Those around the depressed may also be subject to a number of biases that lead them to form rather negative attributions about people who are hurt or suffering. One such bias of observers is described by Lerner's just-world theory (Lerner, 1970, 1971; Lerner, Miller, & Holmes, 1976; Lerner & Simmons, 1966). According to this theory, people need to believe that the world is a fair place where individuals get what they deserve and deserve what they get. When confronted with someone who is hurt or suffering, we convince ourselves that the person somehow earned his or her pain, either by careless and inconsiderate behavior or because of negative personal characterstics. To do otherwise would be to admit that cautious, decent people like ourselves could suffer a similar fate. Other theorists have proposed related concepts, such as the need to see the world as an orderly and predictable place (Chaiken & Darley, 1973; Walster, 1966) or to maintain perceived control (Wortman, 1976), as likewise leading observers to blame and denigrate the unfortunate. These theories, and the research they have stimulated, indicate that factors such as the severity of a person's problem or the likelihood of observers' sharing it can lead others to dislike victims even before they have had any direct contact or interaction (Chaiken & Darley, 1973; Coates, Wortman, & Abbey, in press; Lerner & Simmons, 1966; Sorrentino & Boutilier, 1974). (See also Caplan & Nelson, 1974; and Ryan, 1971; for further discussion of the tendency of observers to blame and derogate victims.)

In addition to these motivational factors, there may be information-processing biases that lead observers to make negative evaluations of the depressed. For example, Jones and Nisbett (1971) have argued that the situational determinants of another's behavior are often not salient to an observer and therefore tend to be ignored by him or her in assigning causality for that behavior. Because information about the situational constraints impinging on others is frequently not available, observers are likely to attribute others' behavior to their personality traits. For example, a woman may become depressed because of the rude and inconsiderate behavior of her husband. The situational forces producing this depression are salient to the woman herself. For observers, her depressive behavior is likely to be far more salient than any situational factors that may have triggered it. Therefore, they may be predisposed to view her depression as the result of her own weakness or maladjustment.

Finally, the failure of others' initial attempts to distract and cheer the depressed person is likely to leave them feeling very frustrated and even resentful. Research on helping behavior has shown that obvious or strong need is a powerful elicitor of aid from others (Schwartz, 1972; Staub, 1970, 1974). However, this research also shows that people become irritated and even angry when their attempts to help fail to prompt any improvement (Brickman, Rabinowitz, Coates, Cohn, Kidder, & Karuza, 1977; Freudenberger, 1974; Maslach, 1976). Several authors (Coyne, 1976b; Salzman, 1975) suggest that a very similar sequence occurs in the depressed's social interactions. They point out that the depressed's behaviors, such as weeping, moping, and verbal descriptions of overwhelming misery, have a very demanding quality to which others are quick to respond. However, when depressed people continue to exhibit these behaviors despite all the attempts to comfort and cheer them, members of the social environment become confused about how to respond to the depressed, upset by the depressed person's lack of improvement, and annoyed by the continuing demands for aid and support.

These feelings of bewilderment, frustration, and irritation may be particularly intense for those who are close to the depressed person, precisely because they care more, and are more concerned by the persistent depression. Based on their counselling experience with spouses of depressed people, Hinchliffe, Hooper, and Roberts (1978) report that it is quite common for family members to feel confused as to what they can do to help the depressed person and angry at the depressed's lack of improvement. Their account from a depressed man's wife illustrates these reactions: "In the beginning, we felt guilty when we were cheerful and Bill was depressed; we did not know how to react for the best—whether to comfort, encourage, ignore, jolly him out of it (impossible!) or what. The family have admitted to feeling angry that Dad was such a wet blanket at times [p. 110]."

Despite the negative feelings that the depressed person's persistent symptoms elicit in others, they will probably try to remain supportive and helpful for some time. Coyne (1976b) specifically indicates that others are likely to feel that the best way to manipulate or control the depressed person's condition is to keep up a positive front and avoid any direct expressions of their mounting negative feelings. Apparently, people do try to conceal their negative feelings and minimize any unpleasant exchanges in their interactions with others who are suffering or depressed (Hastorf, Northcraft, & Picciotto, 1979; Richardson, 1976). In a study by Kleck, Ono, and Hastorf (1966), subjects distorted their earlier stated opinions when interacting with handicapped individuals, evidently in an effort to avoid any disagreements with them. Similarly, both Goffman (1963) and Davis (1961) have provided anecdotal accounts from handicapped and other suffering individuals that indicate how reluctant others are to express negative reactions to them. Coyne (1976b) reports on some data suggesting that people will not directly express hostility to someone they believe is depressed, even when the depressed person is hostile to them. The following account from an interview conducted by Weissman and Paykel (1974) demonstrates that family members will go to considerable extremes to please the depressed person and avoid any unpleasant encounters:

P.N. was a 38-year-old married woman with two children....She became depressed when her husband was planning a family vacation, long desired by him. As she began to prepare for it, she voiced feelings of guilt and inadequacy at not being up to the task....The vacation was not taken and they were unwilling to bring up the subject for fear of producing an exacerbation of symptoms. Her husband, who was very disappointed about not taking the vacation, felt resentful but did not say so directly [p. 92].

Even with all their efforts to be agreeable and to conceal their irritation and annoyance, members of the social environment probably communicate their negative feelings to the depressed in a number of indirect ways. First, although their verbal messages may be supportive and reassuring, their nonverbal behaviors are likely to reveal their discomfort and growing agitation. Research results indicate that able-bodied individuals attempt to maintain pleasant verbal exchanges with handicapped people (Kleck, Ono, & Hastorf, 1966) but also that they show more rigid and controlled motor activity, fewer smiles, greater interpersonal distance, and earlier exits with the handicapped than they demonstrate when interacting with other able-bodied individuals (Kleck, 1968; Kleck, Buck, Goller, London, Pfeifer, & Vukcevic, 1968; Kleck, Ono, & Hastorf, 1966; see Richardson, 1976, for a review). McClean, Ogston, and Grauer (1973) indicate that married depressed people receive very conflicted messages from their spouses and recommend a therapy program to clarify such communications. Hinchliffe, Hooper, and Roberts (1978) made very detailed observations of interactions between depressed people and their mates, and they suggest that there was considerable incongruity between verbal statements and paralinguistic signals such as voice tone. These authors conclude from their observations that "feelings may be expressed covertly in many of our couples [p. 60]."

The depressed are also likely to find that despite all the reassurances and promises of support, others increasingly avoid them. Uncertain of what they can do to help and frustrated by the depressed's persistent misery, members of the social environment may feel that the most comfortable solution is simply to reduce their interactions with the afflicted individual. Home observations by Lewinsohn and his associates (Lewinsohn, 1974a; Lewinsohn & Schaffer, 1971) reveal that family members often shun the depressed person. According to Lewinsohn, Weinstein, and Shaw (1969): "Since most people in the depressed person's environment (and eventually even his family) find his behavior aversive, they will avoid him as much as possible [p. 232]."

Finally, as their frustration and resentment grow, others may begin to show discrepancies even in their verbal replies to the depressed. Both Coyne (1976b) and Salzman (1975) indicate that others' expressions of kindness and concern become increasingly punctuated with angry outbursts and accusations. These temporal discrepancies in others' reactions are demonstrated in this case report from Weissman and Paykel (1974):

> B.P., a 34-year-old housewife, called her husband daily at work for reassurance, talking about her depressed feelings, her inadequacies, and her inability to carry out household chores. Most of the time he tried to reassure her of her competence.... Sometimes he would become quite irritated and demand that she "grow up" and act her age [p. 93].

IMPACT OF AMBIVALENT FEEDBACK

The theorist who has given most consideration to how this discrepant, ambivalent feedback is likely to affect the depressed is Coyne (1976a, 1976b). Coyne argues that depressed people are primarily concerned with gaining social support and that their expressions of dysphoria and other symptomatic behaviors are intended to serve this purpose. According to Coyne (1976a):

> The symptoms of depressed persons are aversive yet powerful in the ability to arouse guilt in others and to inhibit any direct expression of annoyance and hostility from others. Members of the social environment attempt to reduce the aversive behavior of depressed persons and alleviate guilt by manipulating them with nongenuine reassurance and support. At the same time, these same persons reject and avoid the depressed persons. As discrepancies between the reassurance of others and their actual behavior become apparent, the depressed persons are confirmed in their suspicions that they are not accepted and that further interactions cannot be assured. To maintain their increasingly uncertain security and to control the behavior of others, depressed persons display more symptoms and convey more distress, thereby further stimulating the depressive social process [p. 187].

Although Coyne sees the discrepant social responses as the primary factor undermining social support for the depressed, he suggests that other aspects of the depressed person's situation also contribute to this problem. Although he does not specifically label it as such, Coyne indicates that the depressed face an attributional dilemma in evaluating the positive reactions of others. The depressed are uncertain whether others are being kind because they truly care or just because it is the most polite and socially acceptable response to someone in obvious need. Attribution theorists have pointed out that it is very difficult to infer a person's actual intentions from behaviors that are socially desirable (Jones & Davis, 1965) and that any single cause is accepted with less confidence when there are multiple causes for another's behavior (Kelley, 1967, 1971). Several authors (e.g., Goffman, 1963; Schwartz, 1972) have noted that there are strong social norms dictating that people be helpful to needy others. It would seem to follow, then, that people receiving help would often have difficulty deciding whether it is a signal of genuine caring and concern or only the most acceptable, normative response that others can make. Consistent with this reasoning, White, Wright, and Dembo (1948) suggest that visibly handicapped people often feel others' concern and interest is prompted only by their obvious need. These investigators conclude from extensive interviews with disabled soldiers that they often suffer from the "fear that it is not 'me as a person but my injury' that is of primary importance to other people [p. 19]."

As the depressed persist in their symptomatic displays and demanding behaviors, Coyne argues that a series of interactive stalemates are reached. Members of the social environment become increasingly annoyed, and their angry outbursts and hostile retaliations against the depressed become more frequent. The depressed person becomes more aware that others dislike and disapprove of him or her. At the same time, though, those around this individual feel more and more guilty about their rejecting behavior toward someone so blatantly in dire need. As a result, according to Coyne, they tend to follow up their negative reactions with more positive qualifiers, denying any feelings of disapproval and insisting that they still care about the depressed individual. Coyne argues that the depressed are thus provided with mounting evidence that others find them despicable but that they also have no means to determine how they can adjust their behavior to be more pleasing because others deny any negative feelings. The depressed's only recourse is more desperate displays of their intense need for others, leading to more of the same angry reactions and qualifying denials. Coyne indicates that this stalemate continues until members of the social environment withdraw completely from the depressed or have the depressed withdrawn through hospitalization.

Although Coyne offers an intriguing analysis of depression-maintaining social interaction, his analysis may not go far enough. Coyne has fully explored the depressed person's need for social support, and problems in assessing the validity of others' support. However, he has devoted little attention to the need for depressed people to evaluate and clarify their feelings and reactions (e.g., Schachter, 1959; Zimbardo & Formica, 1963). As we have demonstrated, this need for clarification of their feelings may be at the root of many of the depressed persons' interpersonal problems. In addition, Coyne provides only a cursory explanation for the negative response elicited by the depressed person from others. He has noted that the depressed's behavior annoys others, makes them feel guilty, and reduces the reinforcement they experience. We have presented evidence to suggest that the rejection that depressed people encounter stems just as much from the biases and information-processing errors of others as from their own behavior (e.g., Lerner, Miller, & Holmes, 1976).

Coyne leaves the depressed feeling lost and alone, trapped in a web of inconsistent and noncontingent feedback that does not enable him or her to discern how to adjust behaviors to be more socially acceptable. But depression involves more than just confusion and loneliness. Coyne gives no explicit discussion to the role that social interaction may play in fostering other symptoms of the depressed, such as generalized motivational deficits and seriously decreased self-esteem. In the next section, we review evidence suggesting that, at least in some cases, those around the depressed escalate their attempts to control and reduce symptomatic behaviors. Negative reactions to the depressed become more frequent and apparent, and demands for improvement become more insistent. We argue that the afflicted individual does become aware of precisely which behaviors are upsetting others and how these should be corrected. We then consider how others' control attempts can exacerbate the very problems they are designed to correct.

ESCALATED CONTROL ATTEMPTS

As members of the social environment become more frustrated and aggravated with the depressed person's aversive behavior and cries for attention, they are likely to make their dissatisfaction and growing hostility more apparent. Salzman (1975) suggests that others' initial attempts to be kind and helpful are insufficient to meet the depressed's deep need for support, leading the depressed to become more demanding. As a result, "Those who at the outset were interested and considerate to the patient now are angry, impatient, and rejecting [p. 50]." A case study reported by Weissman and Paykel (1974) suggests a very similar sequence of reactions: "R.T. was a 40-year-old married woman.... She communicated her attitudes by... brooding, crying, or withdrawing. While her husband might initially respond to her martyred affect, he eventually resented it and burst into rage [p. 100]."

Others not only become more dissatisfied and hostile, but may also escalate their demands on the depressed to engage in more constructive behaviors. An example of such a demand was provided earlier, where a depressed woman's husband responded to her expressions of inadequacy by telling her to "grow up and act her age" (Weissman & Paykel, 1974, p. 93). Yarrow, Schwartz, Murphy, and Deasy (1955) interviewed the wives of hospitalized mental patients, including depressed patients. Many of these women described their husbands as "spoiled, lacking willpower, exaggerating little complaints, and acting like babies [p. 14]," a situation they would frequently try to correct by insisting on more mature and adaptive behaviors. Weissman and Paykel (1974) similarly suggest that spouses of depressed women may try to "needle" them into actions that the spouses find more acceptable.

There is considerable agreement that depressed people become explicitly aware that those around them are unhappy with their behavior. Depressed patients often report that others are quite demanding and hostile toward them (Schless, Mendels, Kipperman, & Cochrane, 1974). Both Forrest and Hokanson (1975) and Hinchliffe, Hooper, and Roberts (1978) suggest that the depressed may engage in self-blame and other self-punitive behaviors because they believe these behaviors will reduce the derogation and punishment they receive from others. Schrader, Craighead, and Schrader (1978) contend that the depressed have negative expectations about social situations, consistently anticipating that they will be rejected or abused.

Coyne (1976b) acknowledges that members of the social environment become more directly and obviously hostile and even that the depressed become aware that others are angry and rejecting. He argues, however, that the depressed do not know specifically what is bothering other people because others' negative reactions are qualified by later denials and reassurances. We take exception to this view and believe that the depressed learn what behaviors are objectionable to others despite such qualifying comments. We feel that any qualifications or positive statements that accompany this increasingly negative feedback are likely to be dismissed. The attributional dilemma noted earlier provides a reason why depressed people may tend to discount others' kindness, while simultaneously placing a great deal of weight on negative responses. Positive reactions can be attributed to politeness or conformity to social norms. Others' angry outbursts and hostile denunciations are not socially normative, however, especially when the depressed person's distress and need for support are apparent. For this reason, others' negative reactions are much more likely to be seen as genuine. In summary, even if others do qualify their negative responses as Coyne (1976b) has suggested, the depressed may not remain confused about others' feelings. We believe that it becomes unequivocally clear to them that they are strongly disliked by others.

Moreover, in contrast to the view expressed by Coyne (1976b), there is considerable evidence that depressed and suffering people come to learn precisely which features of their behavior are disturbing to others. For example, Glick, Weiss, and Parkes (1974) interviewed widows about a number of issues including their social relationships. These researchers indicate that the bereaved individuals were very aware that others disapproved of weeping, moaning, and other expressions of their misery: "Widows perhaps exaggerated the inability of others to tolerate their grief. Yet they repeatedly reported receiving praise for maintaining their composure, and at most, understanding and indulgence if they broke down [p. 61]." In a similar way, a depressed woman interviewed by Weissman and Paykel (1974) was apparently quite cognizant of others' negative feelings about her failure to maintain her usual responsibilities:

> Following the birth of her third child, Mrs. D. became insecure about her ability to manage the children. She felt her relations watched her with disapproval. Her sensitivity to their criticism... became grossly exaggerated as she became more depressed [p. 84].

EFFECTS OF THESE CONTROL ATTEMPTS

Other Theoretical Perspectives

We have reviewed evidence showing that over time, others escalate their control attempts, making it clear to the depressed that they disapprove of their symptomatic behaviors and demanding more positive action. How are these control attempts likely to affect the magnitude of the depression? Some theoretical perspectives, such as the "secondary gains" analysis, suggest that they may have a beneficial effect. If depressed behaviors are negatively reinforced, they should drop out of the person's repertoire, and the depression should lessen. Other theorists (e.g., Beck, 1974; Rush & Beck, 1977) would expect no particular changes in the depressed person's condition as a result of control attempts by others. According to these theorists, depression is perpetuated not by others' responses but by the cognitive distortions of the depressed themselves (Beck, 1974; Rush & Beck, 1977).

In contrast to these theoretical perspectives, we feel that others' attempts to control or manipulate depressed affect contribute strongly to depression maintenance. We believe that persistent demands for improvement and negative sanctions for depressive displays not only undermine self-esteem and motivation, but can lock afflicted individuals into a situation in which they feel depressed no matter how they respond. Below, we discuss these alternative theoretical statements in more detail and contrast them with our own perspective.

It would seem to follow from several theories of depression maintenance that others' disapproval of the depressed's symptoms and others' demands for behavioral change will result in improvement of the depression. This is the case for Coyne's (1976b) analysis, which maintains that the depressed continue to display their symptoms in order to elicit social support. These displays actually alienate others, but the feedback that the depressed receive is not sufficiently direct or consistent for them to realize that their behavior is counterproductive and self-defeating. However, once others make their disapproval sufficiently clear and obvious, the depressed should be able to learn that they are annoying others with their symptoms. They could then adjust their behavior to be less irritating to others, receive the unambiguous social support they want so desperately, and so become less depressed.

Improvement would also be expected by theorists who believe that depression is maintained by the "secondary gains" that others provide in the form of sympathy and concern (Burgess, 1969). Several formulations of depression (see Eastman, 1976; Liberman & Raskin, 1971, for reviews) have absorbed this concept. According to these views, people reward symptomatic behaviors with their kindness and concern and thus reinforce the depression. However, as others become more negative, hostile, and insistent that the depressed person change, symptomatic behaviors are negatively reinforced. Because depressive displays are now discouraged by others' social reactions, they should gradually be reduced, and the depression should lift.

Lewinsohn's (1974a) analysis also suggests that others' demands for improvement may be beneficial. According to Lewinsohn, depression is caused by a low rate of response-contingent, positive reinforcement. He has argued that an important factor maintaining this low rate of reinforcement is the depressed person's general passivity. Because they are so inactive, the depressed do not exhibit very many reinforceable behaviors. Lewinsohn specifically recommends that therapists encourage the depressed to engage in more activities so that their rate of contingent reward can be increased. This would suggest that by prodding the depressed into more constructive behaviors, others will help the afflicted individuals out of their condition. Other major theorists would hold that increasing the depressed person's activities, or discouraging depressive displays, would have little long-term effect. These theorists believe that depressed people distort feedback and experiences in a way that maintains their depression. Perhaps the most well-known and most thoroughly investigated of these theoretical positions is Beck's cognitive model (Beck, 1974; Rush & Beck, 1977). According to this view, the primary factor in depression maintenance is the "cognitive triad"—a system of inherent negative beliefs that depressed people hold about themselves, their environment, and the future. According to Beck (1974), depressed individuals misperceive and distort their experiences in such a way as to maintain those negative beliefs. They ignore or minimize any positive features of their experience, while magnifying any failures or difficulties. Even if others can prod them to engage in more constructive activities, the depressed will focus on the dark side of things and therefore not feel better. Similarly, although others may reduce the depressed person's unattractive behaviors with negative reinforcement and subsequently offer more sincere support, the depressed will distort this feedback and continue to feel rejected. Others' demands for improvement and punishment of depressive displays may alter the afflicted individual's behavior. However, until the depressed person's cognitive errors and the negative beliefs underlying them are corrected, there is little chance for any genuine improvement in the person's overall condition.

We would agree with Beck (1974) and other cognitive theorists that demands for behavioral change and negative reinforcement of symptomatic behavior are unlikely to be helpful to the depressed. In fact, as will be illustrated, we feel that such demands can be quite detrimental. In our judgment, however, this is not because of inherent negative beliefs or information-processing errors on the part of the depressed. We feel that the depressed may be responding to the feedback they receive from others in much the same way that normals would respond to such feedback. We believe that others' attempts to control the depressed can undermine their self-esteem and motivation and trap them in a situation where they feel more depressed no matter what they do.

Our Theoretical Perspective:
The Futility of Control Attempts

As members of the social environment become more consistent in their negative reactions to any expressions of unhappiness or difficulty, the depressed are provided with strong evidence that they are dealing inappropriately with their problems. Others' responses confirm their worst fears that they are deviant and unlikable. Moreover, they may simultaneously receive negative feedback and demands for improvement from several members of their social environment. The impact of this consistently negative feedback can be devastating and can undermine their self-esteem. Many theorists agree that low self-esteem is commonly associated with depression. However, most feel that this symptom stems from biases in the way depressed people process information about themselves. For example, Beck (1974) has indicated that depressed people maintain their low self-esteem by distorting and misinterpreting their experience and the reactions of others. In our view, lowering of their self-esteem is a very logical response to the pattern of feedback they are receiving. In light of others' increasingly negative reactions, depressed people could perhaps be more correctly accused of distortion if they did *not* lower their self-esteem.

As the social feedback they receive becomes increasingly negative, the depressed may make an effort to be responsive to others' demands. They may force themselves to become more active, and may try to conceal their unhappiness and distress. Many theorists would maintain that such changes will have a positive impact, both because they are rewarding in and of themselves, and because they elicit genuine positive reactions from others. We disagree. We feel that changes that occur in response to others' demands for improvement have virtually no chance of benefiting the depressed. Below, we review evidence concerning the impact of (1) others' demands for improvement, and (2) others' negative sanctions for depressive displays. We attempt to illustrate why these behaviors are not beneficial, and explain how they contribute to depression maintenance.

Reactions to Others' Demands for Improvement

Although no studies have carefully examined how the depressed respond to demands for improvement from relatives and friends, there have been some investigations of depressed people's reactions to encouragement from therapists to be more active. These studies show that such demands seldom improve the depressed person's condition and may even worsen it. For example, Padfield (1976) conducted a study in which one group of depressed women received therapy aimed at getting them to increase their activity level. Another group received nondirective counseling, in which explicit demands were avoided. The results showed no significant differences between these two groups in their level of depression following treatment. Hammen and Glass (1975) describe two similar studies in which one group of depressed subjects were instructed to increase the number of their pleasurable activities, such as going to films or concerts. Control groups received no such instructions. In the first study, the groups told to increase their activities did so but showed no reduction in their depression relative to the less active control groups. In the second study, the instructed group once again engaged in more activities over a 2-week period, whereas the control group maintained their usual behavior level and simply recorded their daily activities. Although the instructed group participated in more pleasurable pursuits, they reported enjoying themselves less and feeling more depressed than the control group did. These results indicate that making clear and explicit demands on the depressed to improve their behavior does not lead to much actual improvement in their condition, contrary to what might be expected from some theories of depression maintenance (Burgess, 1969; Lewinsohn, 1974a).

In our judgment, patients fail to show improvement when they accede to others' demands to become active for one reason: These demands constitute a strong extrinsic pressure to improve, and this pressure undermines any intrinsic motivation to engage in the behavior in question. It is well established in social psychology that the more extrinsic justification there is for engaging in some activity, the less likely we are to see ourselves as intrinsically motivated to perform that behavior (see, e.g., Bem, 1967, 1972). In other words, when there are strong demands or rewards for acting in a certain way, we see ourselves as participating in that action because of the demands or in order to gain the reward, not because we have any real interest in the activity in question. On the other hand, when there are sanctions or even costs associated with taking certain actions, we are more likely to believe we are engaging in those behaviors because we want to do so. Thus the patients who were instructed to increase their activity may have failed to derive much benefit from their improved performance because they attributed it to the therapists' demands rather than to any change in their own interest levels or abatement of their depression. Simultaneously, the patients may have attributed to themselves any behaviors which the therapists discouraged, such as remaining inactive, and so felt more depressed.

In the field of social psychology, a great deal of research has been conducted on the effects of extrinsic pressures on attitudes and behavior. These studies, which have been conducted with normal rather than depressed subjects, have consistently shown that people find activities less enjoyable when there is strong extrinsic reason for engaging in them (see Bem, 1972; Deci, 1975, for reviews). Illustrative of this research, it has been found that: (1) Experimental subjects who are paid $1 to claim that a dull task is interesting subsequently view this task as more interesting than experimental subjects who are paid $20 (Festinger & Carlsmith, 1959); (2) Children who are severely threatened with punishment if they play with a desirable toy show more subsequent interest in playing with the toy than children who receive a mild threat of punishment (Aronson & Carlsmith, 1963); (3) Fraternity pledges allowed free choice about participating in a number-copying task view the task as more enjoyable than pledges who are coerced into participation (Brehm & Cohen, 1962); (4) Children who are rewarded for drawing, an activity they enjoy, subsequently show less interest in this activity than children who are not rewarded (Lepper, Greene, & Nisbett, 1973). This evidence indicates that when one is pressured to engage in certain activities, it is common to show little interest in these activities. Conversely, behaviors that are threatened with punishment may become more desirable. Thus, normals appear to respond much as depressed people do when subjected to strong extrinsic demands.

Of course, Beck's cognitive theory of depression can also account for the finding that depressed people show little improvement as a result of instructions to become more active (Rush & Beck, 1977). Because the depressed hold a negative view of their experiences, increasing their activity without changing their pessimistic cognitions should not leave them feeling any better. According to this model, the depressed will continue to focus on the unfavorable aspects of their experience, thereby convincing themselves that they are miserable. Consistent with this reasoning, subjects in the Hammen and Glass (1975) study who were required to increase the number of "pleasurable" activities found these activities to be relatively unenjoyable. These subjects also reported feeling more depressed, perhaps because their increase in activity only exposed them to more experiences that they interpreted as negative and aversive.

A study by Hammen and Goodman (discussed in Blaney, 1977) provides some basis for distinguishing between the view we have espoused and Beck's (1974) cognitive explanation. Once again, one group of depressed patients was encouraged to engage in a number of specific pleasurable activities. A control group of depressed patients was asked to simply record their activities over a 2-week period. As it happened, both of these groups reported the same increased level of activity during the study period. Because all of the subjects were depressed and all demonstrated a similar increase in activity, it would follow from Beck's model that neither group should show much improvement. Their cognitive distortions and biased interpretations would lead all the patients to see their increased activity as further verifying their negative beliefs. Following from our analysis, however, it might be expected that the depressed subjects who only recorded their behaviors but still increased their activity would feel better. This group could not attribute their increased activity level to the demands and exhortations of the therapist and so would be more likely than the instructed groups to see any improvement in their behavior as intrinsically motivated. The results provide strong support for our analysis. Those people who only recorded their behaviors reported a greater lessening of their depression than did those who increased their activity at the therapists' behest. As Blaney (1977) notes in summarizing these findings: "Apparently the instruction interfered with the inference 'My increase in activity level must mean I'm getting less depressed' [p. 7]."

Considered all together, the available evidence suggests that it is others' demands for improvement, rather than depressed persons' inherent negative beliefs, that undermine their interests and pleasure with constructive or enjoyable activities. By providing the depressed with strong extrinsic justification for any improvement in their performance levels, others lock the afflicted individuals into a depression-maintaining, no-win situation. When depressed people do participate in some constructive activity, they are likely to see themselves as doing so to meet external pressures rather than because of any intrinsic interests or motivation. Beck (1974) himself indicates that this is the case in describing a depressed person's motivational deficits:

> He no longer feels attracted to the kinds of enterprises that ordinarily he would engage in spontaneously. In fact, he finds that he has to force himself into any undertaking. He goes through the motions of attending to his routine affairs because he believes he should, or because he knows that it is "the right thing to do," or because others urge him to do it, but not because he wants to [p. 15].

On the other hand, if the depressed fail to accede to others' requests to become more active, they leave themselves open to continued hostility and further demands to change. So whether the depressed give in to others' demands or not, they are left feeling no better and often worse.

Reactions to Negative Sanctions
for Depressive Displays

We have argued earlier that over time, members of the social environment come to show more frequent and clear negative reactions in response to the depressed person's continuing symptoms. These reactions from others may well lead to a reduction in depressive behaviors, such as weeping and statements of misery or worthlessness. Verbal conditioning techniques applied in clinical settings have been successful in reducing unfavorable self-references and other self-punishing statements of depressed patients (Harsch & Zimmer, 1965; Krasner, 1962). It might seem that by reducing depressive symptoms, these negative social reactions would also help to ease the depression itself. Schulz (1978), for example, has argued that this will be the case. Applying Bem's (1967) self-perception theory, Schulz maintains that as depressed people reduce their symptomatic behaviors, they observe that they are acting less depressed and upset and so conclude that they must be feeling better. To further lighten the depressed's burden, their reduced symptomatic displays could also lead to an improvement in their social situation. As the depressed person's behavior becomes less unattractive, others may offer more sincere social support (cf., Coyne, 1976b).

Unfortunately, however, the depressed may well see themselves as reducing their symptomatic behaviors not because they are feeling better, as Schulz (1978) suggests, but rather because they must do so in order to avoid punishment from those around them. Again, others' negative reactions constitute a strong extrinsic justification for any reduction of symptomatic behaviors. Thus, rather than feeling that their condition is improving, the depressed are likely to feel they must hide their true feelings and problems from members of theif social environments.

Evidence from a variety of sources indicates that the depressed often do attempt to conceal their actual feelings and related difficulties. Several authors have commented on depressed people's apparent inability to communicate their feelings and needs openly and directly (Becker, 1962; Bonime, 1965; Stuart, 1967). Spiegel (Spiegel, 1965; Spiegel & Bell, 1959) argues that depressed people come to express their true feelings covertly if at all in their verbal communications with family members. Prkachin, Craig, Papageorgis, and Reith (1977) videotaped the facial expressions of depressed patients, nondepressed psychiatric patients, and normal controls as they expected to hear an aversively loud noise burst or see a neutral picture. These same subjects then watched the videotapes of others and tried to guess whether the person on the screen was about to receive aversive or neutral stimulation. The depressed were just as capable as the other subjects in correctly interpreting others' facial expressions but were apparently less able to communicate their own affective state in this way. Subjects made more errors in their predictions of which type of feedback the depressed expected than they did in their predictions for the psychiatric and normal control groups. Such communication impairments are quite possibly the result of depressed people learning that they must conceal or disguise their negative feelings in order to avoid hostile reactions from others. Thus, negative feedback is likely to result in impaired communication for the depressed person.

The depressed person's attempts to conceal his or her symptoms may well prompt more favorable reactions from others, but these are not likely to prove very helpful in alleviating the depression. Because the depressed are concealing their problems and feelings, they will probably doubt that others really understand them. Consequently, the depressed are likely to feel that others' kindness is not meant for them as they are, but rather is meant for the more positive image they are presenting. The depressed may well conclude that others would not be so kind if they knew what the depressed know about themselves. Jones and Wortman (1973) present a related argument, noting that the more a person's self-presentation deviates from his or her true feelings, the less signifying value any support they receive is likely to have. Fenichel (1968) has also suggested that the depressed may try to ingratiate themselves to others but feel no less disturbed or miserable as a result of the support they receive in return. Therefore, despite others' positive responses to the reduced symtoms, depressed people are likely to feel as hopeless, isolated, and lonely as ever, because they realize that they receive support only by concealing how they actually feel.

If the depressed attempt to alleviate this problem by trying once again to discuss their true feelings and reactions with others, they are likely to find that things only grow worse. Weissman and Paykel (1974) suggest that depressed women's inability to freely and clearly discuss their problems and feelings with others left them feeling frustrated and dissatisfied. As a result, they eventually became more demanding in their close interpersonal relationships, putting enormous pressure on others to discuss their problems. In turn, this led to increased hostility and more frequent negative outbursts from others. Bothwell and Weissman (1977) interviewed this same sample of depressed patients 4 years after their initial acute episode. Only a third of the sample had managed to remain completely symptom-free, and those who had suffered the most serious relapses differed significantly from the recovered patients in reporting more inhibited communication and greater interpersonal friction. As Bothwell and Weissman point out, their results indicate that any improvement in the depressed person's condition is likely to be temporary at best as long as the depressed cannot openly and comfortably discuss their problems.

Thus, like the demands for increased activity, others' negative reactions trap the depressed person into a depression-maintaining situation. If the depressed respond to these negative reactions by reducing their symptomatic displays, any positive feedback they receive will have little meaning, and they will continue to feel lonely and isolated. Alternatively, if they try to express their feelings and problems, increased interpersonal friction is the likely result. Both impaired communication and interpersonal friction apparently can play an important role in prolonging severe depression or prompting serious relapses (Bothwell & Weissman, 1977).

DIFFUSING PATHOGENIC INTERACTION

We have described an interactional sequence in which members of the social environment contribute to the maintenance of depression by their attempts to control and reduce it. We now turn to interventions that may be helpful in preventing such pathogenic interaction or in counteracting its negative impact.

In the early stages of the depression, it may be quite beneficial to increase the afflicted individual's access to similarly troubled others. By comparing and discussing their reactions with those who share their problems, people can clearly determine the appropriateness of their responses and ways in which incorrect responses can be changed. The available evidence suggests that people who have encountered severe stress, such as cancer patients (Wortman & Dunkel-Schetter, 1979) and widows (Silverman & Cooperband, 1975), often benefit considerably from participating in self-help groups composed of similarly afflicted others. Although the effectiveness of such groups in preventing more serious depressions has not been carefully evaluated, they at least offer the afflicted individuals an alternative outlet for discussing their fears, doubts, and problems. As such, they may considerably reduce the strain on the depressed person's relationships with nonafflicted others.

But even people who do not share the depressed person's problems may be able to help validate his or her feelings and reactions. An important first step in achieving this is to allow the disturbed person to express his or her negative feelings openly rather than trying to distract or cheer the individual. Many observers agree that victims of serious life crises, such as rape (Burgess & Holmstrom, 1974; Gager & Schurr, 1976; Medea & Thompson, 1974) or the death of a loved one (Raphael, 1977), are best served by being encouraged to express their pain. Some authors have even suggested that allowing the bereaved to ventilate their negative feelings freely can prevent or heal more serious depression (Horn, 1974). Distressed individuals may therefore find someone who simply listens to be more comforting than someone who tries to change their mood or outlook.

However, effectively validating the depressed perons's feelings may require more than a patient, understanding listener. The depressed need to know not only that others will tolerate their symptoms but also that others consider the depressive behaviors and reactions to be appropriate under the circumstances. Many psychotherapists have argued that although the perceptions and behaviors of the mentally ill may be quite different from more typical functioning, they are expressions of what the patient sees as reality and as such should be treated with the same respect as any other interpretation of reality (Laing & Esterson, 1964; Rohrbaugh, Tennen, Press, White, & Raskin, 1977). For example, rather than trying to discourage the apparent delusions of a paranoid patient, Jackson (1963) accepted them as genuine and helped the patient look for hidden microphones. The patient was relieved by this response and eventually gave up the delusions when no supporting evidence could be found. Similar approaches may be beneficial for the depressed, as the following quote suggests (Raskin & Klein, 1976):

> A 37-year-old woman was being seen in individual psychotherapy for depressive symptoms. She described her symptoms as painful and dangerous, coming over her suddenly. . . . She was told that her being able to experience and relate such symptoms was useful and that it was time that she learned how to be depressed. She was encouraged not to try fighting against depression, but to face it. Such a statement puzzled the patient, but helped her tolerate her symptoms [p. 553].

As others' attempts to control the depression by being kind and supportive erode into more ambivalent, discrepant responses, the depression is further exacerbated because the afflicted individual is provided with good reason to doubt the sincerity of others' support. An intervention that may be helpful at this point in the interactional sequence has been suggested by McClean, Ogston, and Grauer (1973). In an experiment conducted by these investigators, one group of married depressives were encouraged to use a communication tool for some time each day while interacting with their spouses. The tool consisted of two metal boxes with buttons controlling a red and a green light. Both the depressed person and the spouse were instructed to keep the green light on whenever they approved of the other person's behavior and to turn on the red light as soon as they felt more negative. Such a device would most likely help to clarify communication by providing a single, clear signal of the other person's feelings instead of the more usual jumble of verbal and nonverbal cues. Interestingly, these investigators found that patients who used this mechanical device showed more improvement than a group of depressives who received a wide variety of more conventional therapies, including antidepressant drugs. Perhaps by clarifying communications, this intervention allowed the depressed to trust the positive responses from their mates and prevented the spouses from becoming overwhelmingly negative and demanding in their reactions to the depressed.

Once others have become hostile and angry toward the depressed, it may be possible to bring some relief by informing both the depressed and those in their social environment about certain biases, such as the need to believe in a just world (Lerner, Miller, & Holmes, 1976), that can influence others' evaluations of the depressed. It would be important to stress experimental evidence showing that such biases are widely and commonly held. This should help ensure that those around the depressed do not feel uniquely cruel or guilty because of the interactional problems that have developed. As Hinchliffe et al. (1978) have pointed out, it is obviously desirable to avoid increasing the feelings of frustration, inadequacy, and guilt that members of the social environment are likely to be experiencing. Information about these observer biases, properly presented, could encourage members of the social environment to examine their reactions to the depressed more carefully and to realize that some of the aversiveness they are experiencing may not be due to the depressed person's behavior. The depressed person can learn from such information that the responses of others are not entirely his or her fault. Lamont (1973) found that one group of depressed college students reported improvement in their mood state when they heard a psychology lecture that indicated that people have little influence over the reactions of others, whereas another group experienced more negative feelings when they heard a lecture indicating that people have strong influence over others' responses. Thus, it may be beneficial for the depressed to hear that they are not solely responsible for the way others treat them.

As other people became more demanding, the depressed are likely to show particularly severe motivational deficits. A general goal at this stage is to increase the depressed person's perceived intrinsic interest in constructive or enjoyable activities. One technique which might be useful in accomplishing this goal is having the depressed keep a record of their daily activities. As indicated earlier, Hammen and Goodman (see Blaney, 1977) instructed a group of depressed patients to use this self-monitoring technique and found that they increased their activity level as a result. These patients apparently saw themselves as responsible for the increase in their behavior level, and their motivation and general condition subsequently improved.

A complementary goal would be to increase extrinsic justification for withdrawal and inactivity. This might be accomplished by encouraging the depressed to remain passive. Case study reports indicate that encouraging a variety of psychopathological symptoms and discouraging healthier alternatives often lead to a fairly stable remission of symptoms (Brehm, 1976; Raskin & Klein, 1976). The opposite tack of rewarding increased activity and punishing withdrawal, as is done in token economies, has not proven very successful in effecting any long-term improvement (Kazdin & Bootzin, 1972). Such direct incentives may only be effective in increasing the patients' motivation when they are sufficiently subtle to allow intrinsic attributions for any improvements.

Although for the most part we have discussed special interventions that can be made with depressed patients and their social networks, many of these events may also occur naturally. In the early stages, depressed people may encounter relevant, similar others who can provide the information they need or have close, intimate relationships that serve similar functions in helping them sort out and validate their experiences. Even after the social disruption has occurred, the depressed may be able to find extrinsic reasons for their passivity or intrinsic reasons for increased activity. As the severity of their apparent suffering decreases, the depressed become more attractive to those around them. They can then begin to repair their relationships with others in their social environment, and so the depressions dissipates.

ACKNOWLEDGMENTS

Work on this paper was supported by National Science Foundation grants SOC 75-14669 and SOC 78-04743 awarded to the second author. The authors would like to thank Richard Bootzin, Philip Brickman, and Joan Robinson for critical comments on this chapter.

REFERENCES

Akiskal, H. S., & McKinney, W. T. Overview of recent research in depression. *Archives of General Psychiatry,* 1975, *32,* 285–305.

Aronson, E., & Carlsmith, J. M. The effect of the severity of threat in the devaluation of forbidden behavior. *Journal of Abnormal and Social Psychology,* 1963, *66,* 584–588.

Beck, A. T. *Depression: Clinical, experimental and theoretical aspects.* New York: Harper & Row, 1967.

Beck, A. T. The development of depression: A cognitive model. In R. J. Friedman & M. M. Katz (Eds.), *The psychology of depression: Contemporary theory and research.* Washington: Hemisphere Publishing Corp., 1974.

Becker, G. Affiliate perception and the arousal of the participation-affiliation motive. *Perceptual and Motor Skills,* 1967, *24,* 991-997.

Becker, J. Toward a comprehensive theory of depression: A cross-disciplinary appraisal of objects, games and meanings. *Journal of Nervous and Mental Diseases,* 1962, *135,* 26-35.

Bem, D. J. Self-perception: An alternative interpretation of cognitive dissonance phenomena. *Psychological Review,* 1967, *74,* 183-200.

Bem, D. J. Self-perception theory. In L. Berkowitz (Ed.), *Advances in experimental social psychology,* (Vol. 6), New York: Academic Press, 1972.

Blaney, P. H. Contemporary theories of depression: Critique and comparison. *Journal of Abnormal Psychology,* 1977, *86,* 203-223.

Bonime, W. A psychotherapeutic approach to depression. *Contemporary Psychoanalysis,* 1965, *2,* 48-55.

Bornstein, P. E., Clayton, P. J., Halikas, J. A., Maurice, W. L., & Robins, E. The depression of widowhood after thirteen months. *British Journal of Psychiatry,* 1973, *122,* 561-566.

Bothwell, S., & Weissman, M. M. Social impairments four years after an acute depressive episode. *American Journal of Orthopsychiatry,* 1977, *47,* 231-237.

Brehm, J. W., & Cohen, A. R. *Explorations in cognitive dissonance.* New York: John Wiley, 1962.

Brehm, S. S. *The application of social psychology to clinical practice.* Washington, D. C.: Hemisphere, 1976.

Brickman, P., Rabinowitz, V. C., Coates, D., Cohn, E., Kidder, L., & Karuza, J. *Dilemmas of helping.* Unpublished manuscript, Northwestern University, 1977.

Brown, G. W., Bhrolchain, N. N., & Harris, T. Social class and psychiatric disturbance among women in an urban population. *Sociology,* 1975, *9,* 225-254.

Burgess, A. W., & Holmstrom, L. *Rape: Victims of crises.* Bowie, Md.: Brady, 1974.

Burgess, E. P. The modification of depressive behaviors. In R. D. Rubin & C. D. Franks (Eds.), *Advances in behavior therapy.* New York: Academic Press, 1969.

Cadden, V. Crisis in the family. In G. Caplan (Ed.), *Principles of preventive psychiatry.* New York: Basic Books, 1964.

Caplan, G. *An approach to community mental health.* New York: Grune & Stratton, 1959.

Caplan, G. Patterns of parental response to the crises of premature birth: A preliminary approach to modifying mental health outcome. *Psychiatry,* 1960, *23,* 365-374.

Caplan, G. *Principles of preventive psychiatry.* New York: Basic Books, 1964.

Caplan, N., & Nelson, S. D. Who's to blame? *Psychology Today,* November, 1974, pp. 99-102.

Chaiken, A. L., & Darley, J. M. Victim or perpetrator? Defensive attribution of responsibility and the need for order and justice. *Journal of Personality and Social Psychology,* 1973, *25,* 268-275.

Clayton, P. J., Halikas, J. A., & Maurice, W. L. The depression of widowhood. *British Journal of Psychiatry,* 1972, *120,* 71-77.

Coates, D., Wortman, C. B., & Abbey, A. Reactions to victims. In I. Frieze, D. Bar-Tel, & J. Carroll (Eds.), *Attribution theory: Applications to social problems.* San Francisco: Jossey-Bass, in press.

Costello, C. G. Depression: Loss of reinforcers or loss of reinforcer effectiveness? *Behavior Therapy,* 1972. *3,* 240-247.

Coyne, J. C. Depression and the response of others. *Journal of Abnormal Psychology,* 1976, *85,* 186-193. (a)

Coyne, J. C. Toward an interactional description of depression. *Psychiatry,* 1976, *39,* 28-40. (b)

Darley, J. M. Fear and social comparison as determinants of conformity behavior. *Journal of Personality and Social Psychology*, 1966, *4*, 73–78.

Darley, J. M., & Aronson, E. Self-evaluation vs. direct anxiety reduction as determinants of the fear-affiliation relationship. *Journal of Experimental Social Psychology*, 1966, (Supplement 1), 66–79.

Davis, F. Deviance disavowal: The management of strained interaction by the visibly handicapped. *Social Problems*, 1961, *9*, 120–132.

Deci, E. L. *Intrinsic motivation*. New York: Plenum, 1975.

Eastman, C. Behavioral formulations of depression. *Psychological Review*, 1976, *83*, 277–291.

Ellison, G. D. Animal models of psychopathology: The low-norepinephrine and low-serotonin rat. *American Psychologist*, 1977, *32*, 1036–1045.

Fenichel, O. Depression and mania. In W. Gaylin (Ed.), *The meaning of despair*. New York: Science House, 1968.

Festinger, L., & Carlsmith, J. M. Cognitive consequences of forced compliance. *Journal of Abnormal and Social Psychology*, 1959, *58*, 203–210.

Forrest, M. S., & Hokanson, J. E. Depression and autonomic arousal reduction accompanying self-punitive behavior. *Journal of Abnormal Psychology*, 1975, *84*, 346–357.

Fox, S. S., & Scherl, D. T. Crisis intervention with rape victims. *Social Work*, 1972, *17*(1), 232–241.

Freudenberger, H. J. Staff burn-out. *Journal of Social Issues*, 1974, *30*,(1) 159–165.

Gager, N., & Schurr, C. *Sexual assault: Confronting rape in America*. New York: Grosset & Dunlap, 1976.

Gergen, K. J., & Wishnov, B. Others' self-evaluations and interaction anticipations as determinants of self-presentation. *Journal of Personality and Social Psychology*, 1965, *2*, 348–358.

Glick, I. O., Weiss, R. S., & Parkes, C. M. *The first years of bereavement*. New York: Wiley, 1974.

Goffman, E. The moral career of the mental patient. *Psychiatry*, 1959, *22*, 125–131.

Goffman, E. *Stigma: Notes on the management of a spoiled identity*. Englewood Cliffs, N.J.: Prentice-Hall, 1963.

Gove, W. Societal reaction as an explanation of mental illness: An evaluation. *American Sociological Review*, 1970, *35*, 873–884.

Grinker, R. R. Communications by patients in depressive states. *Archives of General Psychiatry*, 1964, *10*, 576–580.

Hammen, C. L., & Glass, D. R., Jr. Depression, activity and evaluation of reinforcement. *Journal of Abnormal Psychology*, 1975, *84*, 718–721.

Hammen, C. L., & Peters, S. Interpersonal consequences of depression: Responses to men and women enacting a depressed role. *Journal of Abnormal Psychology*, 1978, *87*, 322–332.

Harsch, O., & Zimmer, H. An experimental approximation of thought reform. *Journal of Consulting Psychology*, 1965, *29*, 475–490.

Hastorf, A. H., Northcraft, G. B., & Picciotto, S. R. Helping the handicapped: How realistic is the performance feedback received by the physically handicapped? *Personality and Social Psychology Bulletin*, 1979, *5*, 373–376.

Hinchliffe, M. K., Hooper, D., & Roberts, J. F. *The melancholy marriage: Depression in marriage and psychosocial approaches to therapy*. New York: Wiley, 1978.

Horn, P. Regriefing: A way to end pathological mourning. *Psychology Today*, March, 1974, p. 184.

Jackson, D. D. A suggestion for the technical handling of paranoid patients. *Psychiatry*, 1963, *26*, 396–307.

Jarvis, J. H. Post-mastectomy breast phantom. *Journal of Nervous and Mental Diseases*, 1967, *144*, 266–272.

Jones, E. E., & Davis, K. E. From acts to dispositions: The attribution process in person perception. In L. Berkowitz (Ed.), *Advances in experimental social psychology* (Vol. 2). New York: Academic Press, 1965.

Jones, E. E., & Nisbett, R. E. *The actor and the observer: Divergent perceptions of the causes of behavior.* New York: General Learning Corporation, 1971.

Jones, E. E., & Wortman, C. B. *Ingratiation: An attributional approach.* New York: General Learning Corporation, 1973.

Kastenbaum, R., & Aisenberg, R. *The psychology of death.* New York: Springer, 1972.

Kaufman, I. C. Mother–infant separation in monkeys: An experimental model. In J. P. Scott & E. C. Senay (Eds.), *Separation and depression: Clinical and research aspects.* Washington, D.C.: American Association for Advancement of Science, 1973.

Kazdin, A. E., & Bootzin, R. R. The token economy: An evaluative review. *Journal of Applied Behavior Analysis,* 1972, *5,* 343–372.

Kelley, H. H. Attribution theory in social psychology. In D. Levine (Ed.), *Nebraska Symposium on Motivation* (Vol. 15), Lincoln: University of Nebraska Press, 1967.

Kelley, H. H. *Attribution in social interaction.* Morristown, N.J.: General Learning Press, 1971.

Kendell, R. E. The classification of depressions: A review of contemporary confusion. In G. D. Burrows (Ed.), *Handbook of studies in depression.* New York: Excerpta Medica, 1977.

Kleck, R. Physical stigma and nonverbal cues emitted in face-to-face interaction. *Human Relations,* 1968, *21,* 19–28.

Kleck, R., Buck, P. L., Goller, W. L., London, R. S., Pfeifer, J. R., & Vukcevic, D. P. Effects of stigmatizing conditions on the use of personal space. *Psychological Reports,* 1968, *23,* 111–118.

Kleck, R., Ono, H., & Hastorf, A. H. The effects of physical deviance upon face-to-face interaction. *Human Relations,* 1966, *19,* 425–436.

Klinger, E. *Meaning and void: Inner experiences and the incentives in people's lives.* Minneapolis: University of Minnesota Press, 1977.

Krasner, L. The therapist as a social reinforcement machine. In H. Strupp & L. Luborsky (Eds.), *Research in psychotherapy.* Washinton, D.C.: American Psychological Association, 1962.

Laing, R. D., & Esterson, A. *Sanity, madness, and the family.* London: Tavistock Publications, 1964.

Lamont, J. Depressed mood and power over the feelings of other persons. *Journal of Clinical Psychology,* 1973, *29,* 319–321.

Lazarus, A. A. Some reactions to Costello's paper on depression. *Behavior Therapy,* 1972, *3,* 248–250.

Lepper, M. R., Greene, D., & Nisbett, R. E. Undermining children's interest with extrinsic reward: A test of the overjustification hypothesis. *Journal of Personality and Social Psychology,* 1973, *28,* 129–137.

Lerner, M. J. The desire for justice and reactions to victims. In J. Macaulay & L. Berkowitz (Eds.), *Altruism and helping behavior.* New York: Academic Press, 1970.

Lerner, M. J. Observers' evaluation of a victim: Justice, guilt and veridical perception. *Journal of Personality and Social Psychology,* 1971, *20,* 127–135.

Lerner, M. J., Miller, D. T., & Holmes, J. Deserving and the emergence of forms of justice. In L. Berkowitz & E. Walster (Eds.), *Advances in experimental social psychology.* (Vol. 10), New York: Academic Press, 1976.

Lerner, M. J., & Simmons, C. H. Observers' reactions to the "innocent victim": Compassion or rejection? *Journal of Personality and Social Psychology,* 1966, *4,* 203–210.

Lewinsohn, P. M. A behavioral approach to depression. In R. J. Friedman & M. M. Katz (Eds.), *The psychology of depression: Contemporary theory and research.* Washington, D.C.: V. H. Winston, 1974. (a)

Lewinsohn, P. M. Clinical and theoretical aspects of depression. In K. S. Calhoun, H. E. Adams, & K. M. Mitchell (Eds.), *Innovative treatment methods in psychopathology.* New York: Wiley, 1974. (b)

Lewinsohn, P. M., & Schaffer, M. Use of home observations as an integral part of the treatment of depression: Preliminary report and case studies. *Journal of Consulting and Clinical Psychology,* 1971, *37,* 87–94.

Lewinsohn, P. M., Weinstein, M. S., & Shaw, D. A. Depression: A clinical research approach. In R. D. Rubin & C. M. Franks (Eds.), *Advances in behavior therapy.* New York: Academic Press, 1969.

Liberman, R. P., & Raskin, D. E. Depression: A behavioral formulation. *Archives of General Psychiatry,* 1971, *24,* 515–523.

Marris, P. *Widows and their families.* London: Rutledge and Paul, 1958.

Maslach, C. Burned-out. *Human Behavior,* 1976, *5,* 16–22.

Mayo, P. R. Self-disclosure and neurosis. *British Journal of Social and Clinical Psychology,* 1968, *2,* 140–148.

McLean, P. D., Ogston, K., & Grauer, L. A behavioral approach to the treatment of depression. *Journal of Behavior Therapy and Experimental Psychiatry,* 1973, *4,* 323–330.

Mechanic, D. Some factors in identifying and defining mental illness. *Mental Hygiene,* 1962, *46,* 66–74.

Medea, A., & Thompson, K. *Against rape.* New York: Farrar, Straus & Giroux, 1974.

Mendelson, M. *Psychoanalytic concepts of depression* (2nd ed.). Jamaica, N.Y.: Spectrum Publ., 1974.

Miller, N., & Zimbardo, P. Motives for fear-induced affiliation: Emotional comparison or interpersonal similarity? *Journal of Personality,* 1966, *34,* 481–503.

Misovich, S., Colby, J., & Welch, K. Similarity as determinant of social influence in affective judgments. *Psychological Reports,* 1973, *33,* 803–810.

Overall, J. Associations between marital history and the nature of manifest psychopathology. *Journal of Abnormal Psychology,* 1971, *78,* 213–221.

Padfield, M. The comparative effects of two counseling approaches on the intensity of depression among rural women of low socioeconomic status. *Journal of Counseling Psychology,* 1976, *23,* 209–214.

Parad, H., & Caplan, G. A framework for studying families in crisis. *Journal of Social Work,* 1960, *5,* 3–15.

Prkachin, K. M., Craig, K. D., Papageorgis, D., & Reith, G. Nonverbal communication deficits and response to performance feedback in depression. *Journal of Abnormal Psychology,* 1977, *86,* 224–234.

Raphael, B. Preventive intervention with the recently bereaved. *Archives of General Psychiatry,* 1977, *34,* 1450–1454.

Raskin, P., & Klein, Z. E. Losing a symptom through keeping it: A review of paradoxical treatment techniques and rationale. *Archives of General Psychiatry,* 1976, *33,* 543–572.

Rees, W. D. The hallucinations of widowhood. *British Medical Journal,* 1971, *4,* 37–44.

Richardson, S. Attitudes and behavior toward the physically handicapped. *Birth Defects,* The Original Article Series, 1976, *12,* No. 4, 15–34.

Robertson, N. C. The relationship between marital status and the risk of psychiatric referral. *British Journal of Psychiatry,* 1974, *124,* 191–202.

Rohrbaugh, M., Tennen, H., Press, S., White, L., & Raskin, P. *Paradoxical strategies in psychotherapy.* A symposium presented at the American Psychological Association meetings, San Francisco, 1977.

Rosenthal, S. H., & Klerman, G. L. Content and consistency in the endogenous depressive pattern. *British Journal of Psychiatry,* 1966, *112,* 471–484.

Rush, J. T., & Beck, A. T. *Cognitive approaches to depression: Empirical basis for theory and therapy.* Paper presented at the Loyola Symposium: Progress in the Understanding and Treatment of Depression, Chicago, April 1977.

Ryan, W. *Blaming the victim.* New York: Pantheon, 1971.

Salzman, L. Interpersonal factors in depression. In F. F. Flach & S. C. Draghi (Eds.), *The nature and treatment of depression.* New York: Wiley, 1975.

Savage, C., Leighton, A., & Leighton, D. The problem of cross-cultural identification of psychiatric disorders. In J. Murphy & A. Leighton (Eds.), *Approaches to cross-cultural psychiatry,* Ithaca, N.Y.: Cornell University Press, 1965.

Schachter, S. *The psychology of affiliation.* Stanford, Calif.: Stanford University Press, 1959.

Scheff, T. J. *Being mentally ill: A sociological theory.* Chicago: Aldine, 1966.

Scheff, T. J. The labeling theory of mental illness. *American Sociological Review,* 1974, *39,* 444-452.

Schless, A. P., Mendels, J., Kipperman, A., & Cochrane, C. Depression and hostility. *Journal of Nervous and Mental Diseases,* 1974, *159,* 91-100.

Schmale, H. Adaptive role of depression in health and disease. In J. P. Scott & E. C. Senay (Eds.), *Separation and depression: Clinical and research aspects.* Washington, D.C.: American Association for the Advancement of Science, 1973.

Schrader, S. L., Craighead, E. W., & Schrader, R. M. Reinforcement patterns in depression. *Behavior Therapy,* 1978, *9,* 1-14.

Schulz, R. *The psychology of death, dying and bereavement.* Reading, Mass.: Addison-Wesley, 1978.

Schwartz, D. A. The paranoid-depressive existential continuum. *Psychiatric Quarterly,* 1964, *38,* 690-706.

Schwartz, S. H. Normative influences on altruism. In L. Berkowitz (Ed.), *Advances in experimental social psychology* (Vol. 6). New York: Academic Press, 1972.

Seligman, M. E. P. *Helplessness.* San Francisco: Freeman, 1975.

Shepherd, M., Cooper, B., Brown, A. C., & Kalton, G. W. *Psychiatric illness in general practice.* London: Oxford University Press, 1966.

Silverman, P. R., & Cooperband, A. On widowhood: Mutual help and the elderly widow. *Journal of Geriatric Psychiatry,* 1975, *8,* 9-27.

Sorrentino, R. M., & Boutilier, R. G. Evaluation of a victim as a function of fate similarity-dissimilarity. *Journal of Experimental Social Psychology,* 1974, *10,* 84-93.

Spiegel, J., & Bell, N. W. The family of the psychiatric patient. In S. Arieti (Ed.), *American handbook of psychiatry* (Vol. 1), New York: Basic Books, 1959.

Spiegel, R. Communication with depressive patients. *Contemporary Psychoanalysis,* 1965, *2,* 30-35.

Staub, E. A. A child in distress: The effects of focusing responsibility on children on their attempts to help. *Developmental Psychology,* 1970, *2,* 152-154.

Staub, E. A. Helping a distressed person: Social, personality, and stimulus determinants. In L. Berkowitz (Ed.), *Advances in experimental social psychology* (Vol. 8). New York: Academic Press, 1974.

Stuart, R. Casework treatment of depression viewed as an interpersonal disturbance. *Social Casework,* 1967, *12,* 27-36.

van Praag, H. M. *Depression and schizophrenia.* Jamaica, N.Y.: Spectrum Publ., 1977.

Walster, E. Assignment of responsibility for an accident. *Journal of Personality and Social Psychology,* 1966, *3,* 73-79.

Watzlawick, P., Weakland, J., & Fisch, R. *Change: Principles of problem formation and problem resolution.* New York: W. W. Norton and Company, Inc., 1974.

Weckowicz, T. E., Yonge, K. A., Cropley, A. J., & Muir, W. Objective therapy predictors in depression: A multivariate approach. *Journal of Clinical Psychology,* 1971, Special Monograph Supplement, *27,* 3-29.

Weinstein, F., Yetter, R. J., & Sersen, E. A. Phantoms following breast amputation. *Neuropsychologica,* 1970, *8,* 165-197.

Weissman, M. M., & Paykel, E. S. *The depressed woman.* Chicago: University of Chicago Press, 1974.

White, R. K., Wright, B. A., & Dembo, T. Studies in adjustment to visible injuries: Evaluation of curiosity by the injured. *Journal of Abnormal and Social Psychology,* 1948, *43,* 13-28.

Wortman, C. B. Causal attributions and personal control. In J. H. Harvey, W. J. Ickes, & R. F. Kidd (Eds.), *New directions in attribution research* (Vol. 1). Hillsdale, N.J.: Lawrence Erlbaum Associates, 1976.

Wortman, C. B., & Dintzer, L. Is an attributional analysis of the learned helplessness phenomena viable? A critique of the Abramson-Seligman-Teasdale reformulation. *Journal of Abnormal Psychology,* 1978, *87,* 75-90.

Wortman, C. B., & Dunkel-Schetter, C. Interpersonal relationships and cancer: A theoretical analysis. *Journal of Social Issues,* 1979, *35*(1), 120-155.

Yamamoto, J., Okonogi, K., Iwasaki, T., & Yoshimura, S. Mourning in Japan. *American Journal of Psychiatry,* 1969, *125,* 1661-1684.

Yarrow, M., Schwartz, C., Murphy, H., & Deasy, L. The psychological meaning of mental illness in the family. *Journal of Social Issues,* 1955, *11*(4), 12-24.

Zimbardo, P., & Formica, R. Emotional comparison and self-esteem as determinants of affiliation. *Journal of Personality,* 1963, *31,* 141-162.

Author Index

Subject Index